Tilting at Windmills

Tilting at Windmills

School Reform, San Diego, and America's Race to Renew Public Education

RICHARD LEE COLVIN

Harvard Education Press
Cambridge, Massachusetts

Library of Congress Control Number 2013931902

Paperback ISBN 978-1-61250-564-0
Library Edition ISBN 978-1-61250-565-7

Published by Harvard Education Press,
an imprint of the Harvard Education Publishing Group

Harvard Education Press
8 Story Street
Cambridge, MA 02138

Cover Design: Deborah Hodgdon
Cover Photo: Vicky Kasala/Digital Vision/Getty Images
The typefaces used in this book are Adobe Garamond and ITC Stone Sans

*Dedicated to my parents, Robert Patrick Colvin and
Laura Jean Colvin, who taught me that education and
individual responsibility are the keys to success.*

Contents

Introduction

In March 2012, the Council on Foreign Relations, which assembles panels of experts to examine weighty topics related to national security, turned its attention to the domestic issue of education. The panel's report asserted in the title of its opening chapter that "The Education Crisis Is a National Security Crisis." The report said that the poor performance of the nation's schools threatened "economic growth and competitiveness, U.S. physical safety, intellectual property, U.S. global awareness, and U.S. unity and cohesion."[1] Thirty years earlier, a task force assembled by then–Secretary of Education T. H. Bell issued a similar warning. The famous *A Nation at Risk* report of 1983 declared that the "rising tide of mediocrity" washing through the halls of American public schools would be considered an act of war had it been imposed upon the country by a foreign power.[2]

During the intervening three decades, countless other reports issued similar warnings that the country would face dire consequences without swift and dramatic policy changes to improve public schooling. Much changed during that time. Graduation requirements were raised, states adopted content and performance standards, testing increased, accountability systems were built, the number of teachers per pupil fell, class size went down, salaries and spending rose significantly, teaching fads bloomed and faded, computers were introduced, and the Internet became ubiquitous.

But overall student achievement barely budged, even though some groups of students made greater progress than others. Nine-year-olds in the United States read slightly better in 2008 than they did in 1984, according to scores on the long-term National Assessment of Educational Progress. Thirteen-year-olds and seventeen-year-olds have made no progress.[3] The picture in math is slightly more positive. Nine-, thirteen-, and seventeen-year-olds all perform slightly better than they did in 1982.[4]

Achievement has not gone up, but it hasn't gone down either. That's significant, because some political leaders, perhaps in a well-intentioned effort to motivate their constituents to demand rapid change, talk about achievement in American public schools as if it suddenly plummeted and someone should be blamed. What *has* changed rapidly, however, is the global economy. It has become dramatically more competitive as manufacturing techniques around the world have improved and information technologies have made it easier for a company's workers to be physically located anywhere in the world. Those changes mean that, in effect, standing still is the same as falling back. In that sense, then, the crisis described in *A Nation at Risk* is far more acute today than it was then, even though overall student achievement has not declined.

Remarkably, the concern about public education has remained high for nearly thirty years. Much of that concern has been about student achievement in urban school districts. It is there that the greatest disparities in achievement can be seen and also where the many pathologies that accompany concentrated poverty play out. It is also in urban schools where the nation's latest reform strategy—a set of Common Core academic standards geared to produce students who are ready for college or for the postsecondary training that leads to viable careers—will get its most severe test.

The standards for English language arts and mathematics have been adopted by forty-five states and the District of Columbia. A new set of standards for science is being developed. All three sets of standards emphasize so-called twenty-first-century skills. The English language arts standards call for students to be able to analyze and evaluate what they read, construct arguments using several sources of relevant information, and communicate their ideas clearly and coherently in a manner appropriate for the intended audience. The mathematics standards require students to apply what they know to novel situations, make accurate mathematical models, and analyze situations using their math knowledge. The Next Generation Science Standards focus on understanding concepts and their application rather than memorization of isolated facts.

These skills, of course, are hardly new. They have always been in demand, and those who possessed them have been more likely to succeed, regardless of whether they were artists, craftspeople, professionals, or business executives. But our schools have not been designed with the idea that all students ought to be taught, or expected to learn, these skills. Over the past two decades, changes in the global economy, demographic changes, and advances in digital technologies have made it plain that the United States must educate a far greater percentage of its people to higher levels than ever before, not only for their economic well-being but also for the health of the nation's economy and democracy itself.

Implementing these standards such that they will lead to the outcomes hoped—more students graduating, with more of them ready for success after school—will require systemic changes. The entire district will have to be committed to implementing the standards with fidelity. That likely means a common curriculum, backed up by instructional resources and massive amounts of ongoing professional development. Instructional coaches will likely have to be hired to closely monitor teachers and help them improve. Educators will have to spend more time outside of school and during the summers working on their practice with their peers. Resources will have to be reallocated to pay for the training and the resources. Students who are not ready to meet the greater demands of the standards will need extra help, during longer school days, after school, on weekends, or during the summer. What will be needed is a focused, coherent, sustained, and self-critical effort. That will require strong leadership.

It is this kind of systemwide, all-out focus on improving teaching and learning that Alan Bersin brought with him when he became superintendent of public instruction in San Diego in 1998. The day his appointment became official, he could not have been clearer when he stated that his goal was to make sure that every student across the district, regardless of where he or she lived, would benefit from the highest quality teaching.

Bersin was an unusual choice for the job. He was among the first nontraditional educators to be put in charge of a major urban school district. He was a lawyer who was serving as the U.S. attorney for Southern California, and he'd been tasked by Attorney General Janet Reno with stemming illegal immigration and drug trafficking along the U.S. border with Mexico.

The grandson of Russian immigrants, Bersin had enjoyed and benefited from a rigorous public school education in Brooklyn, New York, preparing him to attend Harvard on a scholarship and become a Rhodes Scholar in England, studying in the same year as President Bill Clinton. He had gotten his law degree from Yale and become a highly successful litigator based in Los Angeles, where he helped the government of the Phillippines recover assets from the estate of former dictator Fernando E. Marcos and worked on complex litigation related to the savings and loan financial debacle, the Alaska Native Claims Settlement Act in the 1980s, and the Treasury bill auction scandal at Salomon Brothers in the early 1990s.

When Bersin was hired, no more than 45 percent of students from grades two through eight were scoring at grade level or above on a national test.[5] The percentage of high school students at grade level dropped well below 40. Only half of the district's Hispanic graduates, by far its largest ethnic group, did well enough in high school to be eligible for California State University or the more elite University of California. But there was a laissez-faire attitude among better-off parents. Their students mostly went off to college, and did fine. In contrast, most of those in the southern half of the district, generally poor Latino or Indochinese immigrants or African Americans, did not. Overall performance had been stagnant for many years, and the district's enrollment was becoming increasingly minority. But those realities were not widely discussed and therefore could not be addressed.

Business and civic leaders in San Diego wanted someone who would shake things up. Bersin was an attractive candidate to the committee appointed by the San Diego Board of Education because he was not an educator, which meant he was not wed to business as usual, and he had a track record of success, having won accolades for the changes he'd brought to the U.S. attorney's office. He brought in a nationally known educator to bolster his education credentials, centralized power over the curriculum and teaching, shifted resources to pay for an unrivaled instructional infrastructure, moved to shut down low performing schools, and didn't let himself get bogged down in making sure every interest group in the city approved of his course of action. His approach made some enemies, most notably the local teacher union and two members of the board of education aligned with the union.

As an outsider who came to be an insider, Bersin maintained a critical, analytical distance from the enormous challenges of the task at hand. He came to understand that while all of the adults involved in the system talk about serving the needs of children, they also are invested in the system as it exists today. Even though unions and superintendents appear to have different, contrary interests, they actually are committed to keeping intact the systems in which they have been encultured. That is one reason that reforms have often amounted to, in the words of Frederick Hess, "spinning wheels" or, as David Tyack and Larry Cuban have expressed it, "tinkering at the margins."

Bersin did not tinker. Instead, he charged ahead rapidly, which generated opposition, especially from the teacher union. Today, the national teacher unions are facing growing opposition not just from anti-union Republicans but also from centrist and even liberal Democrats who believe that the unions are protecting teachers at the expense of the interests of students. For example, the Obama administration has pushed a range of policies—related to evaluations, compensation, tenure, and seniority—that emphasize the importance of educator performance. Bersin, too, emphasized the importance of good teaching and wanted teachers and principals to be evaluated on how well they represented the district's curriculum and its approach to teaching.

That stance generated intense opposition from the San Diego Education Association union, as well as its statewide parent, the California Teachers Association, and even the National Education Association. Bersin was vilified by irate demonstrators nearly every time he spoke publicly throughout his superintendency. He was accused of undermining teacher professionalism, as are superintendents today who are pushing for more rigorous forms of teacher evaluation. In one of the most remarkable episodes in this story, the head of the union asserted in numerous forums that every teacher was equally qualified by virtue of possessing a state teaching certificate. So, when Bersin's top academic officer, Anthony Alvarado, wanted to recruit teachers who were familiar with the curriculum and the district's approach to teaching to help their peers succeed, the union's leadership adamantly blocked the way. The union's position was that those chosen for these highly specialized jobs needed absolutely no training or special skills. They should be assigned as coaches for their peers based solely on seniority. This position demeaned teachers as professionals and treated them as if they were all factory workers who could be plugged into any position on the line.

Bersin also faced battles with the school board, the local media, and various interest groups, such as those representing English language learners and students in need of special education services. But he persevered. He worked to help principals become instructional leaders. He made sure students who needed extra help got it. When all of his efforts failed to improve a few schools, he came up with a strategy for them to try going their own way. High schools posed a special challenge, and he struggled to find a way to improve student achievement. He did not solve the problem, but the story of what he did is illuminating.

Although much has changed in large urban districts since Bersin left his post in 2005, much remains just the same. When Joel Klein became chancellor of schools in New York City in 2002, he sought out Bersin for advice and recentralized power over curriculum and teaching. Klein eventually returned autonomy to schools but held them to very specific performance expectations. When Michelle Rhee became chancellor in Washington, D.C. schools in 2007, she sought him out as well. Bersin advised her to move more slowly than she did to shake things up. But he also encouraged her to push hard to get the contract with the D.C. teachers that she thought necessary. Terry Grier, who was the second superintendent to leave San Diego after Bersin left, lasted there only briefly before he was driven out by some of the same forces that bedeviled Bersin. Now in Houston, Grier takes an approach to leadership that has a lot in common with Bersin's, including high expectations for teachers and principals. John Deasy, who now leads the schools in Los Angeles, has organized the entire district around boosting the performance and skills of teachers, setting a high bar that new teachers have to cross before they gain tenure.

It is evident that Bersin has had a lasting influence throughout urban education, and much of what he did in San Diego is now being done in many large cities. Now, as school districts in all areas—urban, suburban, and rural—take on the challenge of implementing the more demanding Common Core standards, his story and his observations are still instructive.

Bersin's leadership drew attention and praise from national media outlets, major foundations that agreed to back his efforts financially, and policy researchers across the country. His tenure as chief has been well documented in articles, research papers, and books, most notably *Urban School Reform*, a series of scholarly and journalistic essays edited by Frederick M. Hess and published in 2005, the year Bersin left office.

But the story has never been told from Bersin's perspective.[6] The purpose of this book is to do just that—to share his thinking on the seven years he served San Diego as a nontraditional superintendent, why he did what he did, and what he encountered. His story will help leaders both anticipate resistance and identify opportunities to make lasting, real changes that improve the lives of students. Bersin offers his fresh insights into the obstacles to change in our nation's public schools and his thoughts on how to get around them.

But it is not a biography or portrait of Bersin. Rather, it is an honest, introspective, self-critical analysis of a sustained, well-funded, and deliberate reform of a large school district, one that was viewed at the time as one of the most important efforts in the country. By giving the inside story of the process, this book will add a new dimension to the national school reform conversation.

CHAPTER ONE

The Selection

"The Community Wanted a Change Agent"

The process by which school boards choose superintendents is badly flawed and often undermines the potential for lasting reforms even before they begin. Done in public, the process can discourage good candidates from applying. Done in secret, the hiring process can undermine the legitimacy of the candidate selected. Rarely do school boards see hiring a new leader as an opportunity to step back and analyze the needs of the district. Instead, new superintendents are hired, on a split vote or not, and expected to develop a vision for the district once on the job. This makes for short-lived superintendencies, instability, and a lack of continuity. These conditions are key contributors to the unsatisfactory performance of most large city school districts in the United States.

On March 6, 1998, the elected board of education of the San Diego Unified School District announced that it had made an unusual, if not altogether unexpected, decision. The five-member board had voted to hire Alan Bersin, a federal prosecutor who had never spent a single day as a public school administrator, to lead the 143,000-student school district, then the nation's eighth largest. The decision culminated from a secretive process in which a headhunter, a large committee of citizens, and a smaller group of civic leaders chose the two final candidates presented to the board—Bersin and a longtime superintendent from the East Coast. The public vote for Bersin was 4–0, with one abstention. But, in private, only three of the five board members backed Bersin. The divided vote showed that the board's divisions, generated by a bitter teachers' strike two years before, had not gone away.

Though not an educator, Bersin was well known in San Diego. For nearly five years he'd been the United States attorney in Southern California, nominated by Senator Barbara Boxer and appointed to the post by President Bill Clinton, with whom he'd spent time in Oxford, England, when both men were Rhodes Scholars. Attorney General Janet Reno had named him as the nation's first "border czar," giving him the responsibility of coordinating federal law enforcement along the Mexican border to reduce illegal immigration and drug trafficking. In that role, Bersin and his colleagues built unprecedented cooperation among local, state, and federal law enforcement agencies on both sides of the border.

He also crafted a compromise regulating the growth of gaming on Indian reservations in the region, and his office prosecuted three San Diego Superior Court judges for corruption, a first in California. San Diego had long been considered a backwater assignment in the U.S. Department of Justice. But, under Bersin, the office gained a national reputation for innovation and creativity. Felony prosecutions more than tripled, giving the office the highest caseload in the country. Bersin's record of success in that role would be a factor in his appointment in September 2009 by President Barack Obama as Commissioner of United States Customs and Border Protection, a top post within the Department of Homeland Security. But that would follow an unanticipated ten-year stint working in public education.

Back in 1997, Bersin had let it be known that he was ready to take on a new challenge and had explored top-level jobs with the Clinton administration. But no position was immediately available. He had not sought the superintendent's job. But when Malin Burnham, a developer dubbed "Mr. San Diego" because of his civic involvement, approached him through his son, Bersin's neighbor, to gauge his interest. Bersin did not reject the idea.

The first thing Bersin did was to contact Ira Krinsky, a Harvard-trained former superintendent and a managing partner of Korn/Ferry, one of the major headhunters for top education jobs nationally. The two men had never met, but they had much in common. Both had grown up in Brooklyn, both their fathers were pharmacists, and both are Jewish. They agreed to meet at the Jonathan Club in Los Angeles. Bersin, who had been a successful corporate attorney in Los Angeles, had never before been in the exclusive club, where many of the deals that had led to the city's economic and civic development had been made, and which for many years barred Jews from membership.

The two men hit it off immediately and quickly began discussing the specifics of the San Diego search. Bersin was vaguely aware of the school board's dissatisfaction with the previous superintendent, Bertha Pendleton, who had agreed to resign following an awkward attempt to get hired elsewhere, which had come right after she'd been given a generous contract meant to keep her in San Diego. Bersin learned from Krinsky that the board thought too little was happening educationally and that Pendleton, who had risen through the ranks during more than thirty years in the district, was considered to be unlikely to make any bold changes.

That circumstance created a potential opening for a nontraditional superintendent. To be a viable candidate, Krinsky told him, Bersin would have to familiarize himself with the theory of standards-based education. Krinsky ran through the basic concepts: define what students need to know and should be able to do. Develop curricula embodying the standards. Help teachers learn how to teach that material and create more challenging lessons. Assess how well students are learning it. And, finally, use assessment results to hold schools and educators accountable for their performance. Bersin had two reactions to the formula: first, if it really were that easy, why weren't many more schools successful? He also thought it odd that even superficial knowledge of standards-based education could give him enough credibility to be taken seriously as a candidate.

Nonetheless, the talk with Krinsky left Bersin sufficiently interested in the job to conduct an informal due-diligence inquiry. He knew that many in the community shared the school board's frustration with declining student performance. He also knew that many parents worried about violence on campus.

"I wanted to assure myself that the common complaint that the schools were being disrupted by black and brown kids bouncing off the walls in defiance of their teachers was more prejudice than truth," he said later. Indeed, he found that the schools he visited were not rent with violence. That appeared to be a myth. The schools "were quiet," he said. "Indeed, they were too quiet." The teachers and principals "seemed likable enough and were trying hard at their jobs." But Bersin didn't see much excitement about learning. He heard little from the students because their teachers were doing most of the talking. "What I could not tell at that point, but what became crystal clear later on, was that little of educational value was happening in far too many classrooms. The trade-off of peace for mediocrity had been struck in San Diego as well as elsewhere in California and across the country. Many teachers pretended to teach. And many students pretended to learn."

Only one of the schools he visited, Gompers High School, seemed to be out of control, and that was a situation he would eventually have to fix. But his investigation led him to conclude that not only could the school district's problems be addressed, but also that he could help solve them. The school board agreed—or, more precisely, three of its five members did—and appointed him superintendent.

THE COMMUNITY WANTED A CHANGE AGENT

"We chose him because the community spoke clearly with one voice, that they wanted a change agent," board president Ron Ottinger told a television interviewer several days after Bersin's hiring was announced, belying the divisions on the board. "We're looking to focus the whole system on raising student achievement, starting from the teachers in the classroom to the principal to the support staff to the central office. Everyone should be focusing on 'How are we going to get all of our kids to reach a common standard?'"

Sitting beside Ottinger, Bersin echoed his priorities and the desire for change. "This is an opportunity to take a fresh look. What we have to create is momentum for change with one goal in mind for San Diego: student by student, classroom by classroom, school by school, improved student performance. That's the beginning and the end."

Immigration and housing patterns had transformed San Diego schools demographically during the three decades prior to Bersin's hiring. In 1970, 80 percent of the San Diego school district's students were white. By 1998, only 28 percent were.[1] Nearly two in five students were Hispanic, and many of them were not fluent in English.[2] Achievement gaps were growing and the trend in overall test scores was downward. The district's test scores still were generally above those of other urban school systems, leading some to believe that San Diego's schools were succeeding. However, the average scores were higher than most urban districts because San Diego, sprawling along the Pacific Ocean, had retained a substantial number of middle-class students.

The desire for change had been building in San Diego for a number of years. Black and Latino community leaders had been demanding improvements and more equitable treatment. The school district had been sued repeatedly for failing to serve all of its students and had lost every time, but hadn't done much to fix the situation. Business leaders were especially concerned and had mobilized to bring new leadership to the school board. "It really was because businesses felt the schools weren't educating our students, which meant we weren't educating our future work force," said San Diego businessman Mel Katz, explaining the involvement of local executives. "The people coming in to apply for jobs couldn't pass the basics. They couldn't pass a sixth-grade-level math test or literacy test. We felt we were not getting a trained work force and people felt that this was a huge problem."[3]

SCHOOL DISTRICT LEADERSHIP
AND THE FALLOUT FROM A STRIKE

Five years earlier, Pendleton had become the first African American woman to lead the district. She had been deputy to Tom Payzant, who had won a national reputation as superintendent and then left to join the U.S. Department of Education in the Clinton administration. He later would have a successful run leading the Boston Public Schools. Payzant had developed an elaborate reform process that was built on increased community participation and collaboration with the teacher union. But it foundered, in part because of teacher union opposition, but also because of the racial and political divisions in the community. Ottinger had gotten involved in the school district as a community organizer working for Payzant. The difficulties of getting the various parties involved in schools to work together for improvement left him disillusioned. However, he was later enticed to run for the school board by San Diego business leaders.

In 1996, San Diego teachers went on strike for higher wages. Leading up to the strike, teachers picketed school board members' homes, worked to the exact minute their contract required, and refused to do any work outside of class or not specified in the contract. Board members, all Democrats, were determined to resist. As the strike continued, however, one of the board members began telling the union about the board's negotiating strategies. Finally, the board caved in and gave teachers the raises the union demanded.

They also gave away something more precious. The board agreed to set up school site councils that could override many decisions made by principals. "The unions basically took control of the school district," Katz said. "After the strike, Bertha would do nothing without the union's OK. They had won the public relations war and, from that point on, Bertha let them have veto power."[4]

Right after the strike, Pendleton tried to focus on raising student achievement in a dozen or so problem schools that were not making any progress. She created intervention plans for those schools that included reconstituting the faculty. Although she had allied herself with the teacher union, that did not protect her from the anger her plans provoked. As her reward, she "got pretty beaten up for it" by the teacher union, according to Ottinger.[5]

Pendleton abandoned that strategy in favor of a sixteen-point plan for improving overall student achievement. That plan, too diffuse, not easily measured or monitored, and typical of the multifaceted reform plans frequently enacted in large urban school districts, never took off. The power-sharing arrangement with the teacher union slowed any reforms. Infighting on the board also contributed to paralysis. Debt rose. To reduce costs, the board offered an early retirement package for teachers as well as administrators.

In fall of 1996, the business community fielded a slate of reform-minded candidates and backed their campaigns. One of them, Ed Lopez, an emerging Latino leader, defeated an African American longtime board member to become the first Hispanic ever elected to the board. Fearing she'd lost support, Pendleton made it known she would take the buyout and retire. To keep her, the board crafted a more generous compensation package. Soon after, however, the board learned that Pendleton had secretly gone to Dallas to interview for the superintendent's job there. She did not get it. Ottinger had little difficulty in persuading his board colleagues that it was time for her to go.

A SCHOOL BOARD'S MOST IMPORTANT JOB

Hiring a superintendent is a school board's most important job. But the rapid turnover of superintendents nationally suggests deep flaws in the selection process. In 1997, superintendents of the sixty-five large urban districts that participate in the Council of Great City Schools had been on the job an average of less than three years and only one in five had held the post longer than five years.[6] In 2002 the National School Boards Association reported that the leaders of the fifty largest school districts departed after only four and a half years on average.[7] That was not much time to turn around large, complex organizations with thousands of employees, challenging politics, and multibillion-dollar budgets. The average tenure of a departing CEO of a *Fortune 500* company in 1995 exceeded ten years. Even though shareholder pressure had increased, in 2001 CEOs were still serving, on average, more than seven years.[8]

To help them hire superintendents, elected school boards often turned for help to national executive search firms such as Korn/Ferry or Hazard, Young & Attea. A 2000 study found that while only one in four small school districts used a search firm in hiring a superintendent, about half of larger districts did so.[9] Although the price of a typical superintendent search is but a fraction of what it would cost to hire a corporate CEO, it is attractive enough that large national executive search firms, thirty-four state school board associations, and numerous regional outfits all are involved in what is an increasingly competitive business.[10] In 1994, the *School Administrator*, the journal of the American Association of School Administrators, found twenty-three firms conducting superintendent searches. A decade later, it found 233 such firms had advertised positions. Heidrick and Struggles had done just a handful of searches in 1994. A decade later, the firm was doing fifty a year.[11]

A good firm will work closely with the board to determine the needs of the district. That's not always easy. "The most difficult part is getting the board on the same page regarding goals and mission," said Jenne Davis, who ran a Grand Rapids, Michigan, search firm.[12] But some criticize search firms, claiming they care more about getting people hired than finding good matches, so they make safe bets and recruit only experienced superintendents or assistant superintendents climbing the ladder. This inbreeding tends to bolster conventional wisdom and maintain the status quo. Search firms are "limited to rounding up the usual suspects and presenting them as candidates."

Bersin also believed that conducting searches in public limited the field. Many candidates who might otherwise be interested fear that if, like Pendleton, they do not get the job they apply for, their relationship with their current employer will be undermined. "A public selection process," Bersin would later reflect in an interview, "chews people up in district after district. It limits the number and type of individuals willing to apply. Then, when all of the candidates' names are aired and talked about and the candidates themselves are questioned in public, the political free-for-all that results is destructive and tends to drive candidates to withdraw. The process highlights differences and makes consensus more difficult to achieve, whomever is selected."

Bersin, who was already a public figure, did not want to be part of such a process. (Even so, his name surfaced as a potential candidate in a column in the local newspaper, no doubt as a result of his conversations with others in town as he tried to learn more about the job and the school board.) Ottinger also wanted the selection process in San Diego to be kept private. Like Bersin, he worried that a public process would lead to a power struggle involving the teacher union and other powerful special interests and would polarize the school board and alienate the community.

"Polling we had done showed me that the board was held in very low regard, Bertha was held in very low regard, and the system as a whole had lost a huge amount of credibility during the strike," Ottinger said. "It was clear to me that we needed a strong superintendent who would truly come in and make major changes to focus on student achievement, and that the process of choosing a superintendent would have to be arms-length from the board if it was to have any credibility."[13] This reasoning, accepted by board members, led them to appoint a committee of community leaders who would vet candidates and make a recommendation to the board. The trade-off was that this process would deny the board itself a chance to conduct a comprehensive analysis of the district's strengths and weaknesses and then choose someone best suited for the situation.

TURNING TO A CIVIC LEADER

The board wanted a civic leader to take charge of the process. Katz, who chaired the Chamber of Commerce's education committee, suggested to Ottinger that the board ask the head of the highly regarded San Diego Regional YMCA, Rich Collato, to take on the job. "I think the climate was such that they needed someone who was respected in the community, who was looked upon as being apolitical with no bias, and only having the interests of children at heart," Collato said later.[14] The person also had to have a good relationship with San Diego's African American community leaders, because of the tension that had been created when the school board asked Pendleton to resign. "Politically," Collato said, "it was a very, very volatile situation."

Although fearful that the reputation of the YMCA might be tainted if the process became controversial, Collato's sense of civic duty compelled him to help out. He set two conditions, however. The school board had to appoint him unanimously, and it had to agree to accept the composition of a five-member committee he would form to recommend to the board the best possible candidate. The insistence of Collato and Ottinger on independence—although understandable from their perspective—cut school board members out of the process almost entirely.

In addition to himself, Collato's selection committee was composed of Malin Burnham, the developer and civic leader who would later approach Bersin; Alice Hayes, the popular president of a local private university; William Jones, a respected African American business executive who had served on the city council; and Ralph Ocampo, a preeminent Latino physician who had been president of the California Medical Association.

Working with Katz, Ottinger, and other board members, Collato formed a twenty-eight-member committee of business, education, and civic leaders to come up with a list of the ideal superintendent characteristics. Ottinger and Collato asked Ken Druck, a respected local psychologist and facilitator, to help coordinate the outreach. They also personally invited Marc Knapp, the president of the teacher union in San Diego, to participate. But Knapp, a burly, bearded middle school teacher who had been a union leader during the 1996 strike, rebuffed them. He wanted a seat on the more powerful smaller committee that would decide which candidate to forward to the board. According to Collato, Knapp came to his office one day to demand a seat on the selection committee. Told no, Knapp became infuriated and vowed to fight whomever the board chose. Collato, who said he felt threatened, demanded that Knapp leave the office, which he did without further incident. Nonetheless, Knapp vowed to boycott the citizens' committee and announced that none of his union members would take part either. Although some teachers did participate, Knapp declared its deliberations, and the whole selection process, illegitimate. Knapp's unhappiness with the selection process colored his relationship with Bersin even before he met him. Over the next five years, he would oppose Bersin at almost every turn.

San Diegans shared their views about who should become superintendent at three meetings of the citizens committee. The committee's report said the next superintendent should be a "proven successful leader" who knew how to manage money and resources. The superintendent should promote cultural diversity and be committed to "developing a solid plan for raising student performance" in all the schools. He or she should have a track record as a "change agent within a large organization." The only mention of experience as an educator came as a subitem under the last entry on the list of desirable characteristics. Printed almost as an afterthought in a smaller font size, the note said candidates ought to possess "expertise in teaching/learning/understanding of diverse learning styles [and] teaching strategies."[15]

When the committee recommendations surfaced in December 1997, the *San Diego Union-Tribune* published a story headlined: "Wanted: Schools Chief Who Can 'Walk on Water.'" That description came from Collato. "We are going to have to live with this person for a long time," he told the newspaper. "We will try to find that person who can walk on water and possess as many of these characteristics as possible."[16] As a metaphor, that description accurately communicated the expectations that are placed on the shoulders of superintendents in urban districts.

The five-member search committee was unimpressed with the candidates the search consultant Krinsky recommended. He was told to keep searching. The members wanted someone who could bring about big changes. Candidates who had spent their careers working in school districts did not seem to fit the bill. That opened the door for a candidate who had not previously worked in education.

NONTRADITIONAL SCHOOL SUPERINTENDENTS

During the 1990s, attorneys, former military officers, ministers, business leaders, and college professors had been hired in Baltimore, Chicago, Milwaukee, Minneapolis, Philadelphia, Seattle, Washington, D.C., and elsewhere. Rod Paige, the dean of the school of education at Texas Southern University, was elected to the Houston school board in 1990; four years later, he became the district's superintendent of schools. He brought a range of management reforms to the district—decentralizing power, getting more parents involved, improving safety, and emphasizing testing to measure progress. In 2001, he was selected by fellow Republican George W. Bush as secretary of education and also was chosen National Superintendent of the Year.

One of the most prominent of these early nontraditional leaders was Paul Vallas, the former budget director for the city of Chicago, who in 1995 became the CEO of the Chicago Public Schools. Seven years earlier, Reagan administration Secretary of Education William Bennett had declared the Chicago schools "the worst in the nation." Vallas was a tireless, energetic, do-it-all-at-once man who believed school districts could be transformed from the center through smart policies. Vallas would close a $1.3 billion hole in the budget, build seventy-six new schools, and raise test scores. As he left that job for another superintendency in Philadelphia, he was criticized for failing to do much to improve teaching or learning.[17] He later led the Recovery District in New Orleans and then moved on in 2011 to Bridgeport, Connecticut.[18]

Vallas was succeeded in Chicago by another nontraditional choice, Arne Duncan, who had run a nonprofit education organization on the city's South Side and then had briefly run the magnet schools office in the district. Duncan, selected and backed by Mayor Richard Daley, took Vallas's reforms to another level. President Barack Obama, who had gotten to know Duncan in Chicago, chose him as secretary of education in 2009.

Retired Major General John Stanford was appointed superintendent of the Seattle schools in 1996, a year after Vallas. Stanford raised academic standards, improved reading instruction, and curbed the practice of social promotion. He also built a strong relationship with Roger Erskine, the head of the local teacher union.[19]

A year after Stanford was hired in Seattle, the oversight board of the Washington, D.C., public schools hired retired Army General Julius W. Becton to be its head. He found a system in academic and financial chaos. The *Washington Post* reported soon after his appointment that the district had spent $50 million over five years on salaries for employees whose positions had been eliminated. The district bureaucracy had not followed through to stop their paychecks.[20] But in the spring of 1998, only a year and a half after he was hailed as a reformer from outside the insular world of education, Becton resigned. He cited "power politics" and the failure of the district's governing panel to support him. His resignation letter bitterly concluded: "I have had it!"[21]

"School districts tend to look outside for a superintendent only when things have gotten so bad that doing the same old thing just doesn't feel like it's going to work," said Tom Vander Ark, who was a successful businessman before being tapped to lead the Federal Way, Washington school district in 1994.[22] Vander Ark then went on to head up the education division of the Bill & Melinda Gates Foundation, where he supported many nontraditional ideas for improving schools. He later left to start an education-related venture that invests in and advocates the use of digital and online technologies to personalize learning.

It's clear from this list that just hiring someone who does not have a background in education is not a guaranteed solution. Only a few of the nontraditional superintendents who have led school districts in the subsequent years have been given the room to make significant changes. But the lack of experience as educators was not a hindrance.

An alternative source of school superintendents was created in 2002 by the Eli and Edythe Broad Foundation, which is based in Los Angeles. Each year, the Broad Superintendents Academy chooses a small number from hundreds of top business, military, and education leaders, and other government officials who apply, and puts them through an intense ten-month, executive training program that focuses on instructional alignment, operations, and winning support for reform from the teachers and their union, the school board, business leaders, and parents.[23] Academy graduates have held seventy-one superintendencies and over one hundred high-level leadership positions in school districts since the program began. Between 2009 and 2010, Academy fellows were chosen for 36 percent of the openings in large urban districts.

THE SELECTION

After rejecting the candidates Krinsky brought to them, committee members began recruiting others, which led them to Bersin. Collato had wanted to send to the school board a single finalist for an up-or-down vote. But the committee decided it had to send the board two names—Bersin's and that of a veteran superintendent from the East Coast.

Bersin was disappointed in the interview with the board. It was obvious that the board had not been involved in developing the criteria that would inform the crucial choice it had to make.

Ottinger and Lopez talked about the district's achievement gap between white and Asian American students and their African American and Latino counterparts. But Bersin said the discussion was superficial and did not involve any data to quantify that gap. He was told little about the state of the district's finances or academic program or the school board's perspective on it.

"When a new CEO is to be selected, it comes at the end of an extended evaluation process conducted by the company's board. At its core is a thorough review and analysis of the current status of corporate affairs relative to their competition that is prepared by the search team, either internal or external," Bersin said in an interview.

This data then guides the debate as to whether to stay the course and go with an insider or seek significant change by selecting an outsider. The corporate board's interviews with the candidates are based on that analysis. The candidates, operating with the same information, have a basis for determining whether they want the job or are suited for it. The interviews focus on potential strategic directions and initiatives. But that is rarely how superintendents are chosen, and it did not occur in Bersin's case.

Bersin said most of the questions he was asked were what he considered to be "beauty contest questions" about his personal attributes and background, rather than about what he would do as superintendent.

"These were fair questions, to be sure, but by themselves hardly the basis for selection of a chief executive officer for California's second largest school district. Aside from general proclamations about wanting to improve student achievement, there was no 'there, there' in the process."

Bersin was candid about his qualifications. "I don't know how I might have done were more demanded, but the fact remains that there was little press by the school board. While I have since learned an enormous amount about education and instruction, back then I knew virtually nothing. But it turned out that I did fine in discussing the educational issues because they never really came up in any substantive way."

Thinking back, Bersin believed that Ottinger, who did know these issues, deliberately chose not to raise them, for fear of exposing Bersin's weaknesses as an educator. But that didn't explain why John de Beck or Frances Zimmerman, both of whom were highly suspicious of him, did not use the opportunity to press Bersin on his knowledge of education issues. As he got to know them better, Bersin came to believe that, while Zimmerman and de Beck both had been teachers, they were not particularly knowledgeable about curriculum and instruction and not informed much at all about contemporary policy debates and research. "Because there is great breadth but little depth in the knowledge of instructional methods, pretty much anyone can play, and many do, in determining public education policy and operations," Bersin would observe later. Zimmerman was a former substitute teacher and old-fashioned liberal who represented the wealthy neighborhood of La Jolla. Her concerns were political. She asked him repeatedly why the board should choose a Caucasian noneducator to preside over a school district that was increasingly Latino, more than once implying that he was somehow anti-Hispanic. Bersin would later learn that her son-in-law was involved with La Raza, the Latino civil rights organization that had protested against Bersin's work on the border. During the interview, Bersin explained that he had worked with Mexican government officials as well as Latino leaders in the United States to come up with a balanced approach to the immigration problem. He reiterated his belief that quality public education was the surest route available to immigrant children for advancement; this observation was based on his own experience as the descendant of Russian Jews who had embraced education as their path to both survival and success.

De Beck, a board member and retired typing teacher who had been a union negotiator, also was dubious.

Neither de Beck nor Zimmerman voiced strong support, however, for the other candidate. Both wanted to go home and think it through. But Collato feared that anyone who left would consult with the teacher union or other interest groups and might even try to sabotage the entire process so that the committee would have to start over.

After leaving the interview, Bersin was called at home and asked to come back for more discussion. During the second interview Zimmerman, who had attended Radcliffe, asked him whether, while he was at Harvard, he had dated Radcliffe women. It seemed that her question was whether Bersin, whose wife is a former editor of the Harvard Law School Review and at that time a San Diego judge, was willing to work with smart women. His response was jocular. "I told Mrs. Zimmerman that I had dated Radcliffe women, but never successfully."

He thought to himself that in his many appearances before corporate boards of directors, he'd never been asked such a silly question. "What an absurd way to select someone who is arguably the most important civic leader in a community after the mayor and the police chief," Bersin said. "The emptiness of the urban school board–centered selection process, not just in San Diego, but across the country, is really quite astounding."

THE DECISION

It was early Saturday morning when Bersin left the hotel a second time and went home to bed. The board remained split 3–2. Finally, though, de Beck was persuaded to vote in public in favor of Bersin even though in private he was opposed. One reason he blinked, participants said, was that he was told he could help negotiate Bersin's contract. Some became convinced that de Beck thought he could scuttle the selection if he insisted, as he did, that Bersin receive a salary lower than what Pendleton was being paid. Bersin did not know he was being offered a lower salary. Even if he had, he would have accepted the job. Money wasn't what had motivated him to apply.

Zimmerman was persuaded to abstain. But she was not happy. She had bitter, vicious words for both Ottinger and Lopez as they left the hotel. She called Ottinger a "tool" of the business community and Lopez a "box checker," apparently meaning that he was only nominally Latino and that he had acted in a way that was detrimental to the interests of Latinos.

When Ottinger awakened Bersin with a telephone call to offer him the job, he told Bersin he had good news and bad news. The good news was the board had voted in his favor. The bad news was that he had strong support only from three of the five board members. Bersin said that when he relayed the news to his wife, Judge Lisa Foster, she asked, "Which three?" Told that Lopez was on his side, he agreed to take the job.

Bersin's experience as a corporate lawyer and adviser to boards of directors told him that a divided board did not give him a strong foundation on which to construct ambitious reforms. But he believed his experience as a dispassionate negotiator and his long record as a union supporter would enable him to heal the rifts on the board and in the community. He also took heart in the fact that all five of the board members were Democrats and that he had long been active in the party as well.

"While I understood completely that personalities and personal relationships are not enough to bring about change, they often are a necessary condition," he said. "Given my history of brokering truces, assembling coalitions, and bringing people together, I believed that a strong reform program could be developed and a consensus on the board built around it."

This assessment, he would ruefully say later, "turned out to be entirely wrong."

THE ANNOUNCEMENT

When the board announced its decision the next day, Zimmerman expressed her opposition, though she had abstained. "I am deeply troubled by the hurried, pressured, and secretive process the board experienced in making its final decision," she said, though she had voted three times to support that process. She later sued Korn/Ferry unsuccessfully to get the firm to release a full list of the candidates who had been considered and the reasons they were not selected.

The very process that had been designed to be nonpolitical had, in fact, reinforced the us-versus-them divide on the board and left those in the minority feeling shut out. That fueled the unrelenting campaign by de Beck, Zimmerman, and the San Diego Education Association to delegitimize Bersin and have him removed.

The union's opposition quickly became apparent. Even as Bersin and Ottinger stressed the need for change right after the selection was announced, teacher union president Marc Knapp said that the district should keep moving down the path it was already on and that he expected Bersin to follow that lead.

Still, the public meeting at which Bersin was introduced was welcoming and upbeat. "We have no more important issue on the agenda of our community than the education of our children," Bersin said. "Everyone in San Diego and around the country recognizes that our children and their education is what we pass on, what our community will be, and what our country will become."

"I pledge to you my heart, my mind, my soul, my spirit, my energy, and everything else to make your choice what you want it to be in terms of performance and achievement for our children. The situation . . . is full of hope."

Bersin would later say that he not only believed in public service, but he also believed he could draw on all of the talent in the schools to change the system. "I wasn't about to take a job that I thought was undoable," he said. "I was getting too old to go tilting at windmills."

After he'd left the post, he would advise others considering a job offer from a deeply divided board in a district with a hostile union not to accept it. "If one's goal is to be a caretaker and preside over an existing state of affairs, then the political situation on the school board is of less importance. Mounting a major reform, however, should take place in the context of a broad community consensus that is reflected by the school board or mayor and by their choice of superintendent."

To be successful, he would later say, nontraditional superintendents need to have a well-defined point of view, a team largely made up of outsiders, and a political base outside of the school district. "I am glad that I do not have to make the decision about whether, had I known then what I know now, I would have taken the job. I answer that question differently on different mornings. Nonetheless, we did manage to maintain a one-vote majority on the school board for seven years, and this bought time for important change and for the first real existent proof that deep instructional reforms could be achieved in large urban school districts."

CHAPTER TWO

The Transition

"We Will Stumble . . . but We Will Do It"

Superintendents who are new to a school district should request an interim period between the school board's decision to hire them and the day they officially begin working. If the school board has not analyzed the district and its needs, the new leader needs to do that prior to stepping into the office. The tendency is for superintendents to immediately get bogged down in operational details. An interim period allows the leader to find out where the community would like the district to go and how much change the politics will stand. Then the leader needs to lay out a plan of action and hire a talented team prepared to carry it out. Leaders need to be sensitive to internal and external politics and make sure to heed those who can provide insights as to the current needs of the district. But leaders should also look outside for accomplished professionals, whether they have an education background or not.

Bersin was chosen in March, but he would not be sworn in until July 1. Bertha Pendleton would finish up the school year, and he would wrap up matters at the U.S. attorney's office. But Bersin did not intend to just wind down. He knew that he had been given an opportunity to get fully prepared for the duties that lay ahead. He wanted to become familiar with the district, immerse himself in education issues, seek out experts nationally, strengthen his position politically, and create a community-wide sense of urgency. That sense that something had to be done, he hoped, would prepare the community for the magnitude of the changes he needed to make.

"No exceptions, no excuses," Bersin would say at his early public appearances, referring to the need to improve the achievement of all students. Sounding like a trial lawyer giving a staccato closing argument, he said at one such appearance: "We will stumble. We will make mistakes. We will start over again. We will debate fiercely. But we will do it together. Nothing else counts."

In one of his first interviews, Bersin told *Education Week*, the national weekly publication, that he planned to "listen, listen, listen and learn, learn, learn" during his first weeks on the job.[1] That is the standard answer new superintendents give, but that phase usually lasts months, not weeks. Bersin knew that his supporters in San Diego's civic and business community wanted bold action. Bersin's agenda was already clear in his mind. He would focus on improving student achievement first and foremost, while getting the public engaged in the schools and cutting excessive administrative costs.

"Leadership involves imagining a future state, thinking through the steps it will take to get there, and then executing on each of the steps," Bersin believed.

> Flexibility on a firm foundation is critical, because the world often talks back and events rarely play out entirely as imagined. Kicking off change, then, is like playing chess. You have to decide which pieces to move, how and when to move them, and project what is going to happen when they're moved. But such strategic thinking, while critical to political success, is given far too short a shrift in education. Instead, new superintendents allow themselves to become bogged down in day-to-day decisions, and are able to devote little time or energy to the steps necessary to make their well-thought-out plans a reality. Handling the transition well is crucial to setting the stage, establishing expectations, and leaving first impressions.

UNDERSTANDING THE DISTRICT

Bersin took a temporary office at the district headquarters but assured the local newspaper that Bertha Pendleton would be in charge until her last day of work.[2] Pendleton offered to meet with him weekly to discuss district matters, and he accepted. But he didn't think the meetings helped him learn what he needed to know, so he quit requesting them. The only information he was offered to help him get started was a seven-page memo that contained little more than statistics about the district's demographics, size, and scope.

Not getting help from the inside, Bersin brought in a consultant to map out the various district offices and what they did. The district had no money to pay for that help. But, at Bersin's request, local business leaders had set up a management fund to be used at his discretion for such purposes. He also scheduled a dizzying swirl of meet-and-greet visits with civic associations, churches, each of the district's five bargaining units, and ethnic groups in the community. He was met at some of his meetings by protesters from the La Raza Rights Coalition, a group of Latino activists who were opposed to Bersin because of his work as U.S. attorney. Though he was well known, he needed to reintroduce himself to the community in a new role, as an educational leader. He convened town hall meetings in each of the five school board members' districts. At one of the meetings, he compared the school district to a ship's hull encrusted with barnacles. "We must begin the process of scraping off each barnacle, piece by piece," he said.[3]

He also was aware that he was closely identified with the business community, which caused many educators to doubt his understanding of public schools and their purpose. Many educators are ambivalent about business leaders' interest in schools. They welcome gifts from private enterprise, but they resist making schools more businesslike, arguing (as if anyone would disagree) that teaching children is not like manufacturing widgets. They worry that efficiency will result in a bare-bones operation that cannot meet students' needs. That is a legitimate concern. But the problem is that the argument is used indiscriminately to protect programs that add little value as well as those that do. Attempts to cut ineffective programs are greeted by claims that education is being cut, suggesting a failure of will, rather than a decision to use scarce resources in more effective ways.

Bersin didn't have such qualms. While he never thought "education was a business," he also never hesitated to voice his belief that solid principles of management should be applied in school districts. Nevertheless, to counter the instinctive wariness, Bersin did all he could to assure everyone that student achievement, good teaching, and equity were his primary concerns. Naively, he thought that message and his reasonableness would resonate with educators.

As another way to ingratiate himself, Bersin formed a transition committee that included the heads of the teacher union, the nonteaching employee unions, the administrators' group, Pendleton's former deputy, and representatives of parents and ethnic communities. "The committee was a way to bring together the unions and other elements of the community and district to forge a show of unity," Bersin would say later in an interview. "The objective was to calm the potential opposition from the very beginning by reaching out and listening to those who had felt left out."

But the committee met only one time. That meeting, Bersin recalled later, was largely a complaint session rather than a constructive discussion. He laid out the central concepts that guided his plan for reorganizing the district bureaucracy and gave the committee a chance to respond. Having listened to the group, Bersin believed his obligation to the committee, and its usefulness, ended. It had served its purpose, in his view.

Bersin consulted many individual community leaders as well, but only informally. He was wary of creating a formal advisory mechanism. As he was preparing to take over district leadership, Bersin discovered more than one hundred advisory committees with "indefinite missions and undetermined tenures." The advisory committees were useful to previous superintendents because they were seen as proxies for the various racial and interest groups in San Diego and could give district decisions a patina of legitimacy. However, rather than offering authentic input and feedback, Bersin said later, committee members came to see themselves as power brokers who could block action if they protested loudly enough.

"I did not consider them to be the voices that would lead to change," Bersin said. "They had not in the past, and they would not in the future. They were the groups the district bargained with for buy-in. People would say if so-and-so of the Latino Coalition agrees, then the Latino community is with us. If the African American newspaper *Voice & Viewpoint* editorialized favorably, then the African American community was with us. What did that mean? Not very much at all."

"Different groups have different needs," said Bill Flores, a member of the Asian Pacific Islander Advisory Council.[4] Bersin rejected that idea. As he would say many times during his tenure, the best way to advance the interests of any group of students was to give them every opportunity to succeed academically. In his analysis, these groups contributed to the fragmentation of the district and often stood in the way of progress. They established parallel discussions that took time and attention away from the central course of reform. "When you empower a group as an advisory committee, it carries with it a certain grant of authority that should be jealously guarded, particularly in the context of reform," he said. Over his first eighteen months in office, Bersin would disband all of the committees and task forces not required by law.

To build support for his agenda, he formed an Academic Achievement Council that included former advisory committee members, activist academics at local colleges, researchers, and business and civic leaders. He wanted the committee to focus on the district's priorities.

A DEEP FRUSTRATION

In addition to the review by the consultant, Bersin sought information internally by interviewing about twenty of the district's top leaders. In those interviews he learned about such intricacies as how federal Title I compensatory education funds were distributed. He also was learning these individuals' talents and shortcomings, looking to identify those who would be assets in his administration. Not surprisingly, those he interviewed were more forthcoming in private than they were in public, which made clear to him some of the obstacles he would face.

Bersin asked those he interviewed to prepare for him confidential "briefing memoranda" about the district. He also began receiving unsolicited memos, most anonymous, some cynical, and all reflecting a deep frustration. Many of these anonymous messages from teachers as well as administrators communicated "a deep sadness, a disturbing fatalism at the root," he said.

"This district never met an initiative it didn't like."

"Another top-down initiative."

"We have 'tons' of standards handed to the elementary teacher, who responds: 'How am I supposed to address all of these in 54,900 minutes over 180 days? It will take me two months just to read them.'"

"Why do you expect it to be logical? This is San Diego City Schools."

"Another new program! How about support and follow-up for the ones we already have to do?"

"Another planning meeting to plan to plan for planning meetings."

"Do real people work in Human Resources? Even the secretaries have voice mail."

"We establish, in an inclusive manner, and with much 'fanfare,' our district mission statement, goals, and objectives. Then, we set them aside and go about the business of running the district."

Incompetence was tolerated, as if there were nothing that could be done about it. The technology system, which should have provided key data on student achievement and other functions, was nonfunctional; everyone Bersin talked to complained about it, but no one knew how to fix it. (When he asked to see the computer servers, the head of information systems tried to hide the fact that he wasn't even sure where they were. That administrator was fired as of Bersin's start date, a decision that was widely applauded but only in the stairwells or behind closed doors.)

Many of the district employees he spoke with used what Bersin considered to be meaningless buzzwords: freedom and flexibility with accountability, data-driven decision making, "first cabin" human capital development, and "world class" customer service. But these vague concepts did not drive decisions. Moreover, there were no metrics that would define success or even measure progress. One example was the district's career and technical education program. The district was supposed to develop apprenticeship and training programs in partnership with local unions. But these activities were not connected to any other district initiatives and had a life of their own.

BUILT FOR INACTION

Bersin became convinced that, as it was then constituted, the district was incapable of taking bold action. Under Pendleton, seventeen separate organizational functions reported to the superintendent, making the bureaucracy all but unmanageable. Bersin used the metaphors of stovepipes or silos to describe the parallel mini-bureaucracies that carried out their responsibilities virtually independently. The bureaucracies enforced rules in the schools and also served the members of the school board, carrying out their projects and providing them with information. This dynamic led to turf battles and competition for resources. The different parts of the administration ended up working at cross-purposes. "People were unanimous in their acknowledgment of this defect in the organization but clueless as to how they might go about building a coherent system," he said. "The result was a culture of finger pointing that reacted rather than acted. Principals blamed parents, teachers blamed principals, and all of them blamed the kids. Everyone was a victim and no one took responsibility for anything."

Bersin perceived a profound sense of discouragement. The schools were not succeeding, and the people who went to work in them every day knew it. That feeling had grown as the district's demographics had changed from 80 percent Anglo and middle class twenty years earlier to nearly the inverse of that. By the mid-1990s, two of three students came from families living below the poverty line. But the schools and teaching had hardly changed. "There was a sense, not articulated but almost tangibly present, of being overwhelmed by the utter transformation of the district's demographics."

A CULTURAL CHANGE FROM INACTION TO ACTION

Bersin had to change the culture of inaction to one of action. He retitled his position "Superintendent of Public Education," signaling that the person with that title focused on education rather than operations, as the more common title, "Superintendent of Schools," implied. One of his first decisions was to hire no-nonsense retired Marine Colonel Terry Smith as his chief of staff. Bersin had worked closely with Smith on multiagency task forces to fight drug trafficking along the border and regarded him as an exemplar of military discipline and focus. The role of the chief of staff, in Bersin's plan, was to make sure that policy decisions were carried out and to monitor progress. The position was new to the school district and unusual in education. Smith would be put in charge of a small executive committee, and the executive committee would be the mechanism by which Bersin would wield power.

Soon after Smith joined the district, he and Bersin sat through a three-and-a-half-hour meeting of Pendleton's cabinet. The entire meeting was spent wordsmithing reports to be presented to the school board at its semimonthly meetings. It seemed to Bersin like a colossal waste of time.

The lack of action was symbolized, in Bersin's mind, by what he saw when he and Smith happened to enter the rear employee entrance to the district headquarters together. They passed an enormous dumpster, reeking of garbage and swirling with flies. "What the hell is this?" Bersin said to Smith. "This is what greets our people every day? Colonel, you have your first order on day one. Get it out of here!" To Bersin, the interaction embodied the role Smith would play. It also illustrated the district's inability to handle even operational basics in a sensible fashion.

Smith set about interviewing district employees, looking for those willing to reexamine how the district did its business. Karen Heinrich, who was Pendleton's secretary and who would become Bersin's right hand, recalled being interviewed by Smith. "He would ask me straightforward questions and after I'd answered, he'd say, 'What's the foundation for that?' I usually couldn't give him an answer. People had been doing things the same way for such a long time in a certain way, but they didn't know why."[5] Some of the "old guard," who had been with the district for decades, weren't open to change. They got the message and retired or moved on.

On the other hand, a number of Pendleton's top administrators became "crucial members of our team," Bersin emphasized. The chief administrative officer, controller, and budget director all were Pendleton holdovers. All of the top instructional roles also would be filled initially by people from within the district.

Pendleton's top deputy, Frank Till, was one such example. Till had been a candidate for the superintendent's job and was close to Knapp, the president of the teacher union. In the interest of continuity, Bersin asked him to stay on for a year as a critical source of information about the organization. "In exchange for an explicit commitment of loyalty and hard work in the transition, I promised him I'd support him for a superintendency elsewhere," Bersin said. "It was clearly a double-edged sword. But the fact that I kept on Till and the others made it plain for people in the district that I was bringing change, but not ignoring continuity." He fulfilled his promise to Till, who moved on a year or so later to become a superintendent in another district.

BRINGING IN OUTSIDE TALENT

But Bersin also brought in top executives from outside of education to quick-start change. He observed that nontraditional superintendents may have a fresh perspective on education's problems, but that won't matter if they rely only on people who have been professionally acculturated in that world. "My job was to identify first-rank talent in the organization or recruit it from outside, set the strategic direction for the district, establish an ethical tone and a moral purpose, allocate resources, and then get out of the way," he said. "I micromanage only rarely and even then only temporarily. If it happens more often, then I've selected the wrong executive." Such a results-oriented management style intimidated those who had grown accustomed to not being held accountable for their actions.

Over the next few years, Bersin would recruit people such as JoAnn Sawyer Knoll, an administrative law judge and former legal aid attorney, who became the district's general counsel. She would go on to serve as the chief ethics officer for the City of San Diego after the city was humbled by a series of fiscal and political scandals. Lou Smith, a retired rear admiral who had headed up the Navy Seabees, would become chief facilities officer and would successfully manage an enormous rebuilding program that won him national recognition; Admiral Ronne Froman, who as the so-called Navy Mayor had overseen all of the Navy's San Diego facilities, became the district's chief business officer. She would later take an early retirement to head the local Red Cross before becoming the chief administrative officer of the City. The head of catering for San Diego's historic U.S. Grant Hotel, Gary Petill, took over the district's food services and would create a model of efficiency and good nutrition. Bersin hired Deberie Gomez, who had worked in the Fresno and Dallas school districts, as head of human resources. Not only was the team accomplished, it was diverse: by gender, race, ethnicity, and experience.

CHANCELLOR OF INSTRUCTION

The most important job Bersin had to fill was one that hadn't previously existed. He had to find a successful educator to lead the district academically. Bersin was well aware that he was not an educator. He needed someone to help him. And he wanted someone who had a track record and a national reputation, someone who could help him develop a theory for how to attack what he saw as his ultimate goal: improving overall student achievement while narrowing gaps between groups. He knew that he would have to rely heavily on this person and that it was important that he have a strong professional relationship with this individual. He began asking people he respected for recommendations of candidates.

Soon after accepting his position, Bersin traveled with Ira Krinsky, the headhunter, to visit the Harvard Graduate School of Education. Bersin had been an undergraduate at Harvard, and Krinsky had received his doctorate in education there. Krinsky arranged for Bersin to meet several of the education school's best-known professors. Bersin was looking for information about how to overhaul a school district academically and in his efforts had been struck by the paucity of research on the topic. The reforms gaining notice under nontraditional superintendents such as Paul Vallas in Chicago, John Stanford in Seattle, and Rod Paige in Houston seemed to Bersin to be focused on district operations rather than core educational practices. Vallas, formerly the city's budget manager, worked on closing an enormous hole in the Chicago schools' budget. Paige reorganized central office operations in Houston. General Stanford had rebuilt relationships with parents, the community, and the teacher union in Seattle. These were important changes, to be sure, but Bersin wondered about how they could affect student achievement.

While in Cambridge, Bersin met with Susan Moore Johnson, a Harvard professor who authored an important book called *Leading to Change: The Challenge of the New Superintendency.*[6] He learned from her that successful superintendents have to recognize that they have instructional, managerial, and political responsibilities. Larry Cuban, a former superintendent and widely published analyst of school reform, made a similar observation.[7] Citing Cuban, Larry Lashway wrote: "As instructional leaders, they bear ultimate responsibility for improving student achievement. As managerial leaders, they have to keep their districts operating efficiently, with a minimum of friction, yet taking risks to make necessary changes. As political leaders, they have to negotiate with multiple stakeholders to get approval for programs and resources."[8]

The idea of the multifaceted superintendency intrigued Bersin. He was confident he could perform the managerial and political duties. He would assign the instructional work to a chief academic officer who would report to him. During the Harvard visit, Bersin heard from various members of the faculty enthusiastic endorsements of the work of Tony Alvarado, who had briefly been a chancellor of the New York City schools in the 1980s. He had then led New York City's District 2, an economically and ethnically diverse area that stretched up the East Side of Manhattan. Alvarado had developed a national reputation for his focus on coaching teachers and building up principals' instructional leadership skills. Student achievement had risen rapidly, and District 2 had become one of the most successful in New York City. That work had attracted the attention of Harvard professor Richard Elmore and a colleague, Deanna Burney, who were impressed with the fact that Alvarado had shifted a huge share of his available resources to supporting the work of teachers and principals.[9]

Soon after the Harvard visit, Larry Rosenstock, whom Bersin would later help launch the highly regarded, nationally known San Diego charter school called High Tech High, brought Alvarado to see Bersin. Both native New Yorkers, Bersin and Alvarado "hit it off right away, intellectually and viscerally," Bersin said. Bersin then went to New York to visit some of the District 2 schools. "I didn't know precisely what I was looking for, but I liked what I saw—students on task, teachers engaged in questioning, an altogether intelligent view of teaching," Bersin said.

"It is essential to leadership that one never be fearful of hiring people smarter than you are," Bersin said. "It was clear that Tony was a brilliant innovator. I was taken by his singular focus on improving teaching as the vehicle for improving student achievement."

"It struck me that children's difficulties outside of school, whatever they were, were not within the power of the school district to attack or challenge directly. However, teaching was the district's core business and an organization had to be built around improving the quality of it."[10]

In District 2, Alvarado had drastically reduced the size of the central office bureaucracy and had used the savings to put specially trained and highly effective teachers, whom he called staff developers, into all of the schools to work directly with their colleagues. School principals were expected to visit classrooms on daily "walkthroughs" or "learning walks" to observe teachers. Principals were taught to deconstruct the lessons and discuss them later with the teachers. The visits were not evaluations; rather, they were meant to be an opportunity for professionals to collaborate on improvement. What also marked Alvarado's District 2 work was the adoption of a common approach to math and literacy instruction that was designed to build deep student engagement in the subject matter. Alvarado had accomplished all of this in partnership with New York's United Federation of Teachers. Union leaders there lavished praise on Alvarado and recommended him enthusiastically to Bersin.

But it wasn't clear that Alvarado was available. He had already decided to leave District 2. He had applied for the superintendent's job in San Diego. But, when he didn't get it, he decided to join Lauren Resnick at her famed Institute for Learning, which worked with principals across the country to help them become better instructional leaders. Resnick, an expert in cognitive science who was among the founders of the standards movement, had collaborated extensively with Alvarado and the two were good friends. Alvarado was disinclined to move to California. But Bersin was persuasive and accommodating. "I just wouldn't take 'no' for an answer," he said.

Bersin and Alvarado sealed the deal over lunch with Resnick at a restaurant in La Jolla, an affluent community that rises into the coastal hills from a cove on the Pacific Ocean on the north side of San Diego. It also began what would be one of the most talked-about, controversial, and scrutinized partnerships in American education, linking the careers of an outsider to education and a successful, nationally recognized career educator.

Bersin gave Alvarado the title of Chancellor of Instruction, and agreed to pay him the same salary he was earning. He also put him in charge of what he called the Institute for Learning, modeled after Resnick's center. The largely autonomous Institute would develop a districtwide curriculum, establish common teaching strategies, and provide professional development to teachers and principals to help them learn to use those strategies. Alvarado's title, his salary, and the Institute and the special status that came with it all reinforced Bersin's strategy to put teaching and learning in the forefront.

REORGANIZING THE BUREAUCRACY FOR ACTION

Bersin knew he couldn't just create the Institute within the existing bureaucracy and expect it to succeed. He'd noted that different parts of the central office were already competing for resources and were jealous of power. He needed to reorganize the entire management structure to make it leaner and, even more important, supportive of Alvarado's work.

He had studied the organizational charts of more than fifty school districts and concluded that in most of them too many functions of the operation reported directly to the superintendent. He decided to streamline the San Diego schools' management into three major areas. One area would provide administrative and operational support, to be headed up by the chief administrative officer, another new position he created. The CAO would oversee finance, administration, hiring, personnel, and business services, including transportation, food services, and facilities. The second operational unit was the Office of the Superintendent, which would be in charge of communications and community relations, legal services, school police, and educational services such as running libraries and buying instructional materials. This unit also would handle special education, which was operating under a state plan designed to remedy problems that had been the subject of lengthy negotiations. The third unit would be Alvarado's Institute for Learning.

The leaders of these three areas would form the executive committee to be led by Terry Smith, as chief of staff in the Office of the Superintendent. Alvarado and the CAO were coequal with Smith and reported to Bersin but, operationally, they went through Smith.

The chart had an unusual design—the schools were at the top, above the board of education and the superintendent and the rest of the administration. Bersin wanted it to be clear that the administration supported the schools and the work of principals and teachers. That administrative structure would change over time, as reform initiatives evolved. When Bersin unveiled the completed organizational chart, prior to his swearing-in, he said that "there will be two types of district employees: those who teach and those who support teaching and learning;

that's it."[11] This orientation also was reflected in the district's new twenty-word mission statement: "The *mission* of San Diego City Schools is to improve *student achievement* by supporting teaching and learning in the classroom." That statement replaced sixteen goals that had guided Pendleton.

The landscape of school reform is littered with complicated strategic plans replete with multiple goals and tactics. According to Bersin, "the problem with elaborate plans is they lead to confusion over who is to be accountable for interim steps, let alone achievement of the ultimate goal. This diffusion of responsibility means that, at the end, no one is accountable for anything. We chose, instead, to go with 'less is more' at the outset and hammered home the importance of student achievement, improving the quality of teaching, and developing the capacity in the system to provide a standards-based education."

Bersin had taken up his managerial duties by hiring new people and redrawing the organizational chart. He had addressed his educational responsibilities by hiring Alvarado and making the Institute so prominent within the larger organization. His third responsibility, according to Johnson's rubric, was political.

One source of political friction would turn out to be related to Alvarado and Bersin's decision to give him so much power. Alvarado had decided he didn't want to be a superintendent after being turned down for San Diego's top job. He had a fiery temper and was passionately outspoken about the injustices of unequal education. He also was impatient. He believed he'd found the answer to improving student achievement, and he wanted to try that answer out on a larger stage. He agreed to come to San Diego only after Bersin guaranteed him that he wouldn't have to deal with the delicate politics of urban education.

So, Bersin would handle that. In Bersin's view, it was his job to sell Alvarado's reforms to the school board, the union, and the community. "We both wanted him focused exclusively on the instructional challenge," Bersin said.[12]

Alvarado had some reputational baggage, however. He had shown poor judgment a decade earlier when, while head of the schools in New York City, he borrowed $80,000 from subordinates, lied on mortgage applications, and used a limousine service at taxpayer expense to get around town. "There was a time in my life when I engaged in activities that were inappropriate," Alvarado told the *San Diego Union-Tribune* when his hiring was announced.[13] "I made massive mistakes." He hoped that San Diego would give him an opportunity to turn that corner one last time.

But he did little to ingratiate himself. He commuted to San Diego weekly, running up enormous travel costs that were covered by the private fund provided by the local business community. In San Diego, Alvarado lived for free in a condominium in the exclusive area of Coronado Island. All of this was legal and publicly disclosed. But, when Bersin and Alvarado began making significant changes, and critics wanted to weaken them, Alvarado's living circumstances would make him a target.

For the moment, however, Alvarado's hiring, which Bersin announced at a press conference and luncheon in June, before he was sworn in, was celebrated locally and acknowledged nationally as a coup for San Diego.

BUILDING PUBLIC WILL AND ENGAGEMENT

Bersin was joined at the luncheon where he introduced Alvarado by elected officials, top university officials, and community and business leaders. "This is what we want," said Tyler Cramer, chairman of the Greater San Diego Chamber of Commerce education panel. "More accountability, better student test scores, and a lean administration."

Bersin had designed the guest list to show that he had widespread support among community elites. But more needed to be done to bolster his support among parents and teachers.

His strategy for doing that was to lead the campaign to convince voters to back the $1.81 billion school construction and repair bond, known as Proposition MM.[14] By putting himself in the forefront, making the case for Proposition MM, he hoped to gain a honeymoon during which he could launch a plan to improve the district's academics.

San Diego's schools, like those in many communities in California, had been neglected for many years. Falling ceiling tiles, leaking roofs and pipes, rotting wood, and failing electrical, heating, and ventilation systems were the rule, not the exception, at the school sites. Classrooms lacked electrical outlets, and schools were without adequate science labs and libraries. Almost every school was overcrowded, and on some campuses portable classrooms had overtaken playground space.[15] Bersin said the condition of the schools was not only disgraceful, but it also showed students that the community was indifferent to the quality of the learning environment.

Bersin thought that working hard at getting the community to back the bond issue was a way to reconnect them, civically, to the schools. "I was going to have to have a much higher profile," Bersin said of his decision to head up the bond campaign.

The decision was fraught with risk. Under California law, the bond issue had to gain a super-majority of more than two-thirds of the votes to be approved, and many were defeated. It would be particularly difficult in San Diego, which was known for its political conservatism.

Bersin had already spoken to numerous community groups about the bond. He'd gained the backing of key groups, including the San Diego County Taxpayers Association and the Greater San Diego Chamber of Commerce, by promising that if the schools were fixed, the district would commit money in its budget to maintain them.[16]

The bond would pass handily in November. But that victory also extracted a cost for Bersin and his reforms. His focus on getting it passed left him with little time to monitor the progress of the changes Alvarado was moving ahead with swiftly on the education side. This demonstrates once again that superintendents have to juggle their time among three different demands on their attention—instruction, management, and political leadership.

In May, Pendleton's supporters organized a farewell dinner for her and one thousand guests at the Town and Country Hotel in San Diego. It was a black-tie affair that cost $70 per person. Although little had been accomplished educationally under her leadership, speakers praised her without reservation. Naturally, Bersin and his wife, Lisa, attended.

Knapp, who had become president of the teacher union after leading the 1996 strike, lauded Pendleton for her tenure and for the spirit of cooperation he said had been established after the strike.

He joked that "what Alan Bersin doesn't know yet is that there are two superintendents in San Diego." Those in the room laughed, as did Bersin, who turned to Lisa and asked, in mock surprise, "Who's the other one?"

It was a lighthearted moment at an early point in a relationship that over the next five years would often be tense. But it also held portents that Bersin appreciated immediately. Everything he would do as superintendent challenged well-established power arrangements that had an almost geologic history to them. Knapp was issuing a warning to Bersin that he would have to fight to achieve what all those in the district claimed they wanted—the improvement of student achievement for minority and nonminority students alike.

CHAPTER THREE

The First Year

"The District Had Fragmented Into Near Anarchy"

If school district leaders set forth clear and measurable goals, establish a common curriculum, communicate a clear vision of instruction, and create the conditions under which teachers and principals can make that vision a reality in classrooms, they can play a crucial role in improving student achievement. This requires focus and coherence, standards, expectations, effective hiring, professional development opportunities, safe and secure buildings, and adequate supplies. When all of those elements are in place, instructional coherence is possible. When they are not, superintendents who try to impose their vision of instruction will face great resistance. Overcoming this resistance requires recentralization of authority over instruction to bring about coherence and then, through a sequence of decisions, delegation of decision making to the professional judgment of teachers and principals. Over time, a productive tension between the district and the judgments of educators who are held accountable for results should emerge.

As he talked to teachers, principals, and others prior to formally beginning his duties, what Bersin did not hear was a sense of urgency. He did not see a coherent, districtwide, goal-oriented, metric-driven strategy or system for improving teaching or increasing learning. Creating urgency and building such a system had to be his first priority.

But it was hard to know where to start. "Each of the district's 180 schools, and most classrooms within schools, had an instructional program unrelated to what was happening in the next classroom, let alone to classrooms across the district." The schools were using well over one hundred separate reading programs.[1] Students who learned to read in first grade from a teacher who emphasized phonics skills might well have a second-grade teacher who taught them to use picture clues to guess unfamiliar words.

The scattered approach to instruction was reflected in the haphazard professional development opportunities available to teachers. One school district administrator counted three hundred standalone training sessions, most of them one-shot workshops, in a single year, none of which was mandatory. "The fragmentation, atomization, and isolation demonstrated the lack of a district point of view regarding the curriculum or teaching," Bersin said.[2] In fact, the district had ceded decisions over professional development to teacher-dominated school site councils. This was a common situation in many large school districts. Though districts spend tens of millions on professional development, union contracts in many cities make such training optional and allow teachers to earn raises by attending whatever classes they choose. Though this has begun to change in urban districts, it is often still the case.

In San Diego, as in many districts, the instructional program, if one could call it that, was contained in "paper documents strewn all over the district, like so much litter, that offered little of substance. It was a Tower of Babel."[3]

Tony Alvarado put it this way: "The district was fractionalized . . . the different parts of the system were sending different messages. People were doing everything . . . an inch deep."[4]

Bersin said, "In the name of site-based decision making, the district had fragmented into near anarchy."

SITE-BASED DECISION MAKING

San Diego was hardly alone at the time in delegating all educational decisions to the schools, with no common set of expectations or norms. Experiments with site-based or school-based management were under way in Detroit, Minneapolis, Indianapolis, Des Moines, and many other cities.[5] The most radical experiment in devolving power over public education from the district to the schools had come a decade earlier when Illinois legislators, frustrated with a lack of progress in Chicago, created local school councils of parents, community members, and teachers and gave them the responsibility to hire, evaluate, and fire principals; review their school's improvement plan; and approve its annual budget. In 1997, the Illinois legislature, recognizing that school site management had gone too far, gave Chicago's mayor the power to appoint a board of trustees that would exercise oversight. Even so, that left most of the site councils' authority intact.

These arrangements arose from a sense that school districts were obstacles to reform rather than sources of innovation. Most large urban districts were then and continue to be bureaucratized, sclerotic, and bound by rules that stifle meaningful change. It seemed to many principals, policy analysts, and union and business leaders that it would be easier to improve schools than it would be to change a large urban district. Even dysfunctional school districts could boast of islands of success. Such schools usually were blessed with a strong principal willing and able to protect the school and its teachers from distracting central office intrusions. Good research had identified the elements of effective schools—a strong principal, a sense of shared mission among the staff, engagement, goals, and accountability. There was far less certainty at the time about how to make *all* of a district's schools effective.

Some districts, such as Sacramento and Charlotte-Mecklenburg, had gone against the tide in the mid-1990s and had imposed a uniform, districtwide curriculum. But elsewhere educators and business leaders continued to argue that decisions should be made as close to the front lines as possible. William G. Ouchi, a professor of management in the UCLA Anderson Graduate School of Management who was actively involved in school reform in Los Angeles, and who later wrote a book advocating the empowerment of principals, said that "the best way to achieve the goal" of improved student achievement "is through school-based decentralized decision making and increased community involvement in schools."[6]

Ouchi and other advocates of this approach often pointed to the schools in Edmonton, Alberta, in Canada as an example of where site-based management has worked. The leader of Edmonton's schools for many years was Mike Strembitsky, a nontraditional superintendent whom Bersin admired and would later befriend. In Edmonton at the time, principals controlled most of their budgets and could decide how many people to employ and in what jobs. They picked their own reading programs and their own staff training.[7] Attracted by the concept, many American educators and policy makers visited Edmonton to find out its secret.

But what they saw on their visits was a form of site-based management that was quite different from how it manifested itself in the United States. Even though the schools in Edmonton could choose their own reading program, the programs had to be aligned with a detailed curriculum mandated by the provincial government. Site-based management has not been a panacea there. Concerns over the district's graduation rate and less-than-stellar academic performance prompted a rebalancing of power between the schools and the central office. Principals were required to attend monthly, district-led training meetings along with their staffs, and to spend 50 percent of their time on instructional matters.[8] Schools were required to hit performance targets mandated by the provincial government. The district had far more influence in the schools than school-based management advocates in the United States had understood or explained.

Los Angeles, 120 miles to the north of San Diego, provided an example of how school-based management had failed. In 1991, dissatisfaction over poor achievement, racial disparities, and a rising dropout rate had led to the creation of an organization called LEARN (Los Angeles Educational Alliance for Restructuring Now). LEARN's role was to help principals and teachers work together with parents to reform their schools independent of the district office. But it had little effect. Los Angeles also was one of fifteen school-district recipients of a share of the $500 million Annenberg Challenge, the largest philanthropic gift ever to the public schools. As in a number of the recipient cities, the $50 million matching grant was directed toward helping "families" of Los Angeles schools improve their results. The school district itself played but a small role. An evaluation would later find that the project, which had little to do with improving instruction, had had no effect on student achievement. Maria Casillas, the leader of the organization set up to administer the grant in Los Angeles, said, "We would have accomplished more by now" had the organization had "a closer relationship with the [district school board] when we started."[9]

HISTORY OF SITE-BASED DECISION MAKING IN SAN DIEGO

San Diego had begun experimenting with school-site management in 1989, when Tom Payzant was superintendent. The teachers' contract negotiated that year created a joint district-union committee to improve professional development and another committee to review schools' restructuring proposals.[10] Payzant directed his administrative team to keep an open mind about the proposals, no matter how jarring. That contract also created school site governance councils that would accrue more and more power over the years. The 1996 teachers' strike further expanded the school site committees' role.

"Like schools all over the country, the schools got more power and the union prevented any additional accountability," said Ron Ottinger, referring to the local experience with site-based management. Ottinger's first job with the district had been to work with Payzant on the transition to school-based management.[11]

Bersin accepted the fact that in effective schools, just like any organization, the principal and teachers embraced a mission and a set of goals and worked together as colleagues to reach it. He wanted every school to be a learning community in which professionals collaborated with one another to address the needs of every student. The educators, in his view, should use their judgment and work together to enact the curriculum and tailor the specifics of their teaching to the needs of individual students. But he also believed that it was the job of the district to manage instruction. There was no contradiction in Bersin's mind. The district created an environment, or context, within which teaching occurred. That context consisted of standards, expectations, curriculum, and a point of view regarding teaching that was backed by resources and professional development opportunities. Within that context, teachers had to use their judgment, knowledge, and skill to serve the particular needs of their students. It would take a lot to convince the teacher union and many principals that the district had a legitimate role to play in shaping instruction. Indeed, it was the most difficult challenge of Bersin's time as a superintendent.

Bersin's views on education were shaped in large part by his own past. He'd had excellent educational opportunities in the public schools he'd attended in Brooklyn and believed that improving education for all was required for keeping the fabric of American society healthy. For disadvantaged children, who often lack strong adult support outside of school, Alvarado thought—and Bersin learned—that the quality of teaching is "decisive with respect to results." On this point, education research is clear. Teaching, particularly in urban districts, cannot be left to chance. Virtuoso teaching in some classrooms and schools will not suffice. The teaching in all classrooms has to be based on the best available knowledge and information, and must be constantly improving. It was, they believed, the only way to close the enormous achievement gaps in the district between the affluent and the poor, and between most white and Asian students on the one hand and most African American and Latino students on the other.

THE HEART OF THE MATTER IS INSTRUCTION

But most of the public school reforms in the twentieth century have amounted to little more than "tinkering around the edges" of schooling.[12] They failed to affect what Harvard education professor Richard Elmore calls the "educational core" and the University of Michigan's Deborah Ball and her colleagues call the "instructional core," by which both mean the interaction of a teacher and his or her students around academic content.[13]

Alvarado brought with him from New York a distinct view of teaching and learning derived from decades of research by cognitive scientists and other researchers who studied learning.[14] Teachers should set clear, ambitious goals for students and require them to think, not just recall. They should use a variety of strategies to give students many chances to learn and practice challenging material and help them monitor their learning. Teachers should assess students' progress by evaluating not just their answers to questions but also their thinking process and the work they produce. When students begin to fall behind, they should be helped to quickly catch up. Rather than offer lessons aimed at the middle of the ability span, teachers should work to move all children up from where they are to where they should be and beyond.

Just as important as the specific approach, however, Alvarado and others in New York, notably his deputy Elaine Fink, had fostered a culture in which principals and teachers worked together to learn and improve. That culture wasn't created overnight. Rather, it emerged gradually over Alvarado's eleven years leading the district, as he established a strong relationship with New York's United Federation of

Teachers. During that time, the district's academic performance rose from the middle of the city's thirty-one districts to the second highest. As the city became safer and more attractive to families, more affluent parents began sending their kids to the public schools, which contributed to increases in average achievement. There is no doubt, however, that instruction and learning improved.

But District 2 had only 24,000 students in several dozen elementary and middle schools. San Diego had 140,000 students attending 180 schools K–12. No district that large had ever attempted to manage instruction on the scale that was being contemplated in San Diego.

RESULTS HAD TO BE PRODUCED QUICKLY

Bersin anticipated resistance and he got it. The tradition of site-based management in San Diego was but one obstacle. He created another problem by not asking the teacher union to grant him permission to expand the district's role. This decision explains much of the opposition of the union during his tenure. The teacher union, critics in the alternative press, and his opponents on the school board interpreted his strategy of reforming the district from the top, rather than helping it bubble up from the bottom, as a grab for power rather than as a legitimate approach to districtwide reform. To Bersin, it was a step that was unavoidable, if controversial. He couldn't wait for the teacher union to give him the power to pull the district together. He had to take it and get things moving, and overcome the stifling embrace of the status quo. He believed, however, that if the district could get teachers to change their methods, even if reluctantly, they would eventually see results and become converts.

Improving student achievement "would require adult learning and a willingness . . . to engage deeply in that teaching and learning," Bersin said. The educators also had to accept responsibility for student achievement and believe that students "really can learn challenging material and important ideas. It's one thing to talk about it, but it's something else entirely to experience in your own classroom that, if you teach it well, your students will learn it."

Bersin believed that approach made sense instructionally, professionally, and organizationally. But it would work only if the district built an infrastructure to support it.

AN INSTRUCTIONAL INFRASTRUCTURE

It wasn't that the district had no power over schools. In fact, principals reported that, in many ways, they felt hamstrung by a district bureaucracy that strictly enforced rules and made sure every dime was accounted for properly. The district office ordered textbooks, regulated the nutritional value of school lunches, paid employees, operated bus routes, and oversaw as many as fifty education programs supported by public and private sources of funding, under different sets of regulations, in pursuit of specific, sometimes contradictory, goals.[15] None of that, however, had much to do with classroom instruction.

The district had been carved up into five semiautonomous subdistricts, each overseen by an assistant superintendent who, to be effective, had to compete with his or her peers for resources, prestige, and teachers. Bersin was told that, as a group, the assistant superintendents spent between 60 percent and 70 percent of their time responding to the complaints of parents and spent the rest putting out fires—patching a hole in a school budget, interceding in a personnel dispute, or interpreting a central office rule. They were like bureaucratic handymen who knew how to react to any problem that might arise.

The fact that many schools and students under their jurisdiction were performing badly rarely rose high enough on their personal to-do lists to merit their attention. That's understandable because that's not what they were asked to address. Also, improving student achievement was difficult and time-consuming. "They could not accept that as their mission because to do so would saddle them with responsibility for altering failure," Bersin said. "The cultural and political system through which they had risen had inoculated them against any such exposure. The defense mechanisms here, for individuals and the group, are mutually reinforcing and powerful indeed."

The defensiveness of educators about the limits of their effectiveness and uncertainty as to how to proceed is not hard to understand. Lacking a strong professional or technical core, educators cling to the status quo as a comforting refuge, the known as a bulwark against the unknown. Lacking the professional consensus that Bersin was familiar with as a lawyer, teachers are either forced to use materials that reduce their role to reciting a script or are left to their own inspiration and judgment, regardless of how little preparation they have had.

Most teacher preparation programs are not helpful. Teacher preparation at the 1,200 university-based programs (as well as the more than 140 nontraditional programs that have emerged over the past decade or so) across the nation could mean anything. In California, the state board of education had endorsed a set of academic standards, a framework for choosing textbooks that reinforced those standards, and tests to monitor students' progress. But the professors in the teacher education programs within the California State University system, which supplied most of the state's teachers, were protected by tenure and were under no obligation to prepare their graduates in a way consistent with state policy.

ORGANIZING THE DISTRICT AROUND INSTRUCTION

To make the challenge tractable, Bersin and Alvarado reorganized the San Diego district into seven "learning communities," each consisting of about twenty-five schools. The learning communities were not bound by geography. Each group included schools serving poor areas in the southern part of the district as well as schools in affluent areas such as San Carlos, University City, Tierrasanta, and La Jolla to the north.

Each would be led by an "instructional leader," a position Alvarado created. The job of these leaders would be to, literally, lead instruction, unlike the assistant superintendents they replaced, whose duties were largely administrative. They would be "the basic levers for change" to improve teaching.

Alvarado and Elaine Fink, who had been a driving force of reform in District 2 and who was brought to San Diego as a consultant to help establish the Institute for Learning, went looking for particularly effective principals to fill the new positions. Fink had become superintendent in District 2 when Alvarado left, but he and Bersin would soon recruit her to San Diego to work full-time. Fink and Alvarado eventually would marry in a ceremony presided over by Bersin's wife, California Superior Court Judge Lisa Foster.

CHOOSING THE INSTRUCTIONAL LEADERS

Carol Pike, the principal of a year-round elementary school of one thousand one hundred students, was among the first to be hired as an instructional leader. She was told to come to a meeting with Alvarado and Fink, who asked her about the needs of her students and how she met them. Thirty minutes after the interview, she received a phone call and was told she had been chosen to be one of seven instructional leaders, a position that she would hold until the jobs were eliminated in 2005, after Bersin had left the district.

"I hadn't applied for the job, I didn't even know there was a job, and didn't know what the job was," she said. She was told not to say anything to anyone because the school board had not yet approved the positions. But she was also told to be ready to travel the next morning to New York, to visit schools. "We were off and running."[16]

She recalls an image from that intense summer of "these two powerful men flying through the hallways and trying to put this thing together really, really fast."

Another principal selected as an instructional leader, Debbie Beldock, had a year earlier become principal of a school that was stuck in mediocrity. Yet the school's staff thought they were doing just fine. "The staff had been led to believe that it was all about the kids being at fault," she recalled. "But they weren't organized to be efficient or to look as a team at what children were able to do."[17]

Soon after Bersin was selected, Beldock attended a meeting at which he and his new chief of staff, Terry Smith, spoke. Beldock was impressed. "I remember thinking that here's this new superintendent who doesn't have an education background, but his social justice agenda was very clear, and he was very honest about having a different set of eyes and really wanting to make a difference in education." She also sensed that this new team was serious. One attendee asked what would happen if a principal didn't agree with the new approach. She recalled Smith's response: "We'll find replacements!"

When Beldock had what she called "the conversation" with Alvarado and Fink, she was asked "about how I was leading instruction, my strengths, areas where I needed support, how I went about ensuring that teachers took on leadership roles, how I ensured that poor kids were learning, and what I believed about their ability to succeed. I was asked, if I were leading principals, how I would support them. And I remember being asked, if someone wasn't making it, what would I do."

Once chosen as instructional leaders, the seven former principals participated in a whirlwind of preparation sessions that had them working twelve hours a day, sometimes six days a week. After visiting schools in New York they spent two long days in a hotel in Pittsburgh, absorbing the "principles of learning" developed by Lauren Resnick and then talking about how they would put these ideas into place in San Diego classrooms. They interacted with consultants on literacy from New Zealand and Australia who specialized in the approach to reading that Alvarado favored, which he said balanced an emphasis on teaching decoding and word recognition with developing students' writing and comprehension powers. The New York school visits, Beldock said, were "the best thing we could have done because it gave us a picture of what we were trying to get our schools to look like. I remember being so amazed at how engaged the students were and how high-level their discussions were, even though they lived in poverty just like our students."

Bersin went along on the training sessions. "He was allowing Tony to lead the instruction, but I'm certain he was already instilling in us his values," Beldock said.

"We were all so awestruck about everything," she said. "That summer was like euphoria. We had been selected to do this job. We were being appreciated, which was good for the ego. We were on such a learning curve, our eyes just glazed over."

GETTING INSIDE CLASSROOMS

The instructional leaders were working feverishly to, essentially, create their positions. They would be supervising principals who had recently been colleagues and would judge their performance based on how much improvement they saw in the quality of instruction. To do that, they would have to spend time in teachers' classrooms along with the principal and talk about the lessons and how they could be improved. That would require tact and diplomacy and negotiating, as well as firmness.

For all of the attention paid to academic standards, professional development sessions, principals' directives, memos handed down from the superintendent, recommendations from state department of education task forces, and every other effort designed to influence both what is taught and how it is taught, when the classroom door closes, the teacher is on his or her own. Penetrating that barrier must be done delicately. But, given the sense of urgency that Bersin felt, there was little time for the niceties of building consensus about the protocols to be followed.

The instructional leaders were taught to do what Alvarado and Fink had expected principals and staff developers in New York to do: know the approach to teaching well enough to be able to walk into classrooms and critique it in a way designed to spur improvement. These "walkthroughs" or "learning walks" were not part of teacher evaluations. They were meant to foster professional collaboration.

But this was a new job for principals. The instructional leaders had to teach them not only about the pedagogy the district wanted to see, but also what to look for on their classroom visits and a shared language that they could use to talk productively with their teachers. The point was to establish, over time, a shared understanding of good teaching. They anticipated—accurately, as it turned out—that simultaneously teaching the principals while the principals were observing teachers would produce tension and fear.

A NEW ROLE FOR PRINCIPALS

Instructional leadership had long been seen as a part of the principal's job. But what it really meant on a day-to-day basis had not previously been articulated, emphasized, or quantified. The first official discussion of the new role for San Diego's principals occurred during a two-day, back-to-school training session just before the start of school. Prior to that meeting, the principals "did not know that their jobs and their lives were about to change," Pike said. "They weren't going to be only managers any longer. They were going to be instructional leaders, and they would be judged on how much time they spent in classrooms and what their teachers were doing."[18]

Bersin welcomed all of the principals to the meeting at a local hotel and then turned the meeting over to Alvarado, who outlined the new administration's vision, expectations, and beliefs. The principals heard about the role of the instructional leaders, took a forty-five-minute tour through the district's new "literacy framework," and spent a half-hour discussing how to help English language learners. The afternoon was equally packed. That night the principals were treated to a reception and dinner on the yacht of Bill Lynch, a local philanthropist who was committed to improving education in San Diego County.[19]

The principals were told they were to require their teachers to spend no less than three hours each day on literacy lessons. They were to monitor the classrooms to make sure it was happening. They also were tasked with making sure teachers gained a deep understanding of the literacy framework as well as of the specific recommended teaching techniques, to which the principals themselves had just been introduced. In addition to providing training, principals were to spend two hours each day in classrooms, coaching and observing teachers. They were told they would be evaluated each year by the instructional leaders based on how precisely instruction in their school matched the vision of Alvarado and Fink.

"People were walking out bleary-eyed," Pike said of the August meeting. "We probably gave them too much."

CLASSROOM VISITS

When principals began making classroom visits a few weeks later, they stirred fear, resentment, confusion, and protests from teachers. Teachers worried that the principals would be evaluating them on their use of techniques they had not practiced, let alone mastered. The purpose of the visits was to help teachers improve; they were not meant to be evaluations. But the teachers were afraid nonetheless.

Marc Knapp immediately called Bersin to protest, claiming that the teachers' contract prohibited principals from observing classrooms without giving teachers advance notice. He also claimed that a letter Bersin had written to San Diego teachers about the new literacy framework constituted an unfair labor practice because it undermined the union's power. Knapp did not believe that the district had the right to decide which teaching methods or training courses would be most useful. In addition, he said principals could not require teachers to attend any training sessions. Obviously, if Knapp won this argument, Bersin and Alvarado would have to abandon their plans.

Bersin and Alvarado met with Knapp and the union's executive director at the end of September to discuss the union's concerns. In a memo to the district after that meeting, the union suggested that the classroom visits be phased in starting in 1999 after the principals and teachers had been fully trained. The union also wanted teachers to be given copies of any notes taken by the principal or the instructional leaders during their visits. A district legal analysis concurred. But Bersin still trusted his earlier judgment that change had to come quickly: "None of this would seem any less new next year when even more changes would be in store. Delay rarely translates into pain avoidance. To the contrary, the wisdom of Band-Aids suggests otherwise."

There were, in fact, no contract provisions restricting principals from observing classrooms or asserting influence over professional development. Knapp's protests, however, did underline a fundamental disagreement between Bersin and the union that would arise again and again during his tenure. To Knapp, teachers were the only legitimate instructional experts. They knew their students and their needs best. By definition, and by certification, they were qualified to make decisions about how best to help their students and should be empowered to do so. He was right, of course. Teachers are on the front lines in our nation's schools, and their expertise and judgments about what is possible in classrooms are critical to the success of efforts to improve student achievement.

But Knapp defined teacher professionalism with a tautology: a classroom teacher was a professional because he or she was a classroom teacher. Bersin and Alvarado believed expertise and effectiveness mattered. They also believed it was the role of the district to help principals and teachers develop that expertise.

"Rather than teachers operating as private practitioners on their own in their classrooms, we altered the norm to create a districtwide approach to teaching based on a common framework of skill and knowledge," Bersin said. "Quality teaching at scale would result from professional learning—with numerous opportunities for peer assistance, consultation, and review—rather than from even unusually talented teachers confronting challenges on their own."

BATTLE OVER LITERACY COACHES

These issues of control and power played out most explicitly in what became a very public battle over Alvarado's plan to hire expert teachers of literacy to serve as staff developers, as he had done in New York. The union leadership objected because there already was a provision in the union contract under which the district was to set up a system of peer coaches that would be largely controlled by the union. More fundamentally, Alvarado wanted the staff developers to help teachers learn the methods sanctioned by the district. Therefore, he wanted to hire as coaches only teachers who were expert in those methods. The union believed the peer coaches should help the teachers in whatever manner the teachers wanted.

The union leadership insisted that all teachers were essentially the same and that any credentialed teacher, by definition, was qualified for the role of coaching his or her fellow teachers on how better to teach children to read. Therefore, the school site governing councils alone should choose who would serve as a coach, based on seniority. Seniority, of course, is very much under attack now. It comes up in discussions of staff reductions as well as teacher assignments. It is blamed for a cycle that debilitates low performing schools, when more senior teachers leave as soon as they can claim a spot in a school that they prefer.

An agreement on the use of staff developers was finally reached in May, after eight months of negotiations. It was hailed on the editorial page of the local newspaper as a "historical educational reform." But neither Bersin nor Knapp was pleased. Knapp was disappointed that these positions would be used to support the teaching methods Alvarado favored. Bersin believed a potentially powerful lever for improving instruction had been weakened.

But it also taught him a lesson in dealing with the union specifically and public education more generally. As an attorney, he was experienced with tough negotiations that often involved overheated rhetoric. But in litigation, whatever the rhetoric, the evidence and facts ordinarily would determine the outcome. That did not appear to be true in education.

"I learned that you could make arguments based on what's good for kids and pure common sense. You could appeal to third parties, expecting them to decide the matter on the merits, and you could still lose because of outside pressure from the unions which was calculated to bully and intimidate," he said. "It was a turning point for me. In the first year we tried to negotiate solutions to various problems, and I came to realize that if we negotiated everything we'd never get anything done."

PRINCIPALS CONCERNED AND FEARFUL

Teachers and their union weren't the only ones upset with the centralization of power over teaching—principals were worried as well. They shared teachers' fear that they'd be judged on their mastery of something they were just learning to do. A memo from the Administrators Association of San Diego asserted that Bersin and Alvarado were moving too fast, and principals were being denied time to "internalize, digest, and invest in this concept."[20] Principals were stressed, morale was low, Bersin and Alvarado were ruling by "fear and intimidation," and "communication within the district was almost non-existent," the memo said. "It's just slightly possible that 'the way we've been doing things' has a historical evolution which may actually make it the 'right way.'"[21]

In response to the criticisms, Alvarado formed a planning council, whose members included principals, teachers, and representatives of the teacher union and the administrators' association. The first meeting was convened in early October. Afterward, Alvarado circulated a memo that summarized that meeting. "Some reactions to programs and practices of the first 30 days of the school year have shown that we have not done an acceptable job in communicating our purposes and our direction," the memo began.[22]

The memorandum said the school visits by the instructional leaders and principals would continue. But assurances were given that the expectations for teachers would be phased in and that the instructional leaders would be looking only for progress, not perfection, in the use of the new methods.[23]

To that memo was attached another one from the instructional leaders, explaining that the school visits were not meant to be adversarial. They were to be "honest exchanges of perceptions, questions, and suggestions that will build the capacity for all professionals to learn." Even so, the visits also were a way to hold "the principal accountable as an instructional leader" and the instructional leader "accountable as a supervisor."[24] In other words, the instructional leaders were to coach the principals but also evaluate them, based on what was going on in classrooms.

The instructional leaders, however, were themselves uncertain. "It wasn't until we had to get into the schools and implementation that we realized this is hard, and that we were unclear about how to do this," said Pike.

"UNCOMPROMISING MORAL PURPOSE"

Despite those tensions, Ann Van Sickle, one of the original instructional leaders, recalls from the early days a sense of "uncompromising moral purpose" expressed by Bersin and Alvarado. "There was a sense of urgency, that we can't wait, children need immediate attention, and we can't waste a child's life. We had to begin to get better."[25]

Raising student achievement was the preeminent concern. Of less importance was "whether people [were] getting along and liking each other," Van Sickle said. The heightened expectations caused stress. "There was a lot of self doubt . . . and everyone across the system felt that, because the expectations were raised so quickly," she said. "That was the right thing to do. But it did create strong feelings."

Yet, even as Bersin tried to create both urgency and instructional coherence, there were numerous other instructional issues to be addressed. He did not have the luxury of creating a system from scratch. He had to operate the system even as it was changing. This is something that reform-minded superintendents have to keep in mind.

DEALING WITH A MANDATE OVER SPECIAL EDUCATION

One example was a conflict over the district's special education program, which was in state receivership and answered to a special court-appointed master who monitored its adherence to a corrective action plan. The state had intervened the year before because the district program had been instructionally weak and unresponsive to parents of students with special needs.

Compliance dealt mostly with process issues rather than educational issues. Like many others, Bersin suspected that many elementary school students who were considered learning disabled actually were victims of weak instruction. "Eventually, we tamed the politics by focusing on teaching and learning for special needs children in ways that were responsible and that delivered appropriate instruction." Special education programs consumed about 20 percent of the district's budget and served only 10 percent of the students, but, Bersin said, "at least we were getting more identifiable educational benefits for our students."

Even though the district was taking action to improve its special education program, parents and their advocates turned out at most school board meetings in the early years to make long, passionate speeches about the need for more services. A few years later, some parents continued to complain that the school district was not complying with the special education law. The state department of education again sent a team of inspectors to investigate these complaints. They discovered a few violations but no systemic failures. Nonetheless, in response to lobbying by advocates, the state department once again ordered a sweeping remedy.

But Bersin, now confident in the quality of the program, had the district file a lawsuit against the State of California to block enforcement of the new corrective action plans. The district prevailed in significant part on the grounds that the proposed remedy would change practice across all schools and cost millions of dollars without evidence that it was necessary or calculated to improve student achievement. The lawsuit effectively marked the end of massively intrusive state-imposed special education plans in California.

READING WARS

Another controversy arose over the "balanced literacy" philosophy of teaching reading that Alvarado brought to San Diego. The teaching of reading in California had become controversial in the mid-1990s. When the National Assessment of Educational Progress began reporting scores by state, California ranked near the very bottom with Louisiana and Mississippi. The poor showing was blamed on a progressive teaching method known as "whole language" that had been embraced by the state department of education and most school districts, including San Diego. Under this approach, teachers introduce students to reading using books with large pictures that gave them clues to the words on that page. The reasoning was that students would pick up enough knowledge about letters and the sounds associated with them that they would eventually be able to identify new words without using pictures.

The low test scores triggered the so-called reading wars in California and led to state policy decisions in the 1990s regarding standards, assessments, teacher training, professional development, and textbook purchases that elevated the importance of systematic, explicit phonics instruction in literacy lessons. Comprehension, fluency, vocabulary development, and other aspects of reading were not to be ignored but had to be built on a solid foundation of word recognition skills.

Advocates coalesced into opposing camps. The phonics camp had gained control over most of the policy apparatus in Sacramento. But the whole-language crowd held sway in universities and many school districts.

Bersin found himself in a difficult spot. "We understood the importance of decoding and word study, but we couldn't give up the idea that students needed to understand right from the beginning what they were reading and had to be taught to do so," Bersin said.

In Sacramento, Bersin learned that members of the state board of education, including a teacher from San Diego, thought that balanced literacy was just a new name for whole language. This faction pilloried as whole-language advocates two of Bersin's strongest supporters, businessman Bill Lynch and Scott Himelstein, who directed Lynch's charitable foundation and led a "San Diego READS" campaign that would place 1.5 million books into the district's classrooms. Phonics advocates also included a small but vocal group of parents who regularly showed up at San Diego school board meetings and in Sacramento to demand that the district purchase phonics-oriented textbooks to the exclusion of all else.

Bersin was amazed at how ideological the matter had become, describing it as "a modern-day war of the roses between religious sects." He rejected extremism as a matter of politics—"I can't stand witch hunts of any kind"—but as he learned more about the theory and practice of literacy instruction, he decided that as a matter of educational principle he would resist the trap of falling into the camp of one side or the other. He insisted instead on the need for balance and excellent teaching.

Bersin worked hard politically in Sacramento to preserve San Diego's independence on curricular and instructional matters. He asked the state board to give him time and to judge San Diego's literacy efforts solely on the basis of results, agreeing that these could be measured by the state's tests. "The truce with influential state board members was straightforward: as long as progress was occurring on the CSTs (California Standardized Tests), which it did for seven consecutive years, they'd leave us alone. The bargain was made and kept—and kept the ideologues at bay from both ends."

ENGLISH LANGUAGE LEARNERS AND BILINGUAL EDUCATION

Perhaps the most contentious of the curricular issues that arose in the first year of Bersin's superintendency was the question of how to best serve the needs of English language learners. Bersin, a fluent Spanish speaker, believed the best approach was to teach children in both English and Spanish, so that they would be bilingual as adults. That point of view initially made Bersin a hero among advocates of bilingual education, who thought that students could learn academic content in Spanish and gradually become fluent in English. But Bersin later realized the theory wasn't working. As a practical matter, few teachers were able to teach effectively in two languages, and only a handful of students were transitioning from their primary language to English. By Bersin's third year as superintendent, the district was using English language immersion as its approach.

Bersin's change of heart led to many tense meetings with the traditional bilingual education advocates, who were led by professors from the local state university and bilingual teachers in the district whose spoken English was not good enough for them to use it for teaching. They organized scattered protests at school board meetings and later conjured up a purported demonstration of no-confidence in Bersin that attracted little attention. "We had a group of diehards who approached this as ideology coupled with naked employment self-interest. They were more interested in promoting cultural pride and protecting their pocketbook than they were in educational proficiency, and we parted company," Bersin said.

In 2006, after he was no longer superintendent, Bersin was appointed by Governor Arnold Schwarzenegger to the state board of education. By that time, evidence of the best way to teach students not fluent in English had settled the matter. No one in the district or in Sacramento policy circles contended any longer that primary language instruction was a viable educational strategy.

Each of these disputes—over the teaching of reading, special education, and bilingual education—had the potential to undermine the instructional coherence that Bersin and Alvarado were trying to create. "These are consequential matters, and district leaders have to be prepared to keep their focus on building system capacity to deliver good teaching and not to avoid asserting a point of view on curricular issues when something real is at stake," Bersin said. He prevented that from occurring but had to use considerable political capital and substantial energy and time to do so.

FIRST DEVELOPMENT OF EXPERTISE, THEN DELEGATION OF RESPONSIBILITY

By the end of the first year, Bersin and Alvarado had established the district's role in selecting curriculum, teaching methods, materials, professional development for principals and teachers, and even in determining how classroom furniture was to be arranged. But Bersin soon began to realize that once principals and teachers had embraced the district's instructional program, he would have to give them more freedom to apply it to the needs of individual students. A command-and-control approach would only work for so long. "Any centralized reform will falter and eventually fade away, unsustained and uninstitutionalized," Bersin said. Once the district has built up the instructional capacity of educators to teach the district curriculum and made its expectations for student growth clear, "faculty collaboration and collegiality must become the primary drivers of further progress." In other words, Bersin saw centralization as a phase that was necessary but insufficient to achieve the gains in student learning that needed to occur. Eventually, the district had to assume that the educators had developed enough capacity to work on their own, to achieve common aims.[26]

In former Houston school board member Don McAdams's 2006 book, *What School Boards Can Do*, Bersin described the situation as follows:

> The heuristic goal here is to make students the engine of their own learning by teaching them the skills of critical thinking, clear communication, and individual responsibility. Taking the work deep into the classroom and into the marrow of our teachers' practice and students' store of self knowledge can only be accomplished at the school site under the leadership of principals who understand this aim and have mastered their role of implementing continuous improvement.
>
> The work at the school site starts with the development of a school improvement plan derived from data analyses and designed to improve student achievement by focusing on specific instructional strategies for groups of children or individual children as needed. The work at the system level begins with the design, development, implementation, and oversight of a site-based budgeting system. This will have a dramatic effect both on the schools and on the central office, which must develop implementation strategies to transform itself into a service organization. The process must be carefully calibrated and introduced over time so that the framework of site leadership authority, consultation, and shared decision making can mature organically. Any effort to mandate this state of affairs and implement it without underlying capacity is destined to fail. The student-weighted funding system, which we have in mind, ultimately will develop a new paradigm for public education in San Diego.
>
> The crucial component here is to develop the appropriate relationship between oversight and implementation. This necessarily raises the issues of tight and loose coupling of various elements affecting the instructional core. One should err, I believe, always on the side of decisions being made closer to where responsibility resides.
>
> The issue of accountability is central: only with accountability for improvement, measured solely by results reflected in terms of student learning, can this new paradigm retain its integrity and over the long run flourish. The introduction of a district accountability system, as a synthesis of federal and state require-

ments, is required. Such a system will establish, together with federal law, a framework for responding to high or low performance. The challenge before San Diego is aligning district accountability with the requirements of capacity building. Only when people have been provided with the proper tools and training can they be held accountable for results.

The fulcrum for invitation by the center, in terms of accountability, is the failure of the school to achieve expected results for all of its subgroups. The extent of both oversight and intervention depends upon levels of achievement. To the extent that all targets are met, there is less oversight and more flexibility.

This work defines the objective of a "system" of schools rather than a school system. The emphasis must be upon both the center and the schools, with the role and functions of the center determined by the needs of the schools. In this system the district provides a coherent framework and gives principals, working closely with their school community, the freedom to organize the school and expend resources consistent with the needs of the children and results.[27]

Over time, Bersin and Alvarado grew apart over this issue. Bersin wanted to begin devolving power to the schools by the fourth year. Alvarado said the teachers and principals weren't ready yet. He didn't want to let go for fear that instruction would return to what it had been when he arrived in San Diego. By 2002 Bersin wanted to grant high schools, in particular, greater autonomy. He wanted the district to begin encouraging charter schools, to let them try out new approaches. He wanted to turn decisions about how to cut spending over to the schools, figuring they'd know best how to do the least harm. But Alvarado wanted to retain control.

In the summer of 2002, Bersin and Alvarado negotiated Alvarado's departure. In January 2003, Alvarado began to work part-time and then cut ties to the district that summer.

The teacher union had exploited Alvarado's many vulnerabilities—his arrogance, his refusal to moderate his all-or-nothing views on teaching, the fact that he commuted from New York the first two years on the job, and that he was as well paid as Bersin and lived in a subsidized condominium in the exclusive neighborhood of Coronado. Those awkward facts drew attention and may have tainted the ambitious reform effort to which Alvarado was key. On the other hand, the instructional leaders credited Alvarado with helping them learn more about effective teaching than they could have imagined. "Tony's departure left a real void," said Carol Pike.

This ended one of the most important partnerships in American education. A powerful nontraditional superintendent paired with a brilliant educator made such bold moves that a cottage industry of researchers monitored their ups and downs and analyzed the outcomes. Scholars from Harvard, Stanford, the University of California at San Diego, and the University of Pittsburgh and researchers from the American Institutes for Research studied the reforms closely, searching for clues as to what worked and what did not. A number of the studies questioned the speed with which Bersin and Alvarado moved, particularly in the first year, to change what seemed to some as trying to fix everything at once. But all took note of the unprecedented focus on improving instruction.

The debate continues over whether reform needs to wait for teachers to buy in or, as Bersin believed, should proceed while supporting teachers and let the results speak for themselves. Even school principals have to calculate what will lead to greater success: requiring all of their teachers to adopt a new teaching strategy, or working only with those who are anxious to try it. Bersin did not believe that giving reform more time would gain it greater acceptance, especially in the case of San Diego, where the teacher union and a school board minority adamantly opposed any changes at all. He gambled that he would have enough external support in the community to be able to withstand the opposition long enough for the reforms to begin showing results. Then, he believed, the culture would begin to accept the changes and the district could loosen its grip.

Given the chaotic, disorganized, unproductive approach to instruction that he saw in San Diego when he arrived, he believed the district had to assert itself in a manner that demonstrated seriousness of purpose and resolve. He now believes the calculation paid off and that, as teachers and principals became more knowledgeable and skilled, they came to recognize the value of what they'd gone through. The well-known expert on school district change, Michael Fullan, agreed. He observed that Bersin and Alvarado were tough and focused on learning. "But they know that principals and teachers will only be mobilized by caring and respect, by talented people working together, and by developing shared expertise."[28]

"Necessarily, it would take time, but in the end San Diego produced the results we wanted," Bersin would later reflect. "The insistence of the district for three or more years that teachers use research-based practices produced evidence of success when children began to respond eagerly and successfully to these methods. That's when some teachers who were initially resistant changed their views as to how children learn best and what they needed to do to make it happen." Many teachers, of course, never did.

Bersin recalled being in a restaurant after he'd left the district and noticing three teachers sitting together at another table. He recognized two of them as teachers who had been fiercely resistant to the reforms at the elementary school where they'd taught. When they noticed him, they asked the waiter to send him a glass of excellent wine. It came with a note saying that they were now proud of what they had learned and were able to do: "We don't like the way it was done, but we sure like the results and we're much better teachers because of what you did."

Decisions regarding the sequence and pace of change pose the biggest early challenge confronting any reformer. The solution, says Bersin, must be based on the facts of the situation. At the end of the first year of his superintendency, he told Stanford University researcher Amy Hightower that the system in San Diego needed to be shaken up. "There was no other way to start systemic reform," he told her. "You've got to jolt the system. I understand that. You've got to jolt a system, and if people don't understand you're serious about change in the first six months, the bureaucracy will own you. The bureaucracy will defeat you at every turn if you give it a chance."[29]

In other circumstances, he had come to recognize, a series of small jolts might work even better.

CHAPTER FOUR

Principals

"Expectations Were Altered"

The title "principal" is derived from "principal teacher." In the typical large urban school, however, the principal serves more as a site manager than as the instructional leader. The evidence is strong that, of the school-related factors that affect student achievement, a principal's leadership is second only to the quality of teaching. Good leadership is especially important and can make the biggest difference in schools serving the most disadvantaged students. Although principals do not teach, they must themselves be master teachers who are able to recognize strong and weak teaching when they see it and must be able to create the conditions that enable teachers to be effective and students to learn. School districts must ensure that every school has a strong leader. But many university-based leadership programs are weak. So San Diego created its own leadership academy to prepare principals to carry out its expectations. More and more school districts across the country are doing the same.

One of the most important events of Bersin's superintendency occurred within weeks of the end of the first school year that he was in charge. Thirteen principals and two vice principals were placed on immediate administrative leave. They weren't suspended from their jobs because of malfeasance, stealing, or a moral lapse. Rather, they were removed from their posts because they were not doing enough to help either teachers improve their practice or students to learn more.

The school board posted a notice at the district office saying it would be meeting with each of the principals; the principals were then summoned to the district office, told they were being removed from their jobs, informed they could return to the classroom as teachers in the fall, and then directed to clean out their desks. They would have thirty minutes to gather their photos, plaques, stuffed animals, and other keepsakes while a school district police officer watched over them. After they had finished, each was escorted out of the building.

"Never before, or at least not in anyone's memory, had a principal been removed from the San Diego City Schools for poor job performance," Bersin said. "That principals would be removed for lack of leadership skill, or for their disinterest in leading instruction, instead of offered another chance at a different school or assigned to the central office, was simply not contemplated by the culture."

Justified or not, the move was so unusual Bersin feared that, in his words, "one or more of them might go ballistic" upon hearing the news. He'd sought the advice of district lawyers as to how to handle the situation and been told that school police officers in the past had escorted fired principals out of their schools. That comported with his experience in the corporate world, where fired executives are asked to leave the building immediately. But in this case, that move backfired. The names of the principals were leaked to the media and, as the story broke, their names crawled slowly across the bottom of the television screen.

The principals, and many others in the district, felt they had not been given fair warning and that they were being made martyrs so that Bersin and Alvarado could show that they were serious about changing instruction.

"The handling of the situation was a massive miscalculation on my part," Bersin said. "It gave unnecessary support to the charge that the reform was brutal and completely uncaring. It also centered attention on the process of the removals rather than on the crucial accountability point that was being made. Reform opponents always and everywhere focus on the *how* of things rather than the *what*. My stupid decision on the police escort played right into this hand."

As in most districts at the time, and many still, principals in San Diego were considered to be middle managers and expected to maintain order and sustain good relationships with their colleagues and superiors. It was important for them to follow district rules, avoid causing headaches, keep parent complaints to a minimum, and make teachers feel comfortable and valued. Of course, San Diego had many school principals who were successful educational leaders. But, in Bersin's view, many in San Diego saw schools' academic success as more a matter of circumstance than performance. Traits such as congeniality were deemed to be both more important and more authentic. Principals who met that standard, but who were incompetent educators, might be moved from school to school, but they could count on remaining a principal until retirement. Although the phrase seems harsh, that dynamic is still known in urban districts across the country as the "dance of the lemons."

Today, principals in most school districts are expected to be much more involved in leading instruction, and many are evaluated, in part, on students' performance. This has become true in New York City, Washington, D.C., Atlanta, Fort

Wayne (Indiana), and many other districts. But some of the principals in San Diego chose to try to wait out the reforms aggressively pushed by Bersin and his team. And they had lost the wager.

The dismissals marked the low point in the relationship between Bersin and Alvarado and the principals that they considered so critical to their chances of success. "When [Bersin] did the principals, it rocked people's worlds," said former San Diego principal Angela Bass. Bass would later become a key district instructional leader and then go on to become a top education advisor to the mayor of Los Angeles. "For many of us, to go from the excitement of this training we were getting as principals and writing an improvement plan for our schools, to seeing the names on the 6 p.m., 10 p.m., and 11 p.m. news was a tide shifter."

Among those dismissed were "people who thought they were going to get promoted," Bass said. "People loved some of those principals . . . When you define yourself by your job, and it's over, it causes a lot of pain."[1]

SERVING THE NEEDS OF THE ADULTS

Bersin understood this reaction, but it also highlighted for him how much of the district's culture was geared to the adults' interest in keeping their jobs and how little, aside from rhetoric, the educational needs of children mattered. "It's not selfishness as much as it is the fact that the architecture of schooling cultivates and supports the adults who look out for one another," he said. "Children and their families pass through the system over the course of thirteen years. But the on-the-job relationships that are established among the educators last for decades. It's unthinkable for colleagues who grow close to hold one another responsible for the failures of the school. The firings shattered this taboo."

The fifteen administrators did not accept their treatment quietly. They filed a lawsuit claiming that they had a right to their jobs and that the district did not follow its own administrative procedures. The case would wind through the courts for the next six years. Rather than settle, Bersin stood firm, and the district won a precedent-setting legal victory when the U.S. Court of Appeal for the Ninth Circuit ruled that it had the authority to remove them based solely on a superior's professional judgment and did not have to prove they were incompetent.[2] In 2005, under a different school board, the district agreed to settle the matter and pay the plaintiffs $1 million in back wages. But that did not alter the important legal precedent that had been established.

In the aftermath of the demotions, principals in San Diego held a vote on forming a professional union. The principals rejected the idea. To avoid such controversies in the future, however, Bersin established a transparent process for removing poorly performing principals. Principals would be notified confidentially in November that they needed to improve, given a progress report in the spring, and then, if nothing had changed, told well before the end of the school year that they would be returning to a nonadministrative role. Warned that their performance was subpar, many of the principals voluntarily returned to the classroom rather than suffer the indignity of a demotion.

The dismissals had another positive outcome: those who applied for jobs as vice principals or principals from then on recognized that the district was looking primarily for skilled teachers and instructional leaders. "Expectations were altered," Bersin said. "And from then on, the instructional leaders held principals accountable face-to-face. We never had the same uproar again."

During their stints in San Diego, Alvarado and Bersin also addressed the recruitment, selection, training, hiring, evaluation, and professional development of principals.

A LEADERSHIP ACADEMY

Unsatisfied that existing local principal preparation programs put enough stress on instructional leadership and the skills needed to lead school reform, Alvarado and Bersin in 1999 worked with the private University of San Diego to set up an academy to offer customized training and professional development opportunities for principals in collaboration with the university. The program was known as the Educational Leadership Development Academy (ELDA) and, during its first year, fifteen outstanding teachers who had been identified as potentially great principals were selected as interns. The interns would serve as resource teachers in the schools but also take classes and be apprenticed to highly regarded, effective principals. ELDA was established, in part, to help the district recruit principals to replace those expected to retire. A 2001 projection showed that the district would likely have to hire 178 principals and 163 vice principals within five years.

The other reason the district established the program was to develop a cadre of instructional leaders who could enact the curriculum and support the teaching methods introduced by Alvarado and reinforced by Fink. ELDA also developed programs for mentoring new principals and coaching experienced principals, and offered conferences, summer institutes, and other learning opportunities for veteran principals.

"Effective school reform does not occur as a result of program mandates," the ELDA business plan said. "It happens school by school, initiated and guided by capable principals. Thus, while the Blueprint for Student Success provides a means for raising student achievement, the district must also concentrate on developing, selecting, and supporting school leaders to carry out Blueprint reforms."[3] The

Blueprint was the overarching reform strategy that was adopted by the board in the spring of 2000, Bersin's second year on the job.

Although there are now a number of programs around the country similar to ELDA, it was pioneering at the time. When Linda Darling-Hammond studied effective nontraditional leadership programs several years later, she deemed ELDA to be one of the best.[4] The ELDA program, she wrote, was "the most tightly aligned partnership of all those we studied . . . The program emphasizes instructional leadership, organizational development, and change management, and graduates are extremely well-prepared to organize professional learning for teachers and staff in their schools."[5]

Bersin persuaded the Eli and Edythe Broad Foundation to cover the initial cost of the academy. The Carnegie Corporation of New York, the Bill & Melinda Gates Foundation, the William and Flora Hewlett Foundation, and the Broad Foundation would eventually contribute more than $25 million to pay for the academy and the reforms keyed to it.

Between 2000 and 2005, the Academy graduated fifty-three students from its Aspiring Leaders Program and 85 percent of them became administrators. ELDA later started a New Leaders Program to support beginning principals. By the time Bersin left the district, thirty-eight schools in the district were led by graduates of one of the two programs. Of those, thirty-one showed growth on the state's performance measure.[6]

Bersin would continue emphasizing the pivotal role of the principal in school reform after he left San Diego. His experience with ELDA had persuaded him that it was possible to improve school leadership on the scale needed to enact a districtwide reform agenda.

"EXTREMELY INTENSE" PREPARATION

Patricia Ladd was one of the principals who went through the program. She had been a teacher of gifted sixth graders enrolled in an elite academic program at a middle school in an affluent part of the district. She challenged her students academically, offered them a rich curriculum, and gave them freedom to do much of their learning on their own, with her coaching. Bersin visited her classroom when her school reopened after a remodeling project. He later sent her a note thanking her for encouraging him to engage students during the visit. "I've never received anything like that," she said. "If he likes what he sees in the classroom, he sends you a note."[7]

Ladd became a peer coach, working with her fellow teachers on literacy, and then decided to become a principal and was accepted into the ELDA program. As she worked toward her administrator's credential she was assigned to Keiller

Middle School, one of the state's lowest performing, to serve as vice principal. The school enrolled seven hundred students and registered about seven hundred suspensions each year. She was put in charge of student discipline, and the "extremely intense" demands of the leadership academy added to the stress.

Ladd appreciated ELDA's intense focus on instruction but, she said, it did not prepare her to lead a school so dysfunctional that maintaining order took precedence over improving instruction. She planned to take a job as principal in a more affluent, less troubled part of town after she completed the program. At the last minute, however, she reexamined her decision. She became Keiller's principal.

"I just thought, 'Who are you?' 'What do you stand for?' I couldn't let it go. I would look into the faces of the children at Keiller and I thought that if I didn't do something, I'd be a fake. I would be a part of the problem of social injustice. I just couldn't live with myself. I remember Alan quoting Gandhi over and over again. We ourselves had to become the change we wanted to see in the world."[8]

In 2005, the San Diego Board of Education wanted to sever the district's relationship with ELDA, and a long line of principals testified about how the program had benefited them professionally.

"I am a very proud product of ELDA," a principal of a small, start-up high school told the school board.[9] "The academy helped shape and define the leaders' voices. Every morning and every day, our decisions are based on what's good for kids."

Another principal told the school board that the leadership academy had helped him develop "the ability to analyze teaching and learning through the eyes of the students. I now understand what children can and cannot do, based on the teaching practices of the adults."

RECRUITING AND HIRING PRINCIPALS

No matter how good it is, the training of principals won't matter much if performance and knowledge doesn't influence who is hired to lead schools. As in many urban districts, getting hired as a principal in San Diego had previously required passing muster with a school board member. "This placed a premium on politics to the exclusion of skill and knowledge," Bersin said. "Race and gender and personal relationships often trumped all other considerations of merit. This had to end."

But, by considering merit alone, Bersin stirred up racial politics in San Diego.

While he was the U.S. attorney, Bersin had worked closely with George Walker Smith, a prominent San Diego minister who was the first African American member of the school board and the first to chair the National Council of Great City Schools. Smith had taken a special interest in pushing for black teachers to be promoted to principal. Partly because of his advocacy, more than

10 percent of San Diego's principals were black. Under the leadership of Bertha Pendleton, that percentage grew to be disproportional to the enrollment of black students, the city's black population, or the number of black teachers in San Diego City Schools. So, when the district dismissed principals or pressured them to improve, black principals were affected more than others. Bersin got the school board to agree to a new policy for hiring principals that had the effect of reducing the power of Smith and other activists to get certain people hired.

"San Diego had many fine African American principals who flourished, but it also had a fair number who were not very good at all, just as it had incompetents of every racial hue," Bersin said. "But removing any black principal was a serious event because of the struggle of people who had fought discrimination for them to be hired."

The situation caused Smith, who headed up a church that many of San Diego's African American educators attended, to turn against Bersin. "It was painful to me because he and I had been very close," Bersin said of Smith.

Despite the problems it caused him, Bersin believed that the school board's endorsement of using candidates' experience and knowledge as the primary basis for their hiring was one of the board's most consequential decisions in terms of its effect on school improvement.

Donna Tripi, a Chicago principal who moved to San Diego and got hired to lead one of its large elementary schools, said the process she went through to be hired was the most comprehensive she'd ever experienced. She had to pass a written screening test; go through an interview with a panel of teachers, parents, and staff; and then visit classrooms with an instructional leader and other candidates to observe instruction. Afterward, the group shared their observations. "It was truly an authentic situation," she said. "I remember walking out of the interview thinking that they really know me as a principal and know what I can do."[10]

"My job was to ensure the integrity of the process," Bersin said. Over the course of seven years, Bersin would override fewer than a half-dozen recommendations—less than 2 percent of those who were recommended for hiring.

Bersin also won board support for evaluating principals based on their effect on teaching and student achievement. Previously, principals received a cursory review, the outcome of which turned more on how many complaints the school generated rather than how much students learned. The new principal evaluations, performed annually, were done by the instructional leaders who supervised them.

DEVELOPING PRINCIPALS INTO INSTRUCTIONAL LEADERS

Bersin pushed the principals hard, and many were not able to rise to the challenge. But many did. "Alan would say over and over, 'If one child is failing, we're all failing, and we all have to help each other,'" Tripi said. She said she was grateful for the opportunity to work under Bersin. "The seven years I spent with him were . . . the biggest learning and the most productive [period in my career]."[11]

But, as hard as all of the principals and instructional leaders worked, improvement still came slowly. Carole Osborne, who became a principal in 2000 at a large elementary school in an economically depressed neighborhood, said the pace of improvement was frustrating. "So many of us were new principals, and we were learning the content and teaching it. We were learning about leadership and then exercising it the next day. So, the learning curve was quite high for many of us, and the results, while we did see some, were not as dramatic as they could have been."[12]

"We were looking for a high level of interaction, a thinking environment, not just spitting things out," said Debbie Beldock, one of the original instructional leaders, or ILs, as they came to be called. "We wanted to see a sense of lingering, and pondering what the author was saying to you. We wanted to teach these kids to be thinkers and problem solvers."[13] But in her visits to schools, she encountered such teaching only sporadically and not in all classrooms at any school, not even those considered to be the district's very best. She was not seeing evidence that the new teaching techniques the principals were learning—guided reading, independent reading, shared reading, and so on—were being used with fidelity in classrooms.

"Not everyone was able to make connections for people to what we wanted them to do," Beldock said. "How well the principals interpreted the guidance on how best to teach literacy depended on whether they, themselves, understood the techniques."

She agreed with what some independent policy researchers have found, that the efforts to reform instruction in San Diego were uneven, and that much of that unevenness resulted from the variation in the effectiveness of the principals. The lack of knowledge and sophistication of some of the principals early on caused them to act in unthinking, doctrinaire ways.

Beldock said, for example, that the instructional leaders had frequently seen lessons interrupted repeatedly during their school visits. PA announcements, a child bringing a note to the classroom door, a call for a child to come to the office, schoolwide assemblies—all would intrude on lessons. The leaders asked principals to limit the number of assemblies they held so as to allow more time for sustained instruction. Some principals, she said, issued an edict canceling all assemblies.

In another example, one of the instructional leaders commented that children in the upper elementary grades were doing too much coloring instead of writing. One of the principals responded jokingly by saying, "Lock up the crayons!"

Some principals took that statement literally. "They were trying to illustrate that there's a right time and place to have coloring activities, but you certainly can have crayons out," said Marian Kim Phelps, who became an elementary school principal under Bersin.[14] But not everyone got that message.

Beldock also recalled a middle school where the principal mandated that every teacher in every period read to students and discuss the meaning of what was being read. "It didn't make sense" to use the same technique seven periods in a row, Beldock said. But the principal's understanding of good literacy instruction was superficial, and she was unable to exercise professional judgment. Bersin's critics seized on such incidents, saying they proved that the district's reform agenda straitjacketed educators rather than developed them.

MANY MEETINGS FOR PRINCIPALS
TO DISCUSS INSTRUCTION AND LEADERSHIP

The difficult work of trying to build the principals' knowledge of literacy as well their leadership capacity necessitated frequent meetings in addition to the instructional leaders' school visits. The district brought in consultants from New York, Australia, and New Zealand to offer demonstrations and lectures and help them implement San Diego's literacy plan.

But the consultants became controversial because of their cost and contributed to a sense that Alvarado and Bersin considered the educators in San Diego inferior. The district's principals also met monthly as a group for a full-day meeting where they heard from Alvarado, the instructional leaders, and Bersin himself. Bersin wanted to demonstrate that he, as superintendent, thought that supporting good instruction was his most important responsibility.

Bersin always thanked the principals effusively for their efforts on behalf of children even as he emphasized that his expectations were not negotiable. He would mention schools by name and point out something about each one, showing that he not only got out of the office, but that he was also thoroughly engaged when he visited schools. "One year," instructional leader Carol Pike said, "he took all of the principals to the symphony. Principals talked to me all the time about these things."[15] Every new principal appointed received a personal letter from Bersin, enclosing a series of articles and excerpts from research he believed relevant to the work ahead.

"We worked so hard, but we felt appreciated," Patricia Ladd said. "He was introducing accountability, and that's what I thought had been lacking," she said. "So he got my attention right away."[16]

On campus, the principals were expected to meet monthly with their teachers as a group to talk about schoolwide instructional issues. They also were expected to meet regularly with each teacher one-on-one to give them feedback on their teaching and to talk through the progress being made by individual students. In addition, every month, each of the ILs convened the principals of the schools they oversaw. It was a heavy burden.

Some principals considered the monthly meetings to be insulting and believed they already were effective as instructional leaders. But many, although by no means all, considered the monthly meetings to be helpful. Phelps said, "Many of us would walk out of the monthly conferences in awe. You felt inspired. You felt like you'd learned something, and you were pumped up to do the work you had to do, as hard as it was."[17]

At a meeting in December 2000 with the principals she supervised, Carol Pike relentlessly repeated the mantra that the adults were responsible for students' learning. "If you really, really, really believe that learners in the classrooms or learners here are capable, competent people, then if we don't get it yet it's because the instructor has not yet found a way to reach us the way that we need to be reached," Pike told them. She was referring to the relationship between teachers and their students, the relationship between principals and their teachers, and also her relationship with them. She told them that they had made progress but still had a long way to go.

"In general," she told them, "we've given it the old college try, and we've still got some ground to cover." The monthly staff conferences with their teachers were not yet as productive as they had to become. "Time is precious, so you have to maximize those staff conferences to take your staff to the next level, because that's the only way we're going to improve student achievement."

She showed the group a videotape of a meeting run by one of their colleagues. (Oddly, the teachers at the videotaped meeting refused to appear on camera during the meeting. The contract, their union argued, gave them that right.) The principal on the video praised the teachers for their use of guided reading with their students. In guided reading, the teacher supports students as they learn to read using a variety of cues—textual, phonemic, contextual, and visual—to identify words. "I'm pleased that the children are appropriately grouped, that I'm seeing teaching centers where the teachers have everything at their fingertips. I see excellent choices of books, wonderful lessons with focus, and teachers doing all the behaviors that would indicate that they're doing a top-notch group," the principal told her teachers.

Pike then facilitated a discussion during which her fellow principals gave the principal who had appeared in the video a favorable review. Pike herself was not impressed. She thought the principal had offered more praise than was warranted. "I would have focused more on the fact that the teachers are . . . starting out. They're not where they need to be."

The principal who had been recorded said she had praised the teachers so effusively at the videotaped meeting because she saw that they were at least trying to use the district-endorsed methods. The previous year, the teachers had refused to even attempt them.[18]

CHANGING THE CULTURE

Pike reminded the group that the "purpose here is to increase our comfort level" with this type of examination. "It's not about you, it's not about me. It's not personal. It's about changing our culture so that we become comfortable about constantly improving our practice. That wasn't part of the culture we had here before."

Kimiko Fukuda, another instructional leader, was disappointed in her group's progress with improving their staff meetings. "If we're analytical about it, I think it's because we don't yet know how to teach in a powerful way," she told the principals, some of them new, but many of them veterans. "You don't know how to do that, because I haven't taught you."[19]

Principals should open each meeting, she told them, using their "leader voice, the strong voice, to create a sense of urgency and a clear rationale for why this is so important for our kids."

"Ask yourself two questions," Fukuda said. "What is it you want the teachers to learn? And are they going to be able to do it, as a result of whatever it is that I do?' Say that you want them to learn a new technique in teaching reading. 'Is the meeting enough? What if I model the technique? Will that be enough? Have they had time to practice? Will that be enough?'"

Not only were the openings of the staff meetings weak, but so were the closings. "We want the teachers to really know what they're supposed to do . . . They have to hear your leadership voice again. They have to know when they leave your staff conferences that you're clear about what you want them to do and why . . . It's not 'if you'd like to, it would be nice,' or 'I'd really like you to try it, and if you have some ideas about it, and think maybe you'd like to try it sometime,'" she told the principals, an edge in her tone of voice. "That's not the message we want to give. It has to be strong and forceful with a sense of urgency and the passion that so many of you in this room have. They have to know it is important to you."

As the session continued, the principals critiqued staff meetings they themselves had led. "I discovered I was wishy-washy at the end because I was trying to get everyone to share in the decision making," one principal said.

"Did they do what you asked them to do?" Fukuda asked.

"I don't know," the same principal said. "I haven't checked."

Yet the meetings with teachers were not supposed to be coercive. The principals were supposed to lead their teachers in what the Institute for Learning called "collaborative analysis," encouraging them to be as analytical about their teaching as principals were learning to be about their leadership. On the other hand, the principals were supposed to evaluate the teachers, which would likely cause some to be shy about sharing any trouble they were having. Some teachers and union leaders charged that the evaluations were at odds with the coaching. Alvarado insisted on the compatibility of support and judgment, indeed the necessity for combining them. Bersin agreed, on the basis of his professional training and his experience in athletics, from which the coaching model was derived. "Whether in assisting teachers or batters or lawyers, coaches have advice to offer and evaluations to make," he said. "They are dimensions of a single function."

LEADING INSTRUCTIONAL CHANGE

This gets at a critical leadership challenge that faces any superintendent (or principal, for that matter): seeking broad changes in practice. How do leaders make change happen without imposing it? How can they inspire the professionals they supervise to embrace both the need for change, as well as specific changes, without simply invoking the power of their office? Fukuda explained that the principals retained the authority and responsibility to decide on the training and other support the teachers at their school needed most. "We're not going to give you a formula," she told them. "It's not a 'fill in the blank' exercise. It's about our thinking and what we know . . . about our school."

The principals were being told they were professionals and were expected to figure out how to solve problems or move their school forward, drawing on the theories of learning that underlay the district's reform. Professional educators, as with professionals in any field, do not follow a script.

On the other hand, education is a profession still in the making, in part because norms and standards of practice are not highly developed or widely agreed upon. So, Alvarado and the Institute for Learning that he led were offering some—not to substitute for professional judgment, but to inform it. Alvarado's view was that, unless the training was explicit and the principals were taught specific techniques, they could not be held accountable for their performance. Still, to many, it felt like the prescriptions were so precise that neither principals nor teachers had any say in what went on in their schools and classrooms.

Lauren Resnick, the cognitive scientist whose research team provided much of the thinking behind the principal training sessions, acknowledged the challenge the principals were being handed. "Principals have to be instructional leaders, and that means they are the teachers of their teachers," she said. "But there's more and more evidence that there's a certain kind of professional community in schools that work. You can call it various things . . . but the evidence is pretty great. It's the principal's job to create that and sustain that."[20]

Resnick worked with principals nationally for many years on creating such environments, but she said she still saw very few examples of such productive situations. More commonly, she said, she sees principals who spend their time "maintaining order and making sure demands are met and that test scores don't go down. Principals don't spend very much of their time in classrooms working on instruction, even when time is made for that. People do what they know how to do, and if being an instructional leader is something you don't know how to do very well, you're not going to do it."

A recent RAND Education report, commissioned by the Wallace Foundation, which has spent more than $280 million to improve school site and district leadership, examined how effective principals lead instruction.[21] What the study found was that the best principals form instructional teams made up of teachers, coaches, assessment experts, content matter specialists, and others. Rather than dictate changes, principals develop the leadership capabilities of their teams and their teachers and provide them with time to analyze student performance and respond to it.

But such a vision of instructional leadership could not be contemplated in San Diego until it was established that the principals were expected to be instructional leaders.

GETTING BUY-IN

Many teachers resisted the efforts of principals to get them to alter their teaching methods. "That was one of the biggest stumbling blocks, getting teachers to buy into it," said Linda Rees, who retired in 2003 after four years as principal of a small elementary school in an affluent part of town. "I would stand up in staff meetings and say, 'You may not agree with what we're asking you to do, but research is telling us that this is going to make a big difference in our kids.'"[22]

In some schools, she said, the peer coaches Bersin and Alvarado had insisted on—the teachers deployed to help their colleagues—"would go home crying every day because they were supposed to be working with teachers and they'd get into classrooms and see that the instruction was awful, and then the teacher resisted meeting with them or debriefing afterwards."

Getting veteran teachers to view themselves this way, as professionals striving to achieve what might be called a standard of practice, would prove to be difficult. In large measure, that was because the teacher union continually told its members that they were demeaned by any effort aimed at helping them become more effective. New teachers were more receptive.

At a meeting with principals in December 2000, Bersin discussed the importance of the U.S. Supreme Court opinion in *Brown v. Board of Education*. To many at the time, Bersin said, the fact that the 1954 decision outlawing segregation was unanimous was a surprise because the court was known to have been sharply divided between liberals and conservatives. Be assured, Bersin told them, sharp debate and disagreement occurred prior to the decision. However, when it became clear that seven or eight of the nine justices would decide the issue in favor of desegregation, the others went along out of interest for the future effectiveness of the Court. "Unanimity," he said, "was what was required to move on and make progress."[23]

There was a lesson here for the San Diego schools, he said. He'd always encouraged principals and their teachers to disagree on, debate, and discuss the instructional and other changes he and Alvarado were bringing to the district. But, he said, "after that debate comes a time when the improvement of student achievement, which depends first and foremost on the improvement of teaching, requires [that] . . . we come and work together within the framework of a shared professional approach."

He said educators "need to act with integrity and need to know where their own bottom line is, and where they can't go along, to move along." What he was saying, gently but directly, was that if the principals couldn't fully embrace the district's managed instruction program as their own, then they should consider resigning. Going through the motions and saying to teachers that they were asking them to change only because their own supervisors were pressuring them to do so was not a tenable position. If, he said, they were resisting the reforms as a matter of principle, then "you need to make that very individual choice about whether . . . you can . . . move forward on the team."

It's rare in one's personal or professional life that such choices have to be made, Bersin said. But this was one of those times. "We are at a crucial point of change. It is frightening. It is exciting. It is anxiety producing. But we're on our way," he noted.

"Your job is to create an ongoing vision and journey that's yours," Alvarado said at the December 2000 meeting. "If I or Alan were to get up here and say that this is what the board of education wants or that we got a memo from [state superintendent of public instruction] Delaine Eastin and she wants us to do a, b, and c, I think you'd find that less than overpowering as a vision."

The teachers in their schools, Alvarado told them, "have to know and feel . . . that you are put on this earth to make meaning of the chaos in it, and this is the place where you put your two feet down . . . and you have to convince them that it is an honor to be part of this school you are leading."

Some of the harshest critics of the Blueprint and managed instruction reacted negatively to that line of argument. One of the most cynical was Dana Shelburne, the principal of La Jolla High School, who managed to miss the point entirely. To him, it sounded like Alvarado and Bersin were saying, "You will tell your people this, and you will tell them that it's not something we're telling you to tell them. You will tell them that it's your idea and that you support it . . . And if you can't do that, then, I think his phrase was, 'You can vote with your feet.'"[24] Shelburne wasn't the only one who had that reaction. Whether the critics actually misunderstood, or whether they just used this as a way to stir further discontent, was not clear.

Researchers from Stanford surveyed principals during the 1999–2000 school year about the implementation of changes. More than 80 percent of the elementary school principals, nearly 70 percent of the middle school principals, and nearly 80 percent of the high school principals gave the district high marks for setting ambitious expectations, maintaining a commitment to standards, and focusing on teaching and learning.[25]

The survey found that principals and teachers were pleased that they were given greater responsibility for instruction, and they felt leadership capabilities had improved, and the district's instructional approach was more coherent than it had been.[26]

In a 2003 article, Darling-Hammond noted that more than three-quarters of a sample of principals surveyed said the district's priorities were consistent with the principals' goals for their school, and helped the school focus on teaching and learning. More than two-thirds of the principals at each level—elementary, middle, and high school—said the district supported their school's improvement efforts. But over half the principals, and a higher percentage of high school principals, also said the district was too centralized and hierarchical and mandated outcomes and behaviors.[27]

That tension lessened over the years but never did go away, with some principals and many teachers continuing to feel, regardless of what Bersin and Alvarado and the instructional leaders said, that they had little room within which to exercise professional judgment.

Donna Tripi acknowledged that she and her colleagues were not given the freedom to come up with their own set of teaching strategies. But, she said, Alvarado and the instructional leaders made a strong case for their approach.

"The principals who were a little apprehensive were the ones who really didn't get it," she said. "I think they thought, 'We're being asked to do this, and we don't really know how.'"[28]

At a principals meeting in August 2001, Alvarado reported with disappointment that math and literacy scores had not improved from the previous year. Half of the district's students were at grade level. But when measured against performance standards, even in schools in affluent neighborhoods only about one-third of the students were proficient.

"You cannot manage this system into performance, you have to lead it," he said. "The teachers have to feel this is a different ball game." Improvement, he said, would not come from generally better teaching. What was needed was teaching customized to the needs of each student to make sure each one improved.[29]

SUPPORTING PRINCIPALS

Although they were responsible for the quality of teaching in their own school, the principals were not working on their own. The peer coaches (or staff developers) helped them work with elementary school teachers to improve their literacy lessons. Staff developers also were available to help teachers work on math instruction. Content administrators and subject matter experts were placed in the high schools. Vice principals, who traditionally get the not-so-pleasant duty of being in charge of discipline and attendance and handling organizational and administrative duties, began asking to be included in the monthly meetings focusing on instruction. Because all of the members of the instructional leadership team were learning together, they could all help assist teachers. All of these team members became the best source of new principals across the district and in turn recruited excellent teachers to replace themselves. Superior teachers in the past had shied away from administration, not wanting to leave the classroom and their students. Once the paradigm had changed, and good teachers realized they could remain deeply involved in teaching and learning, more and more of them became coaches or content administrators, and many went on to become principals. By the time Bersin left the district, 80 percent of the principals had been hired on his watch.

As a concept, instructional leadership has been around for decades.[30] But it's often been little more than a slogan that meant principals had to "keep their eye on the ball." In San Diego, Bersin and Alvarado made instructional leadership a reality. They attempted to bridge the chasm between quality teaching and administration that continues to exist in most districts. They also tried to embed leadership skills in a culture that made it normal for principals and teachers to talk openly about their performance and how to improve it. Common to other professions, this norm still largely is conspicuous by its absence in education.

If educators don't adopt a new set of values and behaviors as their own, and see them as the new norm for both themselves and their peers, then whatever progress is made will be minimal and evanescent, disappearing with the arrival of a new superintendent or school board and the imposition of a new action plan. Michael Fullan, the well-known expert on change in education, uses the term *reculturing*, noting that "effective leaders know that the hard work of reculturing is the sine qua non of progress."[31]

CHAPTER FIVE

The "Blueprint"

"A Virtual Mission Impossible"

School district reform means little without sufficient resources to pay for it. But windfalls with no strings attached are not likely. Leaders, therefore, must reallocate existing resources—taking money away from efforts that are not producing results and directing it toward new research-based strategies that might. The political environment rarely supports rational, deliberate policy making. To build support for their plans, superintendents have to create a sense of urgency. They then need to manage the conflict that is inevitable, understanding that refashioning the status quo always will be controversial. Bersin would quote philosopher Arthur Schopenhauer on this point: "Every reform passes through three stages. In the first it is ridiculed; in the second it is opposed; and in the third, it is regarded as self-evident."

During their first year in office, Bersin and Alvarado had asserted the district's central role in managing instruction. They introduced powerful new methods for engaging students in literacy lessons. They required teachers to spend at least three hours a day in the elementary grades on literacy, some of that time incorporated into lessons in other disciplines. But that was not enough for some students. Sixth graders who were behind had been assigned to longer literacy classes and were making good progress. High schools had begun spending more time addressing the reading issues of their students. To support those practices, the district had given principals the responsibility for improving teaching and backed up that charge with training and extra help. Teachers had been hired as coaches or staff developers in 115 schools to work in classrooms to help other teachers with the new methods and expectations. Instructional leaders were put in place to support the principals. To pay for the coaches, summer institutes, and other professional development strategies, the district had eliminated more than one hundred jobs in the central office, freeing up more than $8 million.

But Bersin knew that, as important as those changes were, they were not enough to bring about the dramatic student achievement gains that were needed. About 40 percent of ninth graders were already far behind, and would need intensive help to catch up. Nearly a third of San Diego's high school students were dropping out. And 75 percent of those who graduated and enrolled in community college or the state university system had to take remedial classes.

Doing something about these dire statistics would require bold moves and, clearly, more money. Nonfinancial resources, such as time and teacher expertise, would have to be redistributed as well. No program, no matter how good, would do the trick. What was needed was a top-to-bottom reformulation of the district's core business to prepare students for college and the world of work. Changes on the scale needed would meet resistance, but Bersin was willing to stake his superintendency on them. He wanted to make a difference, not just have a job. He felt the urgency of the mission. He had to get others to feel that urgency. That was the leadership challenge that lay before him.

The plan Bersin put together to meet that challenge was what came to be known as the Blueprint for Student Success in a Standards-Based System—or, as most people referred to it, the Blueprint. Conceptually, the Blueprint was a plan for giving every student all the supports the district could muster to help him or her succeed. But it also became a target for Bersin's critics. Whatever complaint any interest group had against a school district policy in subsequent years was directed at the Blueprint. It was too big, too costly, too sudden. Just getting it passed, Bersin would say later, was a "virtual mission impossible."

ENDING SOCIAL PROMOTION

However, the impetus for the Blueprint actually came from a California law that went into effect in January 1999 that required school districts to develop policies to hold back struggling students in grades two through five, at the beginning of middle school, and again before they entered high school. The law was part of a national wave of similar "get tough" policies endorsed throughout the 1990s by President George H. W. Bush, President Bill Clinton, many governors, and district superintendents. The policies were meant to put teeth into the academic standards that federal law required states to develop for what students needed to know and be able to do and how well they were expected to perform. Holding back students who hadn't mastered the required material would show communities that the schools were serious and give the students an incentive to work harder.[1] That was the theory.

The San Diego schools had established just such a policy for holding back eighth graders who did not pass core subjects. Starting in 2000, students were to be required to maintain a C average in the sixth, seventh, and eighth grades in order to go on to high school. But the numbers involved were daunting. In the spring of 1999 it was determined that, had that policy already taken effect, more than one thousand seven hundred students were at risk for being retained, nearly one thousand two hundred of them African American or Latino.[2] Data also showed that about 13 percent of all Latino and 10 percent of African American high school students were already being retained in the 1997–1998 school year, because they had not accrued enough credits.[3]

The new state law required the district to toughen that policy, putting even more students in jeopardy of being held back. Education research is notoriously vague about a lot of issues. But on this point the research was clear, Alvarado and others in the district believed. Holding back students led to more students dropping out.

That was already a major problem. Only 70 percent of San Diego students who entered the ninth grade—six thousand four hundred out of nine thousand two hundred freshmen—received diplomas four years later. The problem was particularly acute for students of color. In the city's highest poverty high schools, 83 percent of African American students and 77 percent of Hispanic students dropped out before graduation.[4] Surely, the poor preparation many students received in elementary and middle school was a significant contributor to the dropout problem. Two community task forces representing the interests of Hispanic students and African American students had analyzed the district's failure to teach these students and demanded swift action.

That was part of the context when Bersin's staff presented to the board in March 1999 a draft version of a toughened district policy. It called for holding back second, third, and fourth graders who were performing far below grade level. The policy set up additional performance gates for students to pass through between elementary and middle school and between middle and high school. An analysis of the potential impact of the policy showed that, had it been in effect and strictly enforced during the previous school year, eleven times as many students would have been retained.

The state law also required districts to provide additional tutoring and summer school for students who were far behind. In the March presentation, the Bersin team briefed the school board on options for satisfying that requirement. The committee that was to examine those options included, in addition to Bersin and Alvarado, four teachers, three principals, and more than two dozen others. Coincidentally, one of the teachers involved in this collaborative effort was Terry Pesta, then an elementary school teacher, who later, as president of the San Diego Education Association, would frequently say that Bersin did not seek others' views, especially those of teachers. He would say that Bersin practiced a "my way or the highway" management style.

The ad hoc committee held a community-wide meeting on the draft policy that spring. Briefings for parents and district advisory committees were offered in April, May, and June. Workshops for principals and union school site representatives were conducted in May. Finally, a redrafted "Student Promotion and Support" policy was submitted to the board for its review in July and approved unanimously.

The policy did not spring, fully formed, from Bersin's head. The teacher union and his two critics on the school board were fully aware of and supportive of the strategies that were approved. Teachers, parents, principals, and community members also contributed to the policy's development. It called for elementary school students to continue receiving three hours of literacy lessons. Full-day kindergarten, which Bersin had successfully advocated the previous fall over the objections of some board members and the teacher union, would continue to be rolled out. Genre Studies, the name Alvarado had given to extended-length high school literacy classes required of students who had fallen behind, would continue. Tutoring after school and Saturday classes would be made available to support students to make sure they didn't need to be held back.

The report to the board on the proposed student promotion policy noted that roughly 20 percent of elementary school students and 30–35 percent of middle school students were not meeting the district's academic expectations. The number was staggering—nearly nineteen thousand students. The report made it clear that this would not be the number of students retained. Rather, it said, "this reveals the number of students for whom support and intervention will need to be provided."[5]

Bersin's financial team advised the school board that the extra cost of all the new services proposed in the promotion policy could be paid for by redirecting money the district received from the state and federal government to meet the needs of disadvantaged students.

None of this was controversial at this juncture. The policy was approved unanimously.

As ambitious as it was, however, it was clear that the policy approved by the board would not succeed. The enormity of the problem was too great. The resources the policy proposed to devote to the problem were too paltry. The weakest part of the effort was that teachers were to receive only twenty hours of additional training to help them accelerate the learning of students who were behind. So the board, even as it approved the policy in order to comply with the state's "no social promotion" law, called on Bersin and his team to develop a comprehensive implementation plan commensurate with the magnitude of the problem. Thus planted were the seeds of the Blueprint, which would later be seized as a symbol of all that the board saw wrong with Bersin.

TOWARD A COMPREHENSIVE PLAN FOR ENDING SOCIAL PROMOTION

Bersin saw the board's directive to create a viable plan for ending social promotion, reducing the dropout rate, and closing the longstanding achievement gaps in San Diego's schools as a political opportunity. He could use it to build support for expanding and making permanent the reforms he'd begun his first year on the job. When Bersin spoke to Alvarado about the strategy, Bersin said, "Tony got it right away."

Bersin asked the seven instructional leaders, Alvarado, and some others to start working on the new plan. They met over the summer and into the fall "hour after hour, day after day, on-site and off-site" with Alvarado and sometimes Bersin sitting in.[6]

A NATIONAL CAMPAIGN AGAINST SOCIAL PROMOTION

Alvarado and the committee looked across the country for insights. But they had not turned up a policy on student retention and social promotion worthy of emulation. "We will not just have a social promotion policy that responds to the call of the general populace for blood in the water," Alvarado told a group of principals in September.[7] He was referring to his reading of the public's sense that schools had grown too lax, that they needed to get tough, and that students had to be made to work harder. He told the principals that twenty years of research had found that such policies did not produce the promised results, had negative consequences for students' well-being, and dramatically increased the likelihood of students dropping out of school.

At the time, schools in Chicago had been getting national attention for a three-year-old policy requiring third-, sixth- and eighth-grade students who were behind to be held back if they did not make sufficient progress in mandatory summer programs. About one in four Chicago students had been required to attend summer school in 1998, and half of those students were not promoted. That number was later reduced after they were given more help but was still substantial. President Clinton, invoking what he said was the success of the Chicago policy, had proposed in his 1999 State of the Union speech to extend that policy nationally. Philadelphia and other cities also were considering adopting similar policies.[8]

The effect of the Chicago policy was analyzed by the Consortium on Chicago School Research in a report published in December 1999.[9] One of the authors of that study was Anthony Bryk, a respected researcher who would later become president of the Carnegie Foundation for the Advancement of Teaching. Bryk and his colleagues had found that the sixth- and eighth-grade students who had been required to attend summer school in Chicago had made impressive gains. Those students who had scored the lowest on tests actually made the most progress.

Unfortunately, those gains did not predict higher performance in the next grade, and the benefits of summer school were less apparent for third graders. Even more discouraging was that only one-quarter of the eighth graders who were held back and only one-third of the third and sixth graders who had been retained made a year's progress the following year, meaning they were continuing to fall further behind.

Alvarado told the principals that he had learned from Bryk that a majority of Chicago's growing population of English language learners and special education students were not subject to the retention policy. In addition, about 40 percent of the students who were supposed to be held back were not, a reflection of the discretion that teachers and principals retained. "The real problem," Alvarado told them, "is that you and I know that, if you set a high enough standard . . . you can hold them over and hold them over and then somebody says, 'Hey, I can't have this eight-foot child in the second grade.' It just doesn't work."

"If we move them on it's a problem, and if we retain them it's a problem," Alvarado continued. "If you don't hold them over, it means there are no standards in the school system. And if you hold them over, you know in your heart the kid is not going to benefit."

Having presented the dilemma, Alvarado threw the floor open to the principals to suggest ways out of it. The suggestions came rapid-fire. One said summer school should be required, not just suggested, for students who were behind. Another said the students needed to get more reading instruction—after school, during school breaks at those schools that operated year-round, or on Saturdays. One principal said that at her school she required teachers who wanted to retain a student to write a detailed learning plan for the student that had to be agreed to by his or her parents and given to the student's teacher the next year. A high school principal said the solution for elementary school students would need to be different from that for middle and high school students. Another said the instruction after school and in the summer had to be customized to the student and related to the school curriculum; it could not be generic. No one in the room spoke in opposition to the idea that students who were behind needed more—more time and more high-quality instruction. And no one doubted that it would require resources.

Indeed, one of the principals noted that the allocation of federal Title I dollars to her school amounted to $220 per student, or $1.60 per child per day. "What do we do with that amount of money to undo all that they haven't learned before they got to school?" she asked Alvarado. She noted that at one time she had run an elementary school that provided preschool to three- and four-year-olds, full-day kindergarten, and 220 days of instruction. "We saw a lot of growth," she said. But those services were expensive. "We cannot continue to fund the schools where kids come to school ready to learn the same way we fund schools where kids are in high poverty and their parents don't have an educational background."

Alvarado agreed that it would take money. "One of our solutions has to be some massive look at extending the school day and year probably at a level that has been systemically unheard of," he said. "It would mean a kid probably would have to go to sessions after school and in the summer for as long as the child demonstrated an academic weakness."

QUALITY TEACHING CRITICAL TO PREVENTION

But, Alvarado said, shifting money from schools serving well-off students to those where students were predominantly poor would set off "internecine battles." In other words, the more active, more affluent parents would not be willing to give up anything to serve the goal of greater equality. He said money had to be found to pay for the extra instructional time for students in the short term. But, he said, the only viable long-term solution was preventing students from falling behind in the first place. "We have to do something about the original teaching that got the kids to where they are now," he told the principals. "This is not about blame. This is about knowledge and skill . . . and that leads back to professional development."

"The horror of Chicago is that they have ploughed $275 million into their retention program, and they haven't spent a penny on improving teacher practice," Alvarado said.

The principals had been hearing from Alvarado and Bersin about the importance of good instruction every month for a year. They had been put on the spot as the linchpin between the district's goals and the improvement of classroom teaching. They now were being told that it was also their responsibility to make sure students didn't have to be retained in grade. The principals continued to offer suggestions. Alvarado assured them that all of their ideas would be taken seriously. The principals were enthusiastic about being part of the solution.

The meeting between Alvarado and the principals illustrated rational policy making occurring in the often irrational and highly politicized environment of a public school district. Directed by the board of education to develop a more comprehensive policy on retention and social promotion, Alvarado and his top instructional lieutenants consulted research, analyzed the national policy environment, identified the challenges, and, in this meeting, asked for ideas from the professionals working in the schools. He told them he wanted their help in coming up with a policy that would actually increase how much students were learning. But this was occurring in private, and whatever approach they put forward had to stand up to scrutiny in the interest-driven environment of public school politics.

HOT-BUTTON ISSUE

The need for a better policy became eminently clear that fall. The policy on retention that was in effect when Bersin took office required that, to be promoted to high school, eighth graders had to pass all of their core courses, either during the regular school year or in summer school. The policy approved in July 1999 had refined and extended that policy, but the eighth-grade requirement was still in place. A report to the board in October said that the policy had been unevenly enforced. About three hundred students had been promoted even though they had failed one or more courses, and they were not receiving any additional tutoring or other help.

Those decisions had been made by principals and teachers, as they had the discretion to do. But that didn't stop school board member John de Beck from blaming Bersin for "an educational disaster" that he said resulted from a "lack of administrative leadership." Frances Zimmerman made similar remarks.[10] Bersin agreed that the situation was a disaster and took responsibility for addressing it, understanding that the situation increased the need for the comprehensive policy that Alvarado and the instructional leaders were developing.

The usually supportive editorial board of the *San Diego Union-Tribune* weighed in, accusing the district of a "shell game" for failing to take a tough, unyielding stance.[11] San Diego's problem was small compared to the situation in Los Angeles. It was announced there that if that district's ban on social promotion were enforced, about three hundred fifty thousand students would not go on to the next grade. But the challenge of eliminating social promotion was being recognized nationally. Michael Casserly, the executive director of the national Council of the Great City Schools, the organization that represents most of the nation's largest school districts, said at the time that the announcements of social promotion policies were usually accompanied by "lots of tough talk about cracking down on kids." As the reality of such policies set in around the country, he said, "the tough talk went away. Nobody has got this down. Everybody is struggling with how to do what the public wants and what is best for students."[12]

In a back-to-school essay published in September 1999, Bersin expressed his thoughts about what was needed. He noted that different schools within San Diego set different standards, with those that served mainly low-income and minority students expecting far less. But he also said the district should not simply demand more of students without giving them extra help.

"For all students to achieve to standard, however, we must be prepared to provide support after school, on Saturdays, into the summer and during intersessions (the breaks at year-round schools)," he said. "In effect, we must extend the school year well beyond 180 days for those students who need the extra time and effort to meet standards."[13]

These supports, he said, would require reallocation of resources. Anyone paying attention should have expected what came next.

"MAJOR SCHOOL OVERHAUL"

In December, Bersin presented to the board a draft version of the Blueprint. A front-page article in the *Union-Tribune* in advance of the meeting called it a "major school overhaul" that proposed adding a fifth year of high school for students not yet meeting graduation standards, providing eleven months of instruction to students who were held back, offering struggling kindergartners extra help during the summer before they entered first grade, creating smaller classes for targeted students, extending reading and math instruction, and making a massive investment in teacher and principal training in mathematics and literacy. The plan was designed to ensure that most students would meet demanding academic standards through the "marshaling of human and financial resources to change the system and put in place a safety net for every child," according to the Blueprint preamble.

"I actually think this will begin to set a national precedent on how to retain and promote kids," Alvarado said. Even Zimmerman was supportive. "For once, we are finally building from the ground up and we are seeing the kind of detail necessary to make a program of no social promotion work," she said. "This is one of the most forward-looking, serious plans that we've ever had in this district for bringing children along academically."[14] Speaking at a board meeting, Zimmerman repeated her support but signaled her concerns as well. "I would be sorry if we drive off a segment of our diverse . . . school population by creating a district that is geared to its low achievers," said Zimmerman, who represented La Jolla, the district's most affluent area. "But I am willing to go along with this idealistic plan."

The board heard the December presentation and asked Bersin to bring back a final plan in the spring. Bersin anticipated that opposition would grow during the interim, as people learned more about the plan and the shifts in spending that would be required. He knew that Marc Knapp, the teacher union president, would protest. "Let's be honest," Knapp told a reporter, "This was not collaboration. This was put together by people in the [administration] and we, the practitioners, have to respond to it."

The substance of the policy was not the problem. Indeed, even the bitterest critics of the Blueprint said they agreed with both its goals and programs. But it sparked strong and sustained opposition for three reasons. First, it was an assertion of power by Bersin, which angered those on the board and in the teacher union who still had not accepted his selection as legitimate. Second, the metaphor of a blueprint suggested that this plan was immutable and therefore inflexible. This fear was misplaced. The Blueprint changed every year, based on circumstances, data, and the money available to pay for it.

Finally, and probably most importantly, the Blueprint was controversial because it called for a redistribution of district resources. Most of the $28 million the district received from the federal Title I compensatory education program, money that had been parceled out to schools to be used however they saw fit, would be reallocated to pay for the higher-impact and more tightly focused services described in the Blueprint planning document. Other special pots of money—for magnet programs, summer school, and libraries—would also be redirected to Blueprint-related purposes. More than six hundred teacher's aides, who worked with students but who in some cases were assigned to supervise playgrounds and work in school kitchens, would be laid off. More than two hundred teachers would be hired to staff the smaller, more intense classes. Another seventy-five teachers would be chosen as staff developers.

GROWING OPPOSITION

The burgeoning opposition was apparent in February, when Bersin and Alvarado appeared on the school district's public affairs channel in a talk show format and took questions from the audience and over the telephone. Bersin did not mince words. He said the district had been carrying out a "deceit on students and a fraud on parents and the community" by passing on and graduating students who had few skills and little knowledge. The Blueprint was an effort to remedy that through "prevention, retention, and successful intervention."

Everyone felt threatened. Mike McCarthy, a part-time writer who was one of Bersin's bitterest and most relentless critics in print, complained that the budget for the Blueprint had not yet been made public. He objected, he said, to the district trying to "ram this down our throats" without saying how it would be financed. Critics made that claim over and over. When the Blueprint was presented in December, Alvarado had said that it "will completely drive the budget" for the entire school district. "I'd like to know what we have to give up for this to work," Knapp had said at the time.[15] John de Beck, the school board member and Bersin critic, called it a "$100 million pipe dream."

A revision of the plan presented in February retained most of the elements and was budgeted to cost $50 million the first year, or about 5 percent of the district's $1 billion budget. None of the money would come out of the general fund budget. Instead, money would be shifted among various state and federal pots set aside for disadvantaged students. Nonetheless, critics would continue for years to argue, inaccurately, that local money was being wasted on unproven strategies. Bersin came to believe that it was the very idea of allocating resources in a different way, more than anything, that his critics objected to most. He repeatedly assured parents and teachers that no schools would lose money because of the plan. But fears remained. As with many public institutions, innovation is paid for only with new money. Existing money, once allocated for a particular purpose, gains a political constituency that locks it in place and can only be freed by brooking fierce opposition. Politics, he told a group of business leaders, has "sometimes kept us from massing our resources."[16]

TRYING TO BUILD SUPPORT

Bersin and Alvarado called meetings with principals, teachers, and parents to try to build support for the plan. But opposition continued to grow. In a public meeting at Morse High School, Bersin felt that he and Alvarado might themselves be in danger, as parents and teachers railed against it. He pleaded for the community to recognize how much help students needed. "It's our responsibility to look the facts in the face and ask ourselves what's happening to our children," he said.[17] "But my greatest concern is the upset that parents and teachers have over" the plan.

A supportive letter to the editor in the *Union-Tribune* said that, whether or not residents agreed with all of the Blueprint's details, Bersin "should be commended for trying to make a difference—something the school board and other elected officials have failed to do. His break-the-mold approach is what districts and municipalities need." But two other letters printed the same day did argue over the details. One, from an instructional assistant, argued that they should not be laid off to pay for the Blueprint. Another letter writer wondered where the additional teachers to be hired would find room to teach.[18]

Bersin also worried about how his own team would react to the growing anti-Blueprint pressure. San Diego was not New York, where political discourse was expected to be rough and tumble. In laid-back San Diego, people were uncomfortable with conflict and saw it as a problem rather than as an inevitable accompaniment to difficult policy decisions. "We were at a perilously early stage of the reform, and, internally, people were trying to figure out where they stood. Polarizing the situation, as the Blueprint was likely to do, would put their internal equilibrium at risk," Bersin said.

In an effort to build momentum, Bersin and Ron Ottinger discussed the plan with Chuck Nathanson and nationally known pollster Dan Yankelovich, two community leaders Bersin had consulted before on challenging political issues. Both Nathanson and Yankelovitch, Bersin said later, pointed to his inability to win widespread support for the Blueprint up front, and concluded that the plan moved "too far, too fast." They urged moderation.

Bersin understood that the pace and scope of change matters and that progress must be closely monitored. But he also understood that there is no natural constituency for change, and that issues of educational inequity had been talked about endlessly for decades, with little to show for it. Moreover, for someone who had spent almost his entire career in the private sector, it did not feel like he was moving rapidly at all. By the spring of 2000, he had been in office almost two years and, while he had made some substantial changes, the Blueprint would cement and extend those reforms. If approved, the Blueprint would be phased in over two years. It would take until 2005 for the Blueprint and the other reforms to produce significant, measurable improvement in academic achievement and dropout rates. How could that be seen as moving too fast? No, it was not time to stop and spend another year meeting to talk over concerns. Besides, the key opponent, the teacher union, was not likely to get on board no matter how long talks continued.

SCHOOL BOARD POLITICS

Part of the backdrop to the public debate over the Blueprint was the upcoming school board election. Zimmerman was seeking a new term, as were Ron Ottinger and Ed Lopez. All three had been previously supported by the San Diego Chamber of Commerce, but Zimmerman had emerged as one of Bersin's most outspoken critics. Behind the scenes, Bersin, Ottinger, and a group of influential business and civic leaders came together to find a candidate who they thought would be more friendly to reform. The Chamber announced in early February that it would not support Zimmerman. But Zimmerman soon had a new ally: the teacher union, which had already registered its opposition to the Blueprint. Thus, Bersin figured that when the Blueprint came to a final vote, Zimmerman would be against it, even though she'd voiced support for it in December.

In the primary election on March 12, Zimmerman came in behind the Chamber candidate, an attorney named Julie Dubick. Ottinger and Lopez won their seats outright because they won the majority of the votes. But Dubick would have to compete with Zimmerman in a citywide runoff in November. To stand a chance of winning, Zimmerman would need the financial backing of the teacher union. Coverage in the local paper of the election had raised the Blueprint as an issue and repeated the claims of critics that it was too costly and disruptive.

THE BIG DECISION

The matter went to a vote two days after the election. Thousands of teachers, parents, and students marched outside the board meeting. Once inside, the protest continued in front of the television cameras. On a videotape of the meeting, Knapp can be seen in the front of the room negotiating with Lopez, the board president, about how to choreograph the spectacle about to take place. Then, several hundred protesters, many of them teachers and most of them white, began trooping through, dropping petitions opposing the Blueprint into a large box. Meanwhile, Knapp was being interviewed at the front of the room by a television reporter. Soon, Lopez had to ask everyone who was not seated to leave the room, at the order of the fire marshal.

When Bersin was given the chance to make his case, he was grave and tense, amid grumblings and even some boos. "I have listened and now I ask to be heard," he said. He recounted the sad litany of statistics, describing a district that was doing far too little for students at the bottom and barely enough for all students except those at the very top. He spoke of the vast differences in performance between children of color and children who were white and Asian. He brought up the fact that so many were lost along the way and that two-thirds of those who graduated had to take remedial classes when they went to college. Bersin blamed no one, but he said the time had long since passed for action. Over and over, Bersin said it was the collective responsibility of the San Diego community to come together and attempt to solve the problems.

He recounted what had happened in the twenty months since he had become superintendent. The district now had a common approach to literacy and math, replacing the hodgepodge of programs that had greeted him upon his arrival. The additional time spent on literacy classes in elementary, middle, and high schools was beginning to pay off in higher test scores, which he attributed to the work of teachers. Principals were learning to be instructional leaders. Thousands of teachers had attended summer workshops, and students had taken summer classes. The district was on the move, and the Blueprint would pull it all together and make sure those needing the most help got what they needed when they most needed it.

In closing his presentation, Bersin read a short essay by a second grader who he said only eighteen months earlier had arrived at school, unable to speak a word of English. "I understand and accept the upset and pain of our teachers," he said. "But when we look at work such as this . . . when we see kindergartners who could not read or write in September who are now doing both, and instead of sixteen out of twenty second graders falling behind in reading, now we have the opposite, we must continue to move ahead and put our money where the results are."

Then, dozens of speakers, each allotted just two minutes, followed him. Most opposed the plan. No matter how many times Alvarado tried to reassure them, they claimed the Blueprint, by reallocating resources, would take away opportunities for their children, especially those who were gifted, musical, or artistic. While this might happen at some schools, he said over and over, it wouldn't be because of the Blueprint. It would be due to the decisions of principals and teachers.

As part of the plan, several elementary school magnet programs where student test scores were abysmal would be converted into schools emphasizing literacy or math. One parent brought her daughter, who attended a marine science elementary school, to protest.

"Marine science has given me an insight into science and will prepare me to tackle more complicated middle school and high school science," the little girl said, reading haltingly from a script. "My dream is to become a marine biologist."

The child's mother couldn't resist speaking. If the plan passed, she said, parents would go on strike. "You're attempting to murder the minds, bodies, and spirits of all of our children."

Bersin was taken aback. "Here I go from being an educational reformer trying to improve reading skills to a destroyer of dreams," Bersin said years later, no longer surprised but still astonished by the characterization.

In these meetings, as in many episodes throughout his tenure, opponents argued from anecdotes against systemic reform. Because one student was inconvenienced, or one teacher felt inhibited from carrying out a favorite lesson, or one principal zealously misinterpreted a broad principle as a hard and fast dictate, the transformation of a school district to refocus on instruction and learning was declared to be unworkable, unfair, and unwise.

UNION OPPOSITION

When he took to the podium, it was clear that Knapp was ready for a fight. He relished the role of spokesman, listing the people who had ceded him their time to

let him represent their views. He said the many prominent people who would tes-
tify in support of the plan were misguided. They were not classroom teachers and
so were not qualified to judge the plan. Because they weren't educators, Knapp
said, "it was an abomination" that they were allowed to register their support. But
the biggest problem with the Blueprint, he said, was not the specifics. In fact, he
said, many of the ideas in the plan were "meritorious and . . . ones that our members have supported for years." But he took issue with "how it's packaged, budgeted, and implemented." He said he could not support it because teachers had
not been asked for their approval and had not bought into it. When his allotted
time was up, Knapp kept shouting until the microphone had to be turned off.

STRONG SUPPORT TOO

Supporters of the plan were passionate as well. John Johnson, the venerable head
of the Urban League of San Diego, had been fighting for improved education for
African American and other students of color for more than three decades and
still, he said, the performance data painted a picture of intolerable neglect. A 1967
lawsuit against the district had found that twenty-three of the district's schools
were racially segregated, and the district was ordered to desegregate them. However, the busing order was successfully challenged. So, instead, the district developed magnet schools and open enrollment policies as alternatives. By 1999, the
white population in the district had dropped from 70 percent to 29 percent, and
the achievement gap was as large as ever. In 1995, a group of minority parents had
filed another lawsuit asking a court to force the district to equalize achievement,
rather than just desegregate the schools. But nothing had been done. "Ladies and
gentleman," Johnson said, "integration, while a good public policy, has nothing to
do with good education."

Johnson, like others who spoke in favor of the plan, was not completely
comfortable with the amount of input they'd had into the process. But, he said,
"while collaborative buy-in is good at times, there are also situations where leaders must . . . exercise leadership. It's difficult to get things done by committee.
We believe Mr. Bersin is doing the right thing. His moves are reformist. And
they are needed."

Jimma McWilson, another African American community activist, said he
didn't understand the opposition to the changes the Blueprint would make in how
money was spent. "Over a billion dollars has been spent on integration over the
past twenty years or so, and it has not elevated those kids or closed the achievement gap," he said. "It may be necessary for the community to march in support
of its own children."

The dynamic of the meeting was clear—most of the teachers and the parents, most of them white and middle class, were opposed to the plan. Most of the leaders of business and higher education, as well as the civil rights activists, favored it. The school board was split, with the two opponents, de Beck and Zimmerman, openly antagonistic.

De Beck asked two principals to talk about the potential effects of the plan on their campuses. But when he did not hear the dire warnings he wanted to hear, he talked over the principals and did not let them respond. He talked about all the opportunities students would be denied and, when Alvarado tried to disagree, he refused to let him speak. "We have a right to have a different point of view," de Beck said. He said he was angry because the administration had not figured out how to pay for it—even though the school board had been presented with a budget that showed how it would be paid for down to the dollar.

Zimmerman launched an angry attack. She said the administration was engaged in "flat-out lying" and that "I know for a fact that a lot of the testimony heard tonight from principals was coerced testimony." She said everyone in the room wanted the Blueprint to succeed but she'd already written it off as a failure, because Bersin had not negotiated its details. She breathlessly listed the Blueprint's flaws, working herself into a full-throated rant that ended with a demand to table the action. Loud applause broke out.

Bersin responded calmly. He noted that, indeed, some aspects of the plan would have to be negotiated with the teacher union. But he called out Zimmerman on her accusation that testimony was coerced. "I ask the media to talk to every principal who appeared here and ask them if they were intimidated," Bersin said. "That is a very serious charge and it has no basis in fact." De Beck came to Zimmerman's defense. "I know that were I a principal and someone called to ask me to report on the Blueprint's success . . . I think I'd come," de Beck said, looking into the camera, a half-smile crossing his lips. He was playing, cynically as always, to the audience.

Ottinger then offered a nine-part motion that directed Bersin to begin to implement the Blueprint, to have it independently evaluated, to report back monthly, and to address a number of other concerns that had been raised. He also reminded the packed room that Bersin had become superintendent only twenty months earlier, and at the time the community had spoken out in favor of hiring a "proven successful leader, a change agent with experience within a large organization, and a leader who insists on high expectations for students."

For too long, Ottinger said, the schools in San Diego—the eighth-largest city in America, yet one that was often parochial and small-minded—had resisted any significant changes, preferring to toy with reform rather than embrace it. Always in San Diego, he said, the impulse was to start small and go slow. Now, he said, it was time for the overhaul that school leaders often promise but only rarely deliver. "This is the first time in my fifteen years in the district we have had presented a comprehensive road map." The Blueprint was approved by a 3–2 vote. The same board members who were in favor of hiring Bersin still supported him.

BLUEPRINT AS TARGET

But, rather than ending the controversy, the approval of the Blueprint made it a target. Bersin's opponents on the board and in the teacher union spent the rest of his time as superintendent attacking it. They would never accept its legitimacy, just as the school board members who originally balked at hiring Bersin refused to accept that he'd been chosen by a majority of the board. Bersin had been unwilling to bow to the politics that had always before blocked any real change. His unwillingness to give in caused a shock to the system that continued to affect it for many years. Bersin's eventual successor, Carl Cohn, and Cohn's successor, Terry Grier, would both be forced to deal with hard feelings that grew out of the passage of the Blueprint.

Soon after the board's decision, parents of Sherman Elementary School students filed a complaint with the U.S. Department of Education alleging that the decision to reallocate federal Title I funds to the Blueprint was improper because parents had not been consulted. The challenge was rejected, and Assistant Secretary of Education Michael Cohen sent a letter to the district in June 2000 confirming that. The letter said that San Diego's proposed use of its Title I funds was proper and, moreover, that "it was the kind of school reform that we wish to see school systems across the country put into place."[19]

That summer, more than thirteen thousand students would attend summer school in San Diego because their math or literacy scores were poor. Kindergartners judged to be behind would attend several weeks of "junior first grade" classes. About one thousand two hundred ninth graders who were behind would get extra help with their reading in a two-hour literacy block. Another thousand ninth graders, who were even further behind, would spend three hours studying literacy when they entered tenth grade in the fall.[20] By that fall, 40–50 percent of middle school students were enrolled in two-hour blocks of time focused on literacy. Nearly twenty-five thousand students reading below grade level in 156 schools were spending extra time in school to receive additional help.

The estimated cost of the Blueprint's first year was $61 million rather than the $49 million anticipated. Planning for the second, even larger, phase of the Blueprint began in earnest in the fall of 2000. The following spring, the school board would approve expanding its strategies to math, at an annual cost of more than $90 million. As a way of reallocating money, the Blueprint was a success. At its peak, the Blueprint's strategies cost $108 million, about 10 percent of the district's spending.

"THE MOST IMPORTANT URBAN SCHOOL REFORM EFFORT IN THE COUNTRY"

Marshall "Mike" Smith, the Undersecretary of Education in the Clinton administration who later joined the Hewlett Foundation and oversaw its investments in education, said at the time that the reforms in San Diego constituted the "most important urban school reform effort in the country . . . If the reforms work here, they will have a national effect because ideas travel."[21] In the fall of 2001, Hewlett and the Bill & Melinda Gates Foundation agreed to commit a combined $22.5 million to support teacher training, literacy, and classroom materials that were part of the Blueprint.[22] Between 2000 and 2004, foundations donated more than $40 million to support Blueprint-related strategies.

Despite the outside funding, the Blueprint remained vulnerable because of its cost. California's budget had a deficit. In 2003, the San Diego schools were hit with a $31 million budget cut. Bersin and his financial team managed to find $100 million in cuts over five years that did not affect classroom spending. By 2004, however, the district was facing a $98 million deficit, and the Blueprint—which had grown to the point that it required resources beyond those that could be redirected—would not be spared.

BLUEPRINT'S EFFECTS

The teacher union continued to do all it could to undermine the effectiveness of the Blueprint and to blame it for the need to make cuts in spending elsewhere in the budget. Not surprisingly, given the union's constant complaint, the first of two studies of the Blueprint by the American Institutes for Research (AIR) found a "climate of fear and suspicion" among educators. "Not only do teachers feel that they are expected to be doing everything now, but they also feel that they are expected to be doing all of it 'right.'"[23]

Many teachers nonetheless supported the change. Hilda Rodriguez, a fifth-grade teacher who had joined the district through a training program designed to get bilingual teachers into classrooms as fast as possible, said she had had no prior notions about teaching. So she, unlike many teachers, was learning the balanced literacy approach for the first time. "It was the milk we were being fed, and I didn't need to shift gears. I felt very, very comfortable."[24]

Implementation of the Blueprint was uneven, a second AIR report said. Teachers in elementary schools told the researchers in a survey that they were using the new methods. But the instructional leaders, who were in charge of seeing that the reforms were carried out effectively, were far less impressed with the quality of teaching that they saw. Teachers also were not convinced that the staff developers, which were costing tens of millions per year, were helping all that much. Because of the depth and complexity of the changes that were supposed to happen, some coaches, principals, and instructional leaders focused on enforcing superficial characteristics of the methods rather than working toward substantive, long-lasting improvements in teaching.

Although the AIR report noted progress in student achievement, it warned that the reforms were still fragile and could easily disappear. "The initial years of the reform effort . . . demonstrate the difficulty of launching and sustaining an ambitious district-wide effort such as that undertaken in San Diego. School reform that involves strengthening the core of educational practice in a large school district is an undertaking that requires stable and supportive leadership, cultivating broad support among all stakeholders, and sufficient time to ensure that practices are put in place in a thoughtful way."[25]

AIR found there was "continued resistance among large numbers of teachers" to the reforms.[26] "The continued dissatisfaction of San Diego teachers with certain Blueprint features, and with the district change process, could ultimately undermine the long-term success of the Blueprint."

PROGRESS OCCURRED

Just as Bersin was leaving office in 2005, the most comprehensive evaluation of student achievement under the Blueprint found mixed results. A team of researchers led by Julian R. Betts, an economist and a senior fellow at the Public Policy Institute of California, found that high school students who participated in extended classes to beef up their skills actually did more poorly than the peers who were not in such classes. In high schools, achievement gaps grew. By then, the Bersin team had recognized these issues and had restructured some high schools and created new, smaller ones. But those efforts did not produce progress in the near-term, in the same way that high school reform efforts nationally that have focused on restructuring high schools have proven initially disappointing.

On the other hand, the Betts team found that the district's success in improving reading performance was "so definitive that San Diego's efforts are well worth a look by other school districts in California and the nation."[27] A significant percentage of the elementary and secondary students who took part in the double- and triple-length English classes, extended school days, and summer school reading programs "showed marked improvement on standardized reading tests." Achievement gaps were narrowed significantly. Retention did not have to be widely used.

Betts and his coauthors concluded that the Blueprint's broad principles—using reading assessments to identify students needing extra help before they fall too far behind, placing these students in extra literacy classes during the school year, and doing everything possible to make sure literacy teachers were highly skilled and well trained—were worthy of national replication.

In a moving 2003 profile of a second grader who was reading at a kindergarten level, Pulitzer Prize–winning editorial writer Jonathan Freedman related how Dee Lyon, a teacher at Encanto Elementary School, asked her principal, Angela Bass, for help with the girl, who had already been held back twice. An Institute for Learning consultant showed Lyon how to change her room for more intensive learning with some students, and Lyon expanded her classroom library to one thousand books. Bass visited the classroom frequently, monitored student progress, and suggested strategies. In one year, the troubled girl advanced the equivalent of more than two years academically.

At the end of second grade, she announced "I can read" and entered third grade the next fall, well prepared.

In 2000, as the school board was preparing to vote on the Blueprint, Bersin was quoted saying, "We must do what is best for students, and not what is most comfortable for adults." There is no doubt that the Blueprint made many adults uncomfortable. They were asked to teach and use resources differently. And it's undeniably true that Bersin, despite his intentions, was unsuccessful in selling the plan to many teachers and principals.

But it's also true that Bersin and Alvarado had proposed a comprehensive plan for addressing the central problems of schools and students—getting resources to those who needed the most help. And remarkably, defying the status quo, they actually implemented a major overhaul to the benefit of many students in a large urban public school district. It was a struggle, but one Bersin believed well worth the effort. Over the years in San Diego, Bersin quoted Frederick Douglass regularly on this point to educators, parents, academics, and to himself:

> If there is no struggle, there is no progress. Those who profess to favor freedom, and yet depreciate agitation, are men who want crops without plowing up the ground. They want rain without thunder and lightning. They want the ocean without the awful roar of its many waters.
>
> This struggle may be a moral one; or it may be a physical one; or it may be both moral and physical; but it must be a struggle. Power concedes nothing without a demand. It never did and it never will.[28]

CHAPTER SIX

The Teacher Union

"This Hostility Is Not Becoming of Professionals"

Among union leaders in San Diego, as well as in some education circles nationally, Alan Bersin is thought of as someone who fought the teacher union throughout his superintendency. Some policy analysts, too, blame Bersin and say he should have worked more collaboratively and built consensus around his reforms. But Bersin believed he needed to build momentum by bringing change quickly. Otherwise, he feared, he might squander the strong support of civic and business leaders. From the beginning, the union's leaders wanted to slow down reform and block any changes they thought would not serve their members' interests. Today, teacher unions are under pressure from Democrats as well as Republicans to be more amenable to a wide range of reforms—including performance pay, accountability for raising student achievement, and changes to tenure and seniority rules. Many union leaders recognize that, in addition to protecting their members, they have a duty to look out for the needs of children. But during Bersin's term, the local union fought all efforts to help teachers improve their practice, even when those efforts were popular with its members. It was behavior such as this that allowed opponents to paint the unions as opponents of efforts to improve schools.

When a San Diego educator was hired for a top job in the Los Angeles school district in 2008, the newspaper reported that she had worked under Alan Bersin, "who was known for nearly ceaseless battles with the teachers union."[1] That is certainly partly how Bersin is still viewed today by union activists and others in San Diego and in some national education circles. Even though he moved one of the nation's largest school districts far along the reform path quickly, he is disdained by some critics, not so much for what he did, but for how he is perceived to have done it. Bersin and other observers believe that the conflict with the union could not be avoided, that he had to choose between moving ahead at a glacial pace, which risked the loss of the momentum created by the circumstances of his selection as superintendent, or moving ahead quickly and, because the union leaders were opposed, creating enmity. He chose the latter course. While the conflict was unfortunate, Bersin believed it was a necessary price to pay and that the benefit outweighed the harm:

> The usual story concerning the San Diego reform is that a confrontational, hard-line, top-down superintendent refused to back down from the teachers union and took no prisoners. This isn't an entirely inaccurate or a completely unfair description. But it was not that at the beginning. This was a war I did not choose and would not fight until it became crystal clear that there really was no middle ground to be reached with the union leadership in place, and its two allies on the school board.
>
> In my previous career I assembled coalitions, built consensus, and resolved disputes. But I also had to try lawsuits when settlement efforts failed. So, when the fight came, I didn't shy away from what I believed in. And, goodness knows, there was a fight to be had in San Diego over school reform. Conflict was un-avoidable because the issues were real and the differences unbridgeable at the time and in the context. The price of getting along here was simply too high.

Bersin believed that social change is always accompanied by a reallocation of power and that conflict is inevitable. If you rule out conflict, you circumscribe change that must occur in stages and the status quo becomes the default position, a starting place and an ending place.

But how much conflict must be or can be endured? Given that there is no natural constituency for change, what incentives are there for leaders to attempt serious reforms or for unions to accept them? Is it even possible to improve education if every change is considered a "give back" in the collective bargaining process? These questions will arise from the local implementation of reforms that eleven states and the District of Columbia have promised to make in return for a total of $4 billion they received from the federal Race to the Top grant competition. To win that money, the states agreed to change their evaluation procedures to take into account student performance and to experiment with new compensation schemes. In many of these states, the specifics of the reforms will be subject to negotiations between school district leaders and local teacher unions. What was promised in the applications may look very different in reality, especially as school budgets continue to be constrained by the slow recovery from the 2008 recession.

That conflict was also at the heart of the Chicago Teachers Union (CTU) strike in September 2012. Similar to Bersin, Mayor Rahm Emanuel decided that the benefits of insisting on evaluating teachers partly based on student test scores and paying successful teachers more than their less-effective colleagues outweighed the costs. The union, for its part, decided that it was not going to back down from its opposition to those policies. Given his previous job in the White House, and the Obama administration's support for those policies, Emanuel became the national face of education reform. Karen Lewis, the CTU's fiery, staunch defender of employees' rights, was committed to standing in the way.

For these reasons as well as many others, Bersin's experience in San Diego remains relevant today. "There is strong resistance to change in the school business, and there are no consequences for failure," former Secretary of Education Rod Paige told the *San Diego Union-Tribune* in a 2002 interview.[2] "Why would they want to change when there's no real reward for success?" He was referring, specifically, to the unwillingness of many educators to have their compensation linked to student performance. But the comment sums up a lot of the resistance Bersin met in San Diego.

The battle against this paralyzing culture is more important than any specific disagreement between a school leader and the local teacher union. It is also larger than disputes over such issues as evaluations, performance pay, seniority rules, or how much teachers should contribute to the cost of their pensions and health benefits. The critical fight is how to change a workplace culture that consistently places the needs of adults ahead of those of students. "I always understood that we needed the hearts and minds of teachers," Bersin said. "But we realized that improving instruction at scale involved massive reform and that the union leadership had decided to stop change in its tracks. We couldn't change the minds of teacher union leaders and, frankly, weren't enamored with their hearts."

A MATTER OF POWER AND PRIDE

Marc Knapp, the leader of the teacher union during the first four years of Bersin's tenure, had been recognized as a teacher who took special measures to connect with his fifth- and sixth-grade students and was named San Diego County's Teacher of the Year in 1991. Knapp had a special love of the desert, and he shared that passion with his students, making it a part of his teaching all year long. At the end of the year, he took his students camping so they could see it for themselves. "I had a kid who turned out to be a herpetologist who had never seen a lizard before I took him out to the sand dunes," he told the *San Diego Union-Tribune* when he received the teaching award. "You sort of make your mark on other people. I'm not going to walk away with a piece of legislation with my name on it, but I'll walk away knowing I had an effect on someone."[3]

Knapp also was a fearless, passionate, articulate, outrageous, passive-aggressive leader who fought Bersin from even before he met him. He had been chief spokesperson for the union during its successful strike in 1996 and right afterward was elected president. He had a flair for the dramatic and a big personality and could inspire a crowd. As a union leader, he participated in the national Teachers Union Reform Network (TURN), a group of progressive union leaders who believed that their interests were better served by a collaborative relationship with school district leaders rather than an adversarial one. But when he returned to San Diego from the meetings, it was clear from his behavior and statements that he believed the collaborative approach advocated by TURN and its members was for him just a change in tactics, rather than a change in perspective. To Knapp, school boards and superintendents could demonstrate they respected teachers by ceding more power to the unions. That, he believed, would benefit students even as it benefited teachers. He did not want to compromise on the tenets of unionism that protected teachers or that sublimated their interests to those of the students. To Knapp, the two sets of interests were identical.

While that may have been consistent logic, there was little evidence that it worked out that way in practice. Knapp never spoke explicitly of the interests of students except in the vaguest of ways. He did not dwell on the importance of teacher practice and skill. He took it for granted that all of his members, by definition, were performing as well as they needed to and the only help required was more encouragement and support. His greatest interest was the process by which policy was decided rather than the policies themselves.

Knapp, who died of cancer in 2007, considered the contract the union won in 1996 to be one of his highest professional achievements. Not only did the union win its salary demands, but it also won for teachers more control over their own professional development activities. Most professional development offered to teachers involves lectures, out-of-class workshops, and demonstrations that researchers have found have little if any effect on the work of teachers. Understandably, teachers don't want to be ordered to attend sessions they don't think are relevant or useful. The contract required the district to negotiate a Memorandum of Understanding (MOU) that would describe how these committees were supposed to work.

As has been already noted, Knapp believed he had a collaborative relationship with Bersin's predecessor, Bertha Pendleton. But his definition of collaboration seemed to mean only that they generally got along well. When Pendleton wanted to restructure a group of persistently failing schools and require the faculty to reapply for their jobs, the union stood in the way and accused her of top-down management. After the one meeting of the transition advisory committee Bersin had formed, Knapp spoke to Bersin privately. "You've got to let me win some and I'll let you win some," Bersin recalled Knapp saying to him. Bersin remembers thinking: "What exactly is he talking about?" He did not intend to go out of his way to antagonize Knapp. But he also didn't plan to horse-trade the interests of students.

CONSENSUS ABOVE ALL ELSE

Five weeks after he was sworn in, Bersin received a union memo describing the relationship it wanted to have with Alvarado's Institute for Learning. The memo matter-of-factly informed Bersin that the district was obligated to reach a consensus with the union before making any changes in curriculum, teaching methods, or professional development.[4] "Everything will be rolled out in collaboration, after being jointly developed," the union memo read. When that did not happen, Knapp began accusing Bersin of using top-down management methods, just as he had in reference to Pendleton.

In August, Knapp wrote in the *Advocate*, the union's newsletter, that the union "has a Memorandum of Understanding . . . that guarantees collaboration on staff development."[5] "So far, SDEA [San Diego Education Association] has not been included in the design, implementation or delivery of the current 'New Idea' and therefore, we are investigating our legal options at this time." This was a common response of the union to any difference in perspective—to immediately go toe-to-toe and threaten legal action.

In a letter to Alvarado a month later, Knapp wrote that SDEA "requests that you halt all activities relating to what you call literacy training and the [Institute for Learning] until such time that the MOU in the contract between SDEA and SDUSD [San Diego Unified School District] can be implemented . . . The district has unilaterally developed and implemented a staff development program that heretofore did not exist. We believe our agreement has been violated."

But Bersin had analyzed the contract language and he did not believe that the MOU was legally binding. That made Knapp furious. Now everything Bersin did was the occasion for a protest. A letter the district sent to all teachers that explained what it was trying to do was labeled as an unfair labor practice. When principals and instructional leaders began visiting classrooms in September, Knapp claimed the visits violated the contract. Teachers, in his view, were to be given advance notice any time the principal wanted to observe classroom instruction. Bersin met with Knapp weekly to try to address their differences. But Bersin said the discussions in those meetings were almost never substantive. Knapp preferred to deal with Bersin through memos, pronouncements, threats of lawsuits, and diatribes in his column in the union's monthly newsletter.

DEFINING COLLABORATION

In his January 1999 column in the *Advocate*, Knapp complained that "the district believes that collaboration means agreeing with them, not finding common ground."[6] To Knapp, collaboration meant conversation and getting along. It did not mean compromise or real change.

Bersin tried to come to grips with Knapp's definition. "Collaboration does not necessarily mean agreement," he said. "There are times we agree and times when we disagree. Collaboration enables the concerned parties to explore, discuss, and debate ideas and proposals together. But the default position cannot invariably be inaction and stagnation."[7]

That seemed to be what the union wanted. Led by Knapp, and his successor Terry Pesta, the union opposed any Bersin proposal that required a change in practice—the introduction of instructional coaches, principals observing teachers for other than evaluation purposes, full-day kindergarten, changes to the bilingual program, a reallocation of federal support dollars, the elimination of many classroom aides, or improvements in the special education program. Any change "brought forth a protest that this was not warranted in the law or in the contract," Bersin said. "The union leaders' attitude is: what's mine is mine, and what's yours is negotiable."

Bersin believes that elevating consensus to the status of a good in and of itself has been disastrous for public education, preventing even commonsense ideas that question existing understandings, practices, and power arrangements from getting serious consideration. Former New York City schools chancellor Joel Klein referred to the practice of putting everything up for a debate and a vote of the "stakeholders" as "the politics of paralysis," because it allows the least common denominator to play a role in weakening or halting important reforms.

A UNION SUPPORTER

For his part, Bersin supported unions then and still does today. He welcomed them as a political force and recognized that their advocacy for good wages and generous benefits had been critical to the emergence of a large middle class in the United States. Teacher unions had forced an end to the practice of paying female teachers, who mostly taught in elementary schools, less than high school teachers, who were mostly male. Union power also sought and won protections so that teachers were not disciplined or dismissed without due process. All of those gains made teaching more attractive for talented young women, especially.

The American Federation of Teachers (AFT) and the much larger National Education Association (NEA) have been in existence for 94 years and 153 years, respectively. The AFT local in Butte, Montana, negotiated the first collective bargaining agreement in 1936. But collective bargaining became widespread and legalized only relatively recently. It wasn't until 1961 that New York City's teachers voted to have the United Federation of Teachers (UFT) bargain a contract on their behalf. A year later, the UFT mounted a strike against the district and eventually won a $995 raise and the right to have a duty-free lunch. Collective bargaining quickly became a national movement in a field characterized by low pay and heavy-handed management.[8]

Knapp and other union leaders repeatedly claimed that Bersin, who came from a family of pro-union Roosevelt Democrats, was trying to bust the union. On the contrary, Bersin admired Albert Shanker, the founder of the New York City teacher union, who led the famous 1962 strike that marks the beginning of collective bargaining in education. Bersin, then a sophomore at Abraham Lincoln High School in Brooklyn, didn't attend school during the strike because "our family didn't cross picket lines."

Still, like critics of teacher unions across the political spectrum, he came to believe that collective bargaining now stands in the way of education reform, and he was more than willing to take on Knapp and the SDEA. Bersin did not accept the power-sharing arrangement that Knapp believed was called for in the contract, later noting:

> What threatened Marc was two things. We were talking about real change and real impact, and we weren't deterred by the usual things that gummed up the works.
>
> We have to move away from the rhetoric of blame and anger between the union and the district. But we must acknowledge the reality that both parties—school boards and their superintendents on the one hand and unions on the other—are usually equally comfortable with the status quo in our public schools. It's so clear that districts and their locals are two partners dancing a tango in history. The modern dance hasn't led to great results, but the dancers have grown accustomed to it and to one another. In the name of collaboration, union and traditional district leadership teams often compose a profoundly conservative force.

On a more fundamental level, union leaders were offended, on behalf of their members, that Bersin and Alvarado thought the quality of instruction had to improve. Knapp often said that the district had been doing fine academically, and parents in most parts of the city were satisfied before Bersin was hired. Knapp believed that the district had "stood on the precipice of greatness; labor, management, and the community were for the first time in decades working together to make things better for the students of San Diego."[9] So, each time Alvarado talked about "instructional improvement," the union leaders heard "teachers need to be fixed." Despite repeated efforts on Bersin's part in subsequent years to reframe the debate, the ideological and psychological chasm between him and the union and many of its members remained deep and unbridgeable.

In an interview with the *Union-Tribune*, Knapp said, "Today we are just hoping we can survive the landslide of despair. I wish I could express this in a way that you could feel our pain at this unfortunate turn of events."[10] The "unfortunate turn of events" was, in his mind, Bersin's leadership.

TEACHERS AS PROFESSIONALS

Bersin and Knapp also disagreed about what it meant to be a professional educator. In the professions of medicine, architecture, or law, standard practice is built on a foundation of knowledge, ethics, independence, efficacy, and accountability. Bersin noted that professionals draw on a body of knowledge and apply it strategically and creatively to specific sets of circumstances. Doctors, for example, are expected to know the best treatment for a broken arm, but not all broken arms are the same. They draw on their knowledge of accepted, research-based, practice-proven treatments and apply that knowledge to the facts of a particular situation. They do not ordinarily invent their own ways of treating an illness, without a foundation in science and previous practice. Were they to do so, they would likely be cited for misconduct or sued for malpractice.

Bersin, the lawyer-educator, believed that educators, aided by researchers, had to develop a similar basis for practice before teaching could be considered a real profession. Decisions about tenure and compensation should be made on that basis, he argued. "Teachers should be reviewed and determinations made as to who properly deserves tenure," he said. "The challenge for teachers is to accept the concept of genuine evaluation; the challenge for administrators is to make that review fair and meaningful. Once tenure becomes a status earned through a respected process—rather than bestowed after two or three years as a job right—the stature and compensation of the tenured teacher will be enhanced. Connecting tenure to productivity is essential to professionalism."[11] Bersin did not try to implement these policies in San Diego. He already had caused enough tension. But, interestingly, this is close to the model for awarding teachers tenure and relating pay to performance in the Race to the Top competition.

Knapp, not surprisingly, had a different view of professionalism. He defined teacher professionalism by position, rather than by skills or training. When Alvarado wanted to hire highly trained literacy instructors to lead after-school and summer tutoring sessions, Knapp wrote a memo saying that all teachers, by virtue of the fact that they possessed a teaching license, were equally qualified for those positions. Whether a teacher had the specialized knowledge and skill to help students improve their reading was beside the point for Knapp. He wanted those positions to be filled based on seniority. That was the same argument he'd made with respect to the selection of the peer coaches or staff developers—no special skills needed.

Knapp and the teacher union staff considered it to be a contract violation to expect teachers to read professional literature when they were not on the clock and rejected the idea that teachers ought to spend time in the summer preparing to teach in the fall. "It really is pretty ridiculous, when you think about it, expecting us to give up so much of our own time, our off time, our unpaid time, to prepare for our paid work time," Knapp wrote in the September 2000 edition of the *Advocate*. "What other profession does that?"[12] One might have responded to Knapp by saying that all other professionals do that, in order to keep up with the knowledge in their field.

In the same column, Knapp celebrated all that teachers know how to do. "We know how to . . . control a class; supervise recess, lunch, passing time; How to take attendance; Know when a child really has to go to the bathroom; Know where the faculty bathroom is and whether or not you need a key; How to contact the office and what to do in an emergency; How to keep fights from happening . . . and how to break them up; What to say to our students that is inappropriate and appropriate; and Lessons that last the right amount of time."

That is the entire comment. Astonishingly, it does not mention anything about teaching. Knapp spoke frequently about teachers and their rights. He complained that the curriculum and teaching methods favored by Alvarado straitjacketed his members. To Knapp, it was more important to let teachers teach based on their classroom experience and personal style than it was to require teachers to base their work on good, accepted research about how to help students learn.

BATTLES OVER PEER COACHES AND THE BLUEPRINT

These three differences in perspective—regarding the terms of the teachers' contract, the nature of collaboration, and what constituted professional teaching—formed the basis of the two largest disagreements between Bersin and the teacher union. The first big dispute, as noted earlier, was over Alvarado's plan to bring in trained instructional coaches to help their peers improve their literacy teaching; the second was over the writing and implementation of the Blueprint for Student Success in a Standards-Based System.

Coaches are now commonplace, and the hiring of tens of thousands of them over the past decade is one of the reasons the ratio of teachers to students has risen far faster than growth in student enrollment. Back then, however, instructional coaches were new and their use isolated. Alvarado had deployed instructional coaches when he led District 2 in New York. San Diego was among the very first to make coaches a centerpiece of its instructional improvement efforts.

Deployed to each school, the instructional coaches' job was to observe and to help their colleagues learn to use the intellectually demanding pedagogical methods Alvarado favored. The coaches would work alongside the principal and instructional leaders but not evaluate teachers' performance.

Knapp viewed this arrangement as a threat to his members. He wanted teachers to know exactly what instructional leaders, principals, or coaches wanted to see and hear so that they could make sure it happened during their visitations. That, of course, would have defeated the purpose. The visits weren't meant to be an enforcement tool. They were supposed to help principals implement the district's approach to literacy. It seems obvious that, if that's the purpose, the teachers hired as coaches needed to know something about that approach.

The union, by contrast, wanted to rename the coach position "staff developer/peer assistor." Rather than helping to implement the literacy plan, the union wanted the "assistor" to help with the "development and implementation of the site staff development plan."

"We believe that any classroom or staff development program must be based on positive comment and support, not on the intimidation and fear that is currently palpable in the district."[13] Knapp wanted the staff developers to "offer praise with regards to classroom work" and help them "hone exemplary teaching practices." The coaches should "work collaboratively to help everyone reach their highest teaching potential."[14] This was an example of what Bersin would learn was the "make nice" culture of education, which required that educators not criticize or even critique one another.

The positions of the union and the district were so fundamentally different that it is difficult to see how any compromise might have been reached. In a way, it is heartening to recognize how much they did compromise.

After eight months of negotiations, Bersin marked up a draft of the agreement. By his tally, eleven of the elements had been proposed by the district, seven had been added by the union, and seven more came from joint discussions. The district, for example, gave up the right to nominate the coach, as long as the nominee attended an Institute training session. But the two sides were still far apart. The union rejected the idea that the district would train the coaches in any way. The union continued to tell its members, in ever more heated language, that the district was resisting all efforts to work together. Showing that he was planning to stall as long as possible, Knapp's March 1999 column in the union newsletter was headlined, "This Too Shall Pass."

Knapp was quoted in an article in *San Diego* magazine by Jonathan Freedman contending that every time negotiators for the two sides reached an agreement, it would be taken to the district and Alvarado or Bersin would reject it. "While a dialogue appeared to be going on, both sides were actually engaged in separate monologues," Freedman wrote. "Knapp was arguing for teachers to have freedom to teach behind closed doors without being snooped on. Alvarado was arguing for teaching to become a public practice with professional standards, as is required of physicians."[15]

In a further compromise, the district agreed to give candidates who failed the Institute's training course a second chance. But the union rejected that and said additional training was optional even if the person was judged not capable of performing the assigned duties. Robin Whitlow, the union's executive director, reiterated that the union would not accept any requirements that the peer coaches/staff developers have any special skills or qualifications. The "site governance teams" referred to in the contract were to decide who would be hired with no formal role for the Institute or the instructional leaders and but a single vote by the principal. "These changes represent 'must haves,'" Whitlow wrote on a cover sheet to a fax to the district. "Hope this seals the deal."[16]

That did not seal the deal, of course. "The single issue blocking this program from becoming a reality is one of quality assurance," Bersin wrote in an op-ed in the local newspaper. "What does quality assurance in this context mean? It means that staff developers must have specific knowledge, skills, and experience beyond that of the teachers they will be coaching if they are to make a measurable impact on student literacy."[17]

In a letter to the union, Bersin wrote that "it remains impossible apparently for Association leadership to deal with the issue of quality because it refuses to differentiate among teacher readiness, knowledge, experience, and abilities. I respect teachers and the teaching profession profoundly but I know there are differentiated levels of knowledge and skill, experience, and need among teachers, as there are among members of any profession. We must see this diversity as a strength on which we can build rather than continue to deny it as a fact with which we cannot deal."

Knapp and Whitlow viewed the district's insistence on deciding who would become a coach as an unacceptable "power play" that represented "the same old paternalistic attitude that produced the staff development problem we are currently saddled with." (By that, they meant staff development that was not designed at each site by the teacher-dominated site governance team.)

By March, Bersin was running out of time. If the dispute went on much longer, it would not be possible to have the coaches on the job by the fall. To force the issue, he declared a state of emergency and set about to choose 85 "curriculum resource teachers" to serve at 115 schools. The position of resource teacher was already part of the collective bargaining agreement, so Bersin intended to resolve the impasse unilaterally by dropping the title "instructional coach."

"This is grandstanding. This is the Alan Show," Whitlow said.[18] "I don't know why anyone sitting up in the Ed Center thinks they know more about what's best for kids than the classroom teachers," Knapp said.[19]

In his last offer before turning the matter to an outsider to mediate, Bersin proposed that if candidates chosen by the school site teams failed the training, they could take the training again and then, if they were still deemed unprepared, they could appeal to an independent panel that included union representatives. Still the union objected. The mediators stepped in and crafted a deal that pleased neither Knapp nor Bersin. The resolution of the matter reinforced Bersin's view that nothing of substance could be accomplished through traditional collective bargaining routes. Collaboration had, once again, led to paralysis—lots of talking, but little movement.

"Union arguments were derived from 'positions' rather than the merits of the controversy," Bersin concluded. "And their positions had nothing to do with the educational needs of children."

CONFLICT OVER THE BLUEPRINT

That was most evident in the union's position on the Blueprint. After the school board approved moving ahead with the plan in December 1999, Bersin and Alvarado asked the union leaders for their help. But Whitlow and Knapp did not want to get involved in developing the sweeping plan.

The union's objections, as always, were about the decision-making process, not about the decisions themselves. "They claim the SDEA was part of the Blueprint design and that we agreed with the draft," Knapp and Whitlow wrote in a letter to their members. "That isn't accurate. We have continued to work toward consensus, but we find that the Institute has been stringing us along."[20]

They said they were reluctant to reopen discussions because the Institute wasn't willing to also revisit and renegotiate every decision that had been made in the previous twenty months. It seemed that nothing was final. The union even asked Bersin to scrap the Blueprint, after the school board had directed him to keep developing it prior to a vote in March. Knapp asked Bersin to start over with members of the community, teachers, union leaders, and others at the table. "Next to a child's parents, his/her teacher knows what's best for their child. Educators understand the desire of the District's administration to make a name for itself by creating a system that receives national attention. We want that to happen for the district as well. Real practitioners (those that work with children) are more than willing to sit down and show them how." [21]

In February 2000, during discussions about the Blueprint, Knapp wrote that any shortcomings in student achievement were "directly attributable to the fact that real practicing educators have NEVER had the opportunity to address much less fix the problem. We have always had some out-of-town guru roll in with the latest, greatest plan; plans that real educators can see have glaring problems. They are expected to make it work in spite of its inadequacies."[22]

Still, Knapp claimed to support the Blueprint's strategies. "SDEA will be the first to say that many of the concepts in the Blueprint make good sense," he wrote in April 1999. "We've been promoting some for years. It is the implementation and educational tradeoffs that cause our members to disagree."

Because of that, he did all he could to prevent it from going forward. After the school board voted in favor of the Blueprint, Whitlow wrote to the district's head of human resources to say that it violated numerous aspects of the contract. "It may be possible that the Superintendent, a newcomer to the culture of education, may not be aware or maybe just plain does not respect that the contract is an instrument that ensures consistency of quality learning and service to students," Whitlow wrote.[23]

One of the parts of the Blueprint that teachers and principals did not like was that it reallocated much of the federal Title I aid within the school district to the central office, which would use it and other federal funds to pay for more teachers, coaches, and other strategies. However, that put the money beyond the power of school site councils to control.

The district asked teachers to help their principals decide how to deal with the reduction in funds. But Knapp directed them not to participate. "Our superintendent wants to be able to say staffs were involved and thereby support this plan. Don't be fooled into cannibalizing your fellow front-line educators."[24]

The union leaders wanted it both ways. They wanted to be consulted. But they weren't willing to do anything that might help the district and Bersin succeed.

The union filed a loudly announced grievance claiming the district refused to bargain. It also worked with the California Teachers Association (CTA) to sponsor legislation that would expand the scope of collective bargaining to include issues of professional development, curriculum, textbook selection, and academic standards and assessments. Designed as an antidote to the San Diego experience, the bill provoked so much opposition statewide that the Democratic-controlled Assembly, which was usually reliably beholden to the CTA and its massive apparatus of campaign contributions, withdrew its support.

RELENTLESS UNION OPPOSITION

In Bersin's view, the Blueprint demonstration and the failed legislative project in Sacramento represented the height of the union's power and influence during his term. But the union never stopped fighting. The angry protests that began within months of his becoming superintendent would continue throughout his seven years in office. Often-raucous union supporters would pack school board meetings. At one meeting, a planned discussion of budget cuts was overrun with teachers wearing red, which they said symbolized the blood that would be shed if cuts were imposed.

"Those were very bitter times," said Robert Kittle, the editor of the *San Diego Union-Tribune*'s editorial page. "The school board meetings were often a circus. I attended a few of them. I wanted to see what the heck was going on. To have the union members sitting up in the back making catcalls, it really was guerrilla theater. It was just shocking that a public body was engaging in this kind of . . . I don't know what to call it beyond guerrilla theater."[25]

When Bersin was invited to talk to a community group, union protesters would show up to demonstrate against him. Knapp casually referred to Bersin in his monthly newsletter columns as dictator, oppressor, and overseer—in effect, condoning the behavior of teachers who carried signs blithely calling him "Der Führer" and Hitler. Such epithets would be disturbing and offensive to anyone; that Bersin and his family are Jewish made the vilification even more egregious.

Untruths about Bersin's compensation, management of the district's real estate, alleged cronyism, administrative spending, and bargaining positions filled the union's monthly newsletter. The messages were amplified by the staunchly antibusiness local alternative press and the anti-Bersin faction on the school board. The drumbeat was deliberate and loud and, over time, affected how the reform agenda was viewed.

The hostilities played out in private as well as in public. Union leaders would refuse to participate in committees to work out solutions to policy differences, walk out of meetings, direct teachers not to participate in brainstorming sessions, harangue Bersin based on anecdotes during weekly meetings to discuss ongoing issues, and rebuff his invitations to district social events. The battle became personal. "They would yell at people, call me vile names, file rote grievances that were rejected, shout false statements, and angrily threaten job actions," Bersin said.

The tensions concerned San Diego business leaders who supported Bersin.[26] Malin Burnham, the prominent San Diego real estate developer, wrote a 2001 op-ed in the *Union-Tribune* headlined "Moving Beyond the Personal Hostility." He criticized Knapp for resorting to "name-calling, unfounded accusations, and even bogus polling" to stir opposition.[27] But Burnham also called on Bersin and Knapp to find a way to work together. "Too much is at stake—the future of our schools, our city, our state, our nation—and especially our children," he wrote. "The stakes are bigger than any one individual."

Bersin says that over time teachers and principals, especially those hired during his tenure, supported him and the measures he'd championed. But for a number of years, teachers who had taken the side of Bersin and Alvarado couldn't speak up in teacher lounges or in union meetings. Their comments would be met with silence and, at some schools, they would find notes accusing them of being traitors or worse on the windshields of their cars. "In the name of union democracy, these SDEA leaders were running a most intolerant institution and doing so with not a little dose of thuggishness," Bersin said. "More generally, it was a source of great frustration and regret, given my political and personal background, to see how the union movement had evolved over time into a very reactionary set of instincts. They stood for the status quo, pure and simple."

In his farewell column as union president in June 2002, Knapp wrote that the administration has "suggested, encouraged, and forced site administrators to harass, abuse, and intimidate educators in every emotional, professional, legal, and sometimes illegal way possible." He cited no specifics and compared Bersin to a tyrant. "After the fall of every dictatorship those conspirators that do the dirty work for the 'boss' always claim they didn't know what was happening, or that they were just doing what they were told to do." Knapp claimed that "hundreds" of principals who had tried to keep their integrity intact had been fired or forced to quit. "I guess dictators in school districts aren't allowed to incarcerate dissidents," Knapp concluded.[28]

The allegation was wild and everyone knew it, but by then not many cared and no one called Knapp on it. That spring, 85 percent of the teachers did not even bother to cast a ballot to elect his successor.

Bersin took the attacks in stride. "For me, it was politics, although much more brutish and primitive than I'd expected. The discourse was more raw and in the gutter than I had seen in the corporate and law enforcement sectors, perhaps in keeping with the passive-aggressive nature of school district culture. That didn't make the politics complex, just uglier and much more routinely untruthful."

In the spring of 2002, Bersin spoke at a San Diego high school about what he viewed as his accomplishments and shortcomings in an unusual "state of the district" speech. He vowed to improve his working relationship with the teacher union, a statement that drew a standing ovation. "We have rumor mills by the dozen, one-liners by the hundreds, demonization by the pound, and gossip by the ton," he said. "No one, including myself, is blameless on this score."[29]

But it did not happen. Larry Cuban observed that San Diego under Bersin was "very teacher-friendly, but it has not been perceived as teacher-friendly." Instead, he said, "it has been perceived as disrespectful and this is part of the tragic story of this district."[30] Cuban later sharpened his critique, saying that the conflict with the teacher union "ran counter to San Diego's history of cooperation" and doomed the reforms.[31] He said that Bersin and Alvarado deserved blame because they "arrived with sledgehammers and bulldozers to renovate San Diego schools" and should have moved more slowly to gain teachers' trust.

Education historian and policy analyst Diane Ravitch, who was appointed as U.S. assistant secretary of education by George H. W. Bush, leveled heavy criticism of Bersin for the way he dealt with teachers in her 2010 book *The Death and Life of the Great American School School System: How Testing and Choice Are Undermining Education.*[32] It is clear from her chapter on San Diego in that book that her main sources were union leaders, who repeatedly made broad and untrue claims about the number of teachers who left the district due to stress. Ravitch claims that the union's assertions were corroborated by a hospital official. But no statistics were cited and no one was quoted on the record on that point. Data from the district does not indicate any increase in resignation or retirements from historical averages.

Cuban and Michael Usdan, another respected analyst of school districts and reform, noted that continual conflicts made reforms slower and smaller-bore than they could have been and needed to be.[33]

San Diego school principals who were asked years later to reflect on Bersin's time said they were grateful for all they learned and nostalgic about a period when they grew greatly as professional educators. But they said they regret the sometimes-hostile resistance of many teachers, particularly at the outset, from 1999 through 2001. Instructional leader Carol Pike said the contentiousness between Bersin and Knapp made her job harder than it needed to be.

"This thing was growing and growing, and I find it difficult to believe that there wasn't someone out there who could help the system get through that," she said in an interview. "That would have had huge implications for the work. There were supporters and detractors and people sitting on the fence and thinking, 'this is what Marc is telling me and this is what Alan is telling me, and I'm a reasonable person and trying to figure out which way to go.'"[34] She later noted, "In retrospect, all of us should have found a way to play better in the sandbox."

As time went on, Bersin and the district's principals communicated more with teachers directly and, as the positive effects of the Blueprint's strategies began to appear in classrooms, tensions at most schools began to ease. To be sure, many teachers continued to oppose the Blueprint, as was noted by outside analysts such as the American Institutes of Research. But, as one study reported, "many of Bersin's reforms were met with interest and success at the school level once they were actually implemented. Teachers found the workshops helpful, and the teacher coaches (no longer the enemy) became an invaluable resource. Mathematics specialists improved math teaching and freed up time for teachers to plan and prepare. Ironically, according to some outside observers, there was no connection in the minds of teachers between these positive changes and their superintendent. Teachers and the union were rarely willing to give Bersin credit for the benefits they experienced in the classroom."[35]

TEACHER SUPPORT NEEDED

Bersin came to recognize that, under existing circumstances, no urban superintendent could enact sustainable critical reforms in the absence of a working relationship with the local teacher union. "It doesn't have to be friendly, but it does have to function."

He also concluded that without a decisive political shift, the collective bargaining process affords little opportunity to explore new ways of working. Bersin mused that perhaps the state of public education in urban school districts wasn't yet dire enough for union leaders to consider new modes of compensation and a new relationship with management, as had been the case in Detroit between the Big Three auto companies and their employee unions both in the 1980s and again after the 2009 federal bailouts.

The situation in San Diego was extreme because of the labor history in the district, the ambitiousness of what was being attempted, the national prominence of the actors involved, and the personalities of the leaders themselves. However, the San Diego situation also upended the conventionally accepted proposition that nothing could be accomplished in school reform in the face of unrelenting union opposition. The union was unable to build a broader anti-Bersin political coalition. So, the administration's reforms moved forward. "That unnerved union leaders who had grown used to huffing and puffing and blocking anything they didn't like," Bersin said.

The union-district tension in San Diego did not end after Bersin's departure. Five years later, mention of Bersin's name to ardent union supporters in San Diego still sparked animosity and resentment.

His successor, Carl Cohn, was hired with a mandate to make peace. He did what he could to improve employee morale and to build a better working relationship with the school board. The SDEA did agree to a policy that weakened seniority as the determinant of how teachers were assigned, especially to low performing schools. But while Cohn's relationship with the union was warmer, it led to little substantive change. Cohn quit in 2007, less than two years after taking the job.

In an interview after his resignation, Cohn said he tried to build a better working relationship with the SDEA. He and the union's leaders attended two meetings of the Teachers Union Reform Network, the aforementioned national organization of union officials who say they favor greater collaboration with school districts. "Basically," Cohn said, "the conversation is, 'How do you throw out all the district rules and regulations and elements of the union contract that impede the district and the union from creating really competitive new schools?'" Cohn said he tried to convince the SDEA leadership that taking this challenge seriously would serve as a credible response to critics who were saying that districts and unions were not doing enough to rescue at-risk kids. The SDEA rejected the effort, just as it had under the more confrontational Bersin, and Cohn said it was a "big disappointment."[36]

The union's relationship with Cohn's successor, Terry Grier, was much worse. Grier, a more committed reformer than Cohn, regularly collided with the SDEA. In the spring of 2009, the union backed a slate of candidates who had pledged they would do all they could to avoid eliminating the jobs of any teachers, even though the school district was facing enormous deficits. Led by Camille Zombro, the union essentially took over school district governance. Grier departed San Diego in 2009, again less than two years after taking the job.

Zombro remains bitterly angry toward Bersin. She was one of nine teachers who Bersin had transferred in 2004 because they deliberately created conflict and disruption at their schools to undermine Bersin's authority. When he briefly considered running for city attorney in 2007, Bersin gave Zombro, who as union president was an important political figure, a courtesy call. Zombro told the *Union-Tribune* that she refused Bersin's offer to have lunch. "The ego of this man to think that he could have anything to say to me other than an apology," she told the newspaper.[37]

WHAT WENT WRONG?

After he left the district, Bersin continued to analyze what had gone awry. He did not blame Knapp or the other union leaders. He believed they were simply doing what they could be expected to do, given the environment in which they had risen to power and operated.

By their very nature, labor contracts look backward. Each new contract attempts to address actual or perceived abuses by enacting language that, from the union's perspective, constrains the district as much as possible. Then, once negotiated, the contract becomes immutable.

"Individual cases of injustice, real or perceived, became a source of work rules that apply across 9,000 teachers," Bersin said. "You could look at the different sections of the contract and see them as a zone in a geological dig . . . Rule after rule was grafted on top of the existing framework. Always the approach was incremental, never comprehensive. And, over time, the district lost what in any rationally negotiated contract would be considered essential management prerogatives necessary to proper functioning of an organization."[38]

This was especially true of the 189-page collective bargaining agreement in San Diego. When Frederick Hess analyzed the collective bargaining agreements of the fifty largest school districts, San Diego's and those of seven other urban districts were judged to be "highly restrictive." That judgment was based on the degree to which the contract restricted the discretion of management. In the same study, Hess and his coauthor determined that the restrictive work rules in San Diego's contract merited a grade of F and the personnel provisions earned a grade of D+.[39]

In San Diego, contract language on seniority and transfers required the district to wait until late August—just a week or two before school started—to hire teachers from outside the district. All teachers within the district who wanted to transfer to a new school, or who were involuntarily transferred, were entitled to jobs regardless of their performance, and had to be assigned before any new teachers could be hired.[40] It was reported that in August 2004 as many as three-quarters of the one thousand new teachers hired that summer still did not yet know where or what they would be teaching. Nearly 20 percent of those teachers would still not know their teaching position in September, when school began.

The New Teacher Project, then headed by Michelle Rhee, the former chancellor of schools in the District of Columbia, and now by Tim Daly, studied the hiring and seniority policies in San Diego, New York, and Miami for a 2005 report. In an interview about the report for National Public Radio, Bersin said, "The students and classrooms most at risk typically don't get the benefits of the very best teaching."[41]

"It is commonly assumed that improving urban teacher quality simply requires more and better professional development," Bersin said in a press release on the study. "The reality is that staffing rules in urban contracts restrict our ability to do what we really need to do to raise teacher quality—attract and hire promising candidates, keep great teachers, and match teachers with students' needs—by micromanaging teacher assignment and transfer processes, and placing an absolute premium on seniority."

After he left the district and became California's secretary of education, Bersin worked with Rhee and then-senator Jack Scott, chair of the Senate Education Committee, to write and enact a bill signed into law by Governor Schwarzenegger that protected the state's lowest performing schools from having to accept teachers who had been "excessed" from other schools, based on their seniority. The California Teachers Association vehemently opposed the measure.

"Union leaders at the state level and site representatives in San Diego would acknowledge privately the damage done by rigid seniority provisions and single salary schedules but disclaim any ability or desire to alter the contract," Bersin told an interviewer. "There was rigid allegiance to the contract, in an almost religious sense: 'This is what we negotiated in the past, and we cannot and will not give any of it back.'"[42]

HOW TO IMPROVE COLLECTIVE BARGAINING

In a 2005 essay he wrote for *Education Week*, Bersin wrote:

> We lack an intellectual framework to create common ground, a shared concept about how we might move collective bargaining from where we are to where we ought to be in order to strengthen public education. On the one hand, proponents of so-called 'new unionism' call for broadening the scope of collective bargaining. According to this view, a reformed union would embrace the tenets of professionalism. The union would be accountable for practice, providing teachers with much more control over the tools of the profession and the application of those tools, and have a significant influence on curriculum, professional development and instructional materials. It would embrace peer review as a mechanism of evaluation and it would place student achievement at the center of the enterprise and at the heart of the labor-management discussion.[43]

But Bersin was skeptical. "This reformist perspective on collective bargaining has been bubbling along for more than 20 years, but always on the margins, and producing more talk than results. So, the potential benefits of this approach remain theoretical at best, with good reason to doubt the theory as well as the pragmatism of expecting unions to play a completely different role from what their organizational nature and history would suggest."[44]

Bersin tried to work out a third way. He expected unions to continue to play their important role of protecting teachers' employment interests while also being flexible enough to consider new ways of doing business, such that schools and school districts would be able to improve their performance.

One idea he espoused was to allow lower performing schools to volunteer to bargain with teachers separately from the districtwide union. The negotiations would retain important protections for teachers to ensure fairness. But the process also would focus on creating a good climate for a turnaround—a superior principal, committed teacher-leaders, a stable faculty, a coherent curriculum, and outreach to parents, who would be encouraged and helped to participate in the education of their children.[45]

In forums across the country, not infrequently in the company of receptive labor leaders, Bersin advocated for the concept of the "alternative contract," or "thin contract," such as that negotiated by Steve Barr, who ran the Green Dot Public Schools charter network in Los Angeles. Based on reciprocal obligations and accountability among the district, the union, and the school, a flexible arrangement would give schools and their teachers the room they needed to innovate. For example, such contracts could make it possible to pay math and science teachers working in inner-city schools a higher salary to make those positions more attractive.

In August 2008, while attending the Democratic Convention in Denver, Bersin visited the Bruce Randolph Middle School, which implemented an alternative contract with the support of former superintendent Michael Bennet (who has since become a U.S. senator from Colorado) and his senior advisor, Brad Jupp, the former Denver teacher union head who now works for the Department of Education in the Obama administration. "As gifted as Bennet and Jupp are," Bersin noted after visiting the school, "the keys have been the leadership of Principal Kristen Waters, and the school union representative, Greg Ahrnsbrak, and their colleagues. The result is predictably magical."

"We don't see this as radical," said Ahrnsbrak, a physical education teacher at the school. "We see this as common sense. We want to be released from this bureaucratic entanglement that will allow us to do better."[46]

In addition to offering schools the chance to adopt an alternative contract, Bersin also talked about establishing what Alvarado had called "separate negotiating zones," which, among other things, would give principals and their faculties greater control over who joined the faculty at their school. Many supporters of charter schools argue that one of the schools' great strengths is that they are able to hire teachers whom the educators believe would be a good fit.

He came up with other ideas to address problems that had arisen in San Diego. One was to create a separate due-process mechanism that would relieve the union of the burden of protecting the jobs of teachers who are clearly incompetent. Such a process would have to be legally sanctioned, such that the union would still be fulfilling its obligation to defend its members' rights. But in Bersin's mind it would have the salutary effect of dealing with such issues, as well as other grievances, outside the collective bargaining process. That way, the contract would not become thick with work rules that then applied to every school and every teacher. The union would not be tied by definition to practitioners and practice inimical both to teacher quality and student achievement.

THE BATTLES OF THE PAST

Bersin concluded that unions, if they are going to continue to be relevant, must stop refighting the battles of the past, move beyond their industrial union roots, and embrace a version of teacher professionalism that values skill, knowledge, training, accountability, and performance:

> Unions are unable to embrace features of innovation that would both raise sala-
> ries across the board and provide for incentive compensation, which is a sine
> qua non of high-end professional earning. The grand bargain here leaves the
> union political monopoly in place in exchange for flexibility and contractual
> choice for teachers at the school level. Absent that bargain, teacher unions seem
> incapable of avoiding the lemming-like march off the edge that doomed manu-
> facturing unions unable to face up to competition from abroad. Their leaders
> believe that teaching jobs cannot be "exported," without grasping, apparently,
> the significance of both charter schools and vouchers to that end, in the public
> schooling context.

Bersin quoted Albert Shanker in support of this new way of thinking. "Collective bargaining has been a good mechanism, and we should continue to use it. But now we must ask whether collective bargaining will get us where we want to go . . . I am convinced that unless we go beyond collective bargaining to the achievement of true teacher professionalism, we will fail in our major mission to preserve public education in the United States and to improve the status of teachers economically and socially."[47]

In the end, however, Bersin was skeptical. "I still cannot conceive of any step our team might have taken—save abject surrender—that could have avoided the union struggle in San Diego," he said. "Political advantage in the short term, revolving around preservation of the existing order of things, trumps all else in the usual teacher union calculus. Typically, it is always and only about the adults in the system."

He said rare union leaders, such as Randi Weingarten, now the president of the AFT, understand that the status quo is not in the long-term survival interest of the public education franchise. "But Randi, whom I like very much, has yet to demonstrate that she is a leader willing to rise up above the noise to take real risks on behalf of real reform. And even Shanker himself could not force the changes in collective bargaining he knew were necessary to move teaching from the industrial occupation it is mostly today to a profession."

PARTY POLITICS

Like many other observers today, Bersin believes the teacher unions pose a problem for the Democratic Party. It is the traditional constituents of the Democrats, African Americans and Latinos, who are losing out educationally. But teachers and their unions also are among the largest blocs of reliable Democratic voters.

Unionized teachers dominate party conventions and "get out the vote" campaigns. Union resistance to reform—exemplified by the refusal of many district union locals to participate in the Obama administration's Race to the Top competition, and the Chicago Teachers Union strike—has weakened their alliances with parent groups. Many African American and Hispanic parents and community leaders now embrace market-based alternatives to chaotic, poorly run traditional public schools that seem hamstrung by weak leadership and restrictive union contracts. Low-income parents want their children to get a good education as much as middle-class parents do. And they're not wed to the idea that public schools run by school districts and overseen by boards of education are the only place their children can get that education. That is one reason charter schools are thriving in many cities.

The key organization helping Democrats reposition themselves on education issues is Democrats for Education Reform, known as DFER. Funded by New York entrepreneurs, and led by former journalist Joe Williams, DFER is pro-charter and does not accept that teacher unions always have the interest of children at heart: "For too long, we Democrats have not allowed ourselves to even talk about some of the messy issues surrounding the improvement of our schools, while [most] Republicans in office have done nothing but talk," Williams has written. "Millions of our nation's children have slipped through the cracks in the process."

Bersin became a board member of DFER because he agreed that Democrats had to find a way to be more responsive to students' needs for better schools, and that meant being less responsive to employee groups.

Bersin often said that the very best teachers should be paid $150,000 or more, based on their performance. To him, the essence of professionalism was that the best performers could count on being well compensated for the time they had spent improving their practice.

It was ironic, except to him and those who knew him, that the superintendent who for seven years was accused by the local teacher union of disrespecting teachers remained throughout a passionate advocate for them, supporting teacher professionalism and high salaries as the potential salvation of public education—with, or if necessary, without unions.

CHAPTER SEVEN

The School Board

"The Reason for the Crisis in American Education Is That No One is Accountable"

Bipartisan school boards emerged out of the Progressive Era in the early twentieth century as a reform meant to insulate the schools from the patronage of machine politics. They attracted leading citizens willing to serve as guardians of the education of the community's children as well as the pocketbooks of their parents and other taxpayers. Over the past century, school boards shrank in importance due to the centralization of state education policy and finance, an expansion of the role of the federal government, and, more recently, globalization. During the same period, the reputation of urban school districts declined as a consequence of middle-class flight and the weak academic record of low-income and minority students. Voters lost interest as school boards became less important. Teacher unions used their resources to help elect sympathetic board members. At times, business interests have tried to exert influence over school board elections. But their efforts usually are short-lived. In many cities and towns, schools board meetings have become a stage on which narrow, local, political struggles to play out. Education issues often take a back seat. That is what Alan Bersin experienced as he spent seven years trying to bring about major changes when two members of the five-member board opposed him at every turn. Bersin believed that, instead of being guardians of schools, elected boards have become major obstacles to education reform.

The applause and boos that drowned out school board members during an October 2004 meeting would not be tolerated by most other elected governing boards. But this was a frequent occurrence at meetings of the San Diego Board of Education before, during, and after Alan Bersin's tenure as superintendent. Mostly, those making the noise were teachers mobilized by their union to support Bersin's critics on the board.

Egged on by the behavior of Frances Zimmerman and John de Beck, the audience this night was more hostile than usual—even though Bersin himself was not in attendance. Finally, school board member Ed Lopez had had enough. Over the past six years, he said, "we as adults have spent way, way too much time . . . focusing on the needs of adults." He noted the bitter partisanship in the crowd and said, "It's sad to note that in all the time I've been here . . . there has not been an equal dedication of time, energy, and resources to discussing the actual issue of student achievement."[1] His comments were greeted by more boos.

The issue on the table had nothing to do with education. Rather, the focus of the meeting was the proposed censure of Zimmerman for a remark she'd made at a meeting two weeks earlier. Frustrated by the district's failure to improve the performance of nine schools on the district's South Side, Bersin had asked the board to use provisions of the No Child Left Behind Act of 2001 (NCLB) to invite for-profit and nonprofit companies and organizations to submit proposals to operate the sites as charter schools. The San Diego teacher union was opposed. Zimmerman saw an opportunity to attack. Should his proposal pass, she had said, Bersin and his team would be abandoning more than ten thousand students enrolled in those schools to an uncertain educational fate. She likened Bersin to a *Gauleiter*, whom she (inaccurately) said were "Jews who worked for the Nazis [to shepherd] their own people onto the trains" to the concentration camps.[2]

It was hardly the first time that Zimmerman used Nazi allusions when talking about Bersin. She'd been doing just that for four years, echoing and emboldening teacher union leaders to make similar comments. This time, Bersin registered his disgust at her comment. "My God, Mrs. Zimmerman, you have really hit bottom this time," Bersin said to her at the meeting. She also offended board president Ron Ottinger, who is Jewish as well. "Finally, my patience is at an end with these kinds of personal attacks," Ottinger said in a statement. "As a human being, I deplore it. And I call upon those who are perpetrating it to renounce it and to ask their supporters to do the same."

Instead of apologizing, Zimmerman brought her attorney and supporters to the censure meeting and claimed her rights to free speech and due process were violated by the board even considering the motion. She wrote a letter to the newspaper saying that Bersin should be the one censured for what she considered to be the crime of sending children "out of the District to an uncertain future and most probably a second-rate education or, perhaps, to no education at all."[3]

Zimmerman did not acknowledge that, run by the district, the schools at issue were educational failures. Students were not learning. Teachers were ineffective or distracted by disruptions. The schools were perennially on the district's list of low performing schools in spite of Bersin and Alvarado's concentrated efforts to improve them. Teachers moved in and out of the schools, in a constant churn of dismay and failure.

But Zimmerman did not want to talk about that. As long as Bersin had been superintendent, she had rejected any suggestion that instruction needed to improve as an insult to teachers' professionalism, just as union leaders did. In her outrage, Zimmerman asserted it was she who was looking out for the children's interests.

Lopez continued despite the jeers. "Where we are now clearly is repeating the past, in that we'd like to attack one another rather than . . . end the status quo and improve education for our children," he said. That touched off further shouting, and Ottinger ordered the auditorium cleared.[4]

A BAD WORKING RELATIONSHIP

The meeting represented one of the lowest points in a difficult seven-year relationship between Bersin and his two opponents on the board. That relationship became nationally famous when Sue Braun, one of Bersin's three supporters on the board, frustrated by such meetings, showed poor judgment in writing an email in which she joked that the only way to deal with Zimmerman and de Beck was to "shoot both of them." She was relieved of her duties as board president but, because Bersin needed her support, he did not push for her to resign, until the next election, when she did not run.

"It was hard to take the school board seriously because of the way it conducted itself," said Robert Kittle, the *San Diego Union-Tribune* editorial page editor. "The majority members didn't handle the criticism very well either. The personal enmity on the school board . . . and with Alan, were just getting in the way of rational policy making."[5]

EARLY WARNING

Bersin had had clues about the board's dysfunctions even before he took office. The board members also were aware that their behavior was unproductive and had hired a psychologist to help them work out their differences. Ottinger said the group therapy sessions temporarily improved the working relationships on the board. "We don't have to love each other," he said. "We don't even have to like each other, but we do have to operate professionally."[6]

Ken Druck, the psychologist whom Bersin had consulted on his handling of the Blueprint controversy, said Bersin's hiring stirred up tensions even further.[7] Before he was sworn in, Bersin met with the board and Druck and described how he believed board members and the superintendent should act in meetings. "Board meetings should be educational functions for us to explain, not discuss, issues for the first time," he told the board. "No more ambushes, no more surprises."[8] Two months later, he proposed new procedures designed to make board meetings more efficient, observing that board members sometimes spent hours on an issue without making any progress or decision.

But, within months, Zimmerman ignored the new guidelines. Without advance warning, she proposed that parents participate in the selection of new school principals. She had arranged for a steady stream of parents, many of them African American, to endorse that policy and to attack the district for having failed to routinely involve them in those decisions. Bersin defended himself, saying he was "committed to full parent involvement in every aspect of our children's education, from the selection of principals to the discussion of standards."[9] He said to suggest otherwise four months into the new administration was "grandstanding."

Zimmerman also was angry about Bersin's directive to principals that they report to him or to his chief of staff any direct orders or requests that came to them from school board members. This was intended to discourage board microman-agement, which was then endemic in the district. Zimmerman took it as an un-warranted affront to board authority.

A few months later, the teacher union published in its newsletter a full two-column attack on Bersin by Zimmerman.[10] The board-superintendent relation-ship "is supposed to be based on mutual respect, common ground, and democratic dialogue," she wrote. "Now there are only adversarial proceedings."

But Zimmerman wanted the board meetings to be even more adversarial than they were. She criticized her fellow board members for not opposing Bersin more often, saying, "Some are hoping to ride his 'gnarly political wave.'" If Zimmerman and de Beck opposed a policy endorsed by the three-member majority, they would not accept the decision as final. Instead, they would condemn the board vote as a "rubber stamp" and continue to speak out and organize opposition. "It was a breakdown of majority rule and dissent by nullification," Bersin said. Although they were clearly frustrated with their marginalization, Zimmerman and de Beck continued to contribute to it with their behavior.

Bersin offered to meet with Zimmerman weekly to discuss her concerns. But she met with him only four times in seven years. Instead, Zimmerman and de Beck met regularly with union leaders to strategize how to undermine support for Bersin among parents, teachers, voters, and the media.

Bersin regarded de Beck and Zimmerman as a "fifth column" that regularly relayed private discussions to the teacher union and to the alternative media. De Beck supplied the union with copies of confidential email messages he exchanged with the district's head of human resources, continuing his ex parte communica-tions with the union that had been going on for years.

A number of observers have said that Bersin bore part of the responsibility for the sour relationship with the board minority. Michael D. Usdan analyzed that relationship in a chapter he wrote for the 2005 volume *Urban School Reform: Lessons from San Diego*.[11] He said Bersin and others tried, and failed, to get the board to behave more like a corporate board of directors. As a corporate lawyer, Bersin knew that CEOs, who often also chair the governing board, decide on how much information to share and are accountable for making the appropriate judgment. Bersin "reported to his board only as things happened that concerned it in his view of their policymaking and oversight roles."[12] The three members in the majority accepted that "it seemed to be the way a massive system should run with a capable leader at the helm," but the two dissenters rejected this approach out of hand. For them, according to Bersin, the board was in charge of the district and entitled to participate in "everything that went on in it."

But, whatever Bersin's responsibility in the matter, the San Diego board continued to engage in unproductive behavior long after he'd left. In September 2008, the school board approved a policy designed to prevent its members from criticizing the superintendent. Board members were not to take personnel matters into their own hands, were to set policy and not meddle in the day-to-day operations of the district, were not to pressure school principals to do their bidding, and were to avoid trying to steer hiring decisions toward the candidates they favored. Furthermore, the rules said that board members should not interrupt one another or pander to the audience, and they should practice "acceptable body language."[13]

It was in many ways a silly policy. But it was revealing as well. Most of the members of the board recognized that collectively they'd gotten out of control and they were trying to rein themselves in as the district tried to cope with enormous budget cuts. But then a few weeks later, shortly before the November general election, the incumbents wanted to be able to criticize the superintendent, Terry Grier, on behalf of the teacher union. They rescinded the policy as "inappropriate" and "unworkable."

GOVERNING PUBLIC EDUCATION

Education has always been regarded as a largely local enterprise in America, going back to Puritan communities that believed that teaching children to read the Bible was part of their covenant with God.

In a 2005 book he edited, political scientist William G. Howell examined the changing role and politics of school boards. In the early days of American public education, "school boards became the engine that drove the most rapid expansion in educational opportunity the world had ever seen," Howell wrote.[14]

School boards were the central governing institutions of public education throughout the nineteenth century.

But as early as the 1830s, Horace Mann, who served as the first secretary of the Massachusetts Commission to Improve Education, became concerned that localism had led to vast differences in school quality from town to town. Immigration to the United States was growing fast, and more of the new arrivals were from Germany and Italy and other Catholic countries. Mann believed that the schools should help transmit the American culture to the immigrants. But he knew that many of the schools attended by immigrants were terrible. He believed it was in the interest of the state to do more to ensure the quality of the schools. So, he recommended that the state begin training teachers to ensure that they were qualified.

He recognized, however, that he had no direct power over local schools. "Mann understood the critical dimension of communities feeling a sense of proprietorship in their schools, as a means of transmitting not only knowledge and skills, and culture and values, but also responding to local labor market demands," Bersin said.

At the turn of the twentieth century, efforts to "professionalize, homogenize, and organize common schooling threatened highly prized local control." School boards, which were usually made up of leading citizens appointed to the job, were being asked to deal with rising immigration and the growing demand for skilled workers in the industrializing economy, Howell observed.[15] "Businessmen, professors, and politicians lobbied for the transformation of an agrarian, decentralized pattern of schooling into a bona fide public school system that promoted the values of centralization, efficiency, modernization, and hierarchical control."

During the Progressive Era, schooling became the province of professional educators, and states pushed for the consolidation of schools into districts and districts into larger districts. In 1936, the nation had nearly one hundred twenty thousand school districts; sixty years later, there were only about fifteen thousand two hundred.[16] Not only did that mean fewer boards of education but also many fewer elected members, as the number of seats on boards was reduced, to make governance more efficient. It also meant that bureaucracies grew in power and complexity relative to the capacity of school boards to oversee them.

In the two decades after the 1954 U.S. Supreme Court decision in *Brown v. Board of Education*, courts exercised greater control over schools with their rulings on desegregation cases. In the 1950s and 1960s, the courts ruled as well on the appropriate place of religion in the schools and the rights of disabled students, which led to the 1975 federal Individuals with Disabilities Education Act. The federal government's influence over curriculum grew as the federal government spent hundreds of millions of dollars on teacher professional development in math, science, and languages in response to Russia's *Sputnik* launch in 1957. The 1965 Elementary and Secondary Education Act further inserted the federal government into local education issues, because it limited how those funds could be used to aid disadvantaged students.

In the 1980s, site-based management began to be seen as the antidote to large, slow-moving, rule-bound bureaucracies that had become the norm in large city school districts. It also had the effect of reducing the power of school boards. Another form of decentralization, in this case one that sought to establish competition as a lever to get school districts to seriously embrace reform, arrived in the form of vouchers in just a few cities—Milwaukee, Cleveland, and more recently Washington, D.C. Charter schools, which first appeared in 1991, also undermined school board power by reducing the number of schools they oversaw directly.

The post-war growth of suburbs, the antiblack reaction of many white families to city busing and desegregation programs developed in response to the *Brown* decision, the civil rights movement, state and local housing policies, and other decisions all fueled the flight of middle-class families from city schools. As the performance of students in city schools declined, so did confidence in school boards. In Baltimore, Boston, Detroit, Cleveland, Philadelphia, Chicago, Newark, New York, and Washington D.C., mayors and states dissatisfied with school boards' ineffectiveness, cronyism, and apparent distance from schools' problems moved to eliminate or constrain their powers.

The state role in public education also had undermined school board control, as it took over teacher credentialing, construction regulations, content and performance standards, curriculum, textbooks, and, perhaps most importantly, school finance.

Plaintiffs in various states won lawsuits that challenged the inequities that resulted when schools were paid for mostly with local property tax revenues. One of the earliest decisions was the *Serrano v. Priest* case in California, which led to a series of rulings in the 1970s that had the effect of shifting responsibility for financing schools to the state capitol in Sacramento. Proposition 13, the 1978 antitax measure in California—in part a reaction to *Serrano*—further shifted responsibility for school funding to the state because it severely restricted the ability of local and county governments to raise tax rates to pay for school operations. Decisions that had been up to local school boards were now under the purview of the state legislature.

By the 1980s, what Mann thought that he could not have—the power over local school districts—states were assumed to have. The state role in education continues to grow, even though there is little evidence showing that the trend has improved educational outcomes. The Obama administration's Race to the Top competition required states and local districts to sign on to ambitious reform plans. Districts, then, were required to come up with their own detailed plan for how they'd implement what they'd already committed themselves to doing. More than forty states also have adopted a set of Common Core standards that are supposed to drive not only curriculum but also state assessments.

"Once the local school boards lost taxing power, the stage was set for vast political change in not only who ran for the office but how the elections were conducted," Bersin said. "The school board became less important to voters, and civic leaders with community standing no longer ran for seats." Instead, single-issue candidates (running to restore funding to the marching band or bring about a change in the reading curriculum, for example) began to vie against former teachers, as well as those who saw the school board as a stepping-stone to higher political office.

"Until relatively recently, local urban school board elections provided accountability and made sure schools were responsive to the needs of the community," Bersin said. The campaigns could be rancorous, and having money or monied backers certainly increased one's chances of being elected, but "that's the way democratic elections work." The outcome would affect voters' property taxes, the quality of schooling their children received, the preparedness of the local work force, and the value of their homes. Local governance of public school had also had another advantage, in his view. It allowed for innovative approaches to education to be tried out and tested locally, on a small scale, which could help avoid huge mistakes by imposing a particular curriculum or teaching method on all the schools in the state.

In the past, elections had meted out what he called "democratic rough justice," in the sense that voters got the school board members they backed, and board members who failed to listen could quickly be unelected. But, for a variety of reasons, elections no longer worked that way.

SCHOOL BOARD ELECTIONS

During the Progressive Era of the early twentieth century, school board elections were made nonpartisan, and the timing of elections was shifted to separate them from elections in which legislatures, governors, members of Congress, and the president are chosen. It is often the case that choosing the school board is the only question that goes before the voters in such elections. But the effect of these moves has been to reduce voters' interest in such contests. With smaller turnouts, it's easier to control such elections.

"You end up with a completely different set of school board members beholden to a different set of interests, and it obviously changed how they act and govern," Bersin observed.

In urban districts, one special interest came to dominate the political landscape: employee unions. Terry M. Moe studied California school board elections and found that teacher unions were the single most significant influence on who wins elections and which policies boards support. Incumbents endorsed by teacher unions win 92 percent of the time, according to his research.[17] By 2009, for example, the school boards in every large urban district in California—Los Angeles, San Diego, San Francisco, Sacramento, Long Beach, and Fresno (excepting Oakland, which had been taken over by the state)—were dominated by employee-group-elected majorities.

"From a democratic standpoint, the rise of teachers unions is troubling, because it may give one special interest group too much power in the politics of education while other groups, particularly broad-based ones like parents and taxpayers, have too little," Moe wrote.

But teachers who are politically influential through their union are not just political actors. They also are employees, and, Moe writes, "as such they have vested interests—in areas such as job security, higher wages and fringe benefits, costly pensions, restrictive job rules, bigger budgets, higher taxes, lax accountability, limits on parental choice, and many others—that may often conflict with what's good for children, schools, and the public interest."[18]

When the elected officials are allied with the adults, rather than with the students, the process seems unfairly skewed. "Where else do employee groups have the right to elect their own board of directors?" Bersin asked. Or, as Moe told a Pittsburgh reporter, "The unions get to pick the people they're going to bargain with. It's an unbelievable thing, isn't it? What a break."[19]

SCHOOL BOARD ELECTIONS IN SAN DIEGO

All five members of the San Diego board at the time were Democrats, as was union president Marc Knapp and Bersin himself. Bersin had grown up in a staunchly Democratic household that supported unions. He had first walked precincts in Hubert Humphrey's 1968 campaign and chaired Bill Clinton's election committee in San Diego in 1992. Initially, he believed that his long history as a Democrat would help him build a good working relationship with the board and with the union. But his party activities turned out to carry little weight.

"Though we all claim to be Democrats, this is a very partisan board," Zimmerman told an interviewer. "The nicest thing I can say about them [referring to Braun, Ottinger, and Lopez] is that they are not axe murderers."[20]

The first election during Bersin's superintendency came in 2000, when Ottinger, Lopez, and Zimmerman were all up for reelection. Bersin and his supporters knew that Ottinger and Lopez had to win, or the nascent reforms they had launched would likely be killed and Bersin would be ousted. Such a development would set back the cause of urban school reform not just in San Diego but nationally. They also wanted to pick up a fourth supportive member, in order to give Bersin more maneuvering room and to discourage the union and other critics. This was the election that occurred during the controversy over the Blueprint, and the San Diego Chamber of Commerce and its Business Roundtable had decided to back Julie Dubick, then a lawyer in private practice, in hopes of helping a Bersin ally win.

Although a lot was at stake for Bersin, superintendents are limited in how involved they can get in local elections. Bersin thought it was an unfair fight. Employee groups could campaign for their candidates, but he could not do so directly for his. "They play politics 360 days a year, and superintendents are supposed to implement and defend reform without being political," Bersin mused. That separation is understandable, of course. He did, after all, report to the board.

Bersin had reason to be careful about getting too involved in the election. In the fall of 1998, he'd signed a letter to voters that described the poor condition of many schools and urged support for the construction bond issue. An antitax citizens group sued him personally for misuse of school district funds to send out the mailer. The district settled the case and conceded that the letter may have crossed the line into advocacy.

Even so, Bersin was unwilling to stay out of the March 2000 election entirely. He and Ottinger and a core group of civic leaders began meeting prior to the primary to discuss election strategy and began raising money on behalf of Dubick, who had never before run for public office. Dubick won more votes than Zimmerman in the primary but did not get enough to avoid a November runoff. Bersin's allies began planning strategy to mount an "independent" campaign to make sure she won.

They worked with a local political consultant named Larry Remer, who had managed the successful campaign to get Proposition MM passed. Bersin had worked behind the scenes to raise more than $1 million in support of the measure, and Remer urged him to once again put his fundraising skills to work. Bersin brought in six-figure donations from John Moores, the owner of the San Diego Padres; John T. Walton, the late Walmart heir and San Diego resident; Qualcomm founder Irwin Jacobs; and local businessmen Malin Burnham and Mel Katz. It was later revealed that Eli Broad, the Los Angeles billionaire, also contributed a large amount, but funneled the money through East Coast foundations.

The campaign raised $720,000, $500,000 of which was spent on a negative television ad campaign that urged voters to "tell Fran Zimmerman to stop voting against back-to-basics reform, because it's working."

It wasn't as if Zimmerman was just bringing in small donations from her neighbors, however. The teacher union backed Zimmerman with about $200,000. But many observers, including Bersin, believed that the unprecedented amount of money spent to defeat Zimmerman had made Bersin and business leaders look power hungry. It was so large that she could credibly argue that she was a populist underdog who was being attacked in order to elect a "Chamber of Commerce puppet."[21] She eked out a narrow victory over Dubick.

"I think people were shocked about the kind of money that was spent," Zimmerman told the *Union-Tribune*. "People really don't like this kind of interference with their public schools. Mr. Bersin and his rich friends, they really pushed too hard."[22]

Bersin regarded the campaign as a "total disaster" and, while he was not involved in the day-to-day decision making, he took responsibility for the fiasco. In private meetings, he had argued constantly against the strategy, but he did not pull the plug on the campaign. "I knew it was going on and I should have just put my foot down. I thought it was going to backfire and we didn't even need it. Dubick would have won without it."

Bersin saw that election as a key turning point in his superintendency. He was confident that, had he obtained a 4–1 majority on the board, he would have been able to work more productively not just with the board but also with the employee unions. The teacher union would have recognized it had lost power, and would have been more amenable to serious negotiating. Instead, the union and Zimmerman and de Beck would continue fighting him at every turn, knowing that if they could take control of one more board seat, they'd be able to get rid of him. Bersin also had little incentive to change course.

"There was no capacity to work out differences, so differences escalated to the point where it was virtually impossible to move forward in tandem. Absent a decisive political mandate, each side believed and acted as though victory (in the form of a solid majority) was right around the corner," Bersin said.

"We didn't move forward because we couldn't resolve the political impasse."

The 2000 election ensured that Zimmerman would become an "unusually rabid enemy rather than merely a staunch political opponent," he said. Another consequence of the election was that it discouraged business leaders in San Diego from continuing their involvement. They'd spent heavily in two consecutive elections and influenced the selection of a superintendent who had launched an important set of reforms. But they had been burned badly by adverse publicity and mostly withdrew after 2000 from school board politics.

THE 2002 ELECTION

In 2002, the teacher union tried to exact its revenge in an all-out $800,000 effort to elect its own board majority. Two seats were open because incumbent Sue Braun decided not to run, after the controversy she'd caused the previous year. The California Teachers Association and the National Education Association, the national and state parent organizations of the San Diego union, contributed more than $400,000 to the campaign on behalf of de Beck and Jeff Lee, a retired Navy officer who was an outspoken Bersin opponent.

But Bersin got two lucky breaks. First, the union broadcast its own negative television ad, attacking the integrity of pro-Bersin school board candidate Katherine Nakamura. The ad suggested that Nakamura's husband, an architect who had worked on district construction projects, had gotten a $5 million sweetheart deal, which turned out to be untrue. The ad was inspired by a story in the *San Diego Reader*, which was crafted by Matt Potter, a close friend of Zimmerman's. The story was false and the ad was quietly withdrawn, which undermined the integrity of Zimmerman's backers even though the local media did not take note.

The second break came when Nakamura's campaign learned about and publicized a report, entirely true, that Jeff Lee had been dismissed as a Navy commander over charges that he'd physically and mentally abused those under his command.[23]

Nakamura won the election narrowly, preserving Bersin's majority. De Beck won as well, which ensured that the 3–2 split in Bersin's favor would continue.

THE 2004 ELECTION

In 2004, in the run-up to the final election during his tenure, Bersin sensed that he and the school district had turned a corner. Satisfaction with the schools was rising, most of the principals were new and had been trained to be instructional leaders, and many teachers had been hired under Bersin and supported the district's curriculum and teaching methods. "We approached the 2004 election in terrific shape," he said. "We had finally organized ourselves politically on the outside and inside as well. We were gaining momentum; the schools had turned," he said.

But events outside his control were occurring that would thwart him once again. The city was nearly bankrupt due to some badly handled, ill-advised, and arguably illegal dealings with the city's pension fund. Voters were disgusted with the city's political leadership. The mayor resigned. Unrelatedly, school board members Ottinger and Lopez had chosen not to run for reelection. Not a single establishment candidate won, including those supported by the teacher union and the business community alike. Of the three insurgent board members elected in 2004, only one of them would be reelected in 2008.

"We want the schools to be integrated into a larger political context, such that the entire community, and not just parents and teachers, care about the schools' fate," Bersin reflected. "But in 2004 in San Diego, the larger political environment hurt us. Ironically, the voters decided the school district was part of the city's broader problems, along with the mayor, rather than the one bright spot, an area of government that was finally starting to work well and serve its clients."

THE ELIMINATION OF SCHOOL BOARDS

Cleveland, Chicago, Boston, New York, Philadelphia, and Washington D.C., among other large cities, have eliminated elected school boards. In New York City, Michael Bloomberg ran in 2001 on a promise to improve the city's schools, even though he did not at the time have much power over them other than to establish the budget and appoint some school board members. After winning, Bloomberg got the New York state legislature to allow him to disband the school board and run the schools directly. Chancellor Joel Klein had only one boss: Bloomberg. That made it possible for him to carry out enormous changes—starting dozens of charter schools, breaking up large comprehensive high schools, and incentivizing principals with generous bonuses based on a complex school accountability system that estimates how much they help their students gain academically. Klein also was able to negotiate more effectively with the UFT teacher union, because its leaders could no longer turn to sympathetic school board members and urge them to pressure the district on the union's behalf. Bloomberg then sought and won a change in state law that allowed him to run for a third term, and to retain near-absolute control over the schools. When Klein left in the fall of 2010, Bloomberg chose a replacement, magazine executive Cathie Black, without consulting anyone else. She lasted only briefly before being replaced by Dennis Walcott, who had advised Bloomberg on education issues.

MAYORAL CONTROL

There is little proof, however, that mayoral control improves school district performance. As a structural change, of course, the outcome is only as good as the ways that the leaders in charge utilize the power and authority that the structure gives them. Education professor Kenneth Wong has studied districts where the mayor is in charge and student achievement has risen substantially. But Frederick M. Hess says there is no one form of governance that is the best. He thinks, however, that when a mayor assumes power over the schools it represents an opportunity to "jump start" significant reforms. In dysfunctional districts, where the school board has abandoned its responsibility for holding the school district accountable for performance, mayors offer a chance for renewal.

"If the schools succeed, the mayor gets the credit. If they don't, the mayor takes the blame," U.S. Secretary of Education Arne Duncan, who as leader of Chicago's schools reported to Mayor Richard Daley, has said. "In districts run by boards, the accountability isn't as clear. For cities that need to take bold action to improve their schools, creating a clear line of accountability to one person is an important step in turning around the schools."[24]

When Adrian Fenty was elected mayor of Washington, D.C., schools in 2006, he, like Bloomberg, persuaded the city council to give him control of the public schools. He hired Michelle Rhee in 2007 and she immediately shook things up, making few friends locally along the way. In 2010, Fenty lost a reelection bid, in large measure because of animosity toward Rhee, which was fueled by several hundred thousand dollars spent on the campaign by the Washington Teachers Union. During the campaign, Rhee made clear her opposition to Fenty's successor, Vincent Gray. She resigned soon after Gray's victory.

Bersin placed his own conflict with his local school board members in the context of a larger tension that he believed was pulling the Democratic Party in opposite directions on school reform issues. He believed a split had developed in which one segment believed that school districts could be made far more efficient and effective through good policies, and the "supply side" view that entrepreneurship and competition would best serve the interests of children.

For his part, Bersin thought both that school districts should not have a monopoly over public education and that they could become dramatically more effective. He asserted that competition could play a crucial role in the education sector. He embraced letting outside groups run failing schools, giving parents a choice as to whether to send their children to them, and requiring the traditional schools to compete for students. "I never perceived school improvement activities and entrepreneurial efforts to build from scratch as incompatible. Traditional educationists may choke on the distinction, but there is really no difference in their objectives. Properly understood and executed, the two strategies are quite complementary."

It was that position that had made Zimmerman so angry and that had prompted her outrageous comment that Bersin was like Jews who sent their own people to death chambers. Bersin took a larger significance from her outburst and staunch opposition. He recognized that Zimmerman was like much of the Democratic Party, caught in the middle between her support for unions and the district's ineffectual efforts to improve its worst schools. Bersin believed that this political tension would have to be resolved. And he was confident that it would not be long before elected school boards would fade from the scene of urban education.

CHAPTER EIGHT

The Media

"The Myths Started Very Early On . . . and We Were Unable to Get Rid of Most of Them"

Community support and understanding is critical to the success of urban education reform. To build that support, superintendents must be able to communicate their goals and strategies and provide regular progress reports to parents, teachers, school board members, and the larger community. But the conventional approach to journalism highlights tension and conflict, especially in breaking news stories, and conflict benefits those who would maintain the status quo by drawing attention away from the substance of the reforms. That's exactly what happened to Alan Bersin, and he was unable to educate the media and the community about the challenges and opportunities of systemic reform. The decline of print newspapers and the rise of both blogs and online news organizations add to the communication challenge. Digital media make it easier for districts and their critics to reach audiences directly. The multiplicity of news sources and commentary, however, tends to fragment school and community constituencies and to exert centrifugal forces that can adversely impact district reform efforts.

A week after Alan Bersin's appointment, the education beat reporter for the *San Diego Union-Tribune* published a generous front-page profile that laid out his priorities and sensibilities. Among the challenges: attracting experienced teachers, improving special education services, getting a bond issue passed, serving the growing population of language minority students, and reducing the large racial and linguistic achievement gaps in the district. These issues, the reporter noted, were similar to those facing urban schools nationwide.[1]

The new superintendent was confident and laughed easily but was serious about making progress. He was open to experiments. He knew he had a lot to learn as an educator but was clear on his goal and role. "My job is to lead and manage and to work with teachers and principals," he said. "But there is a commitment to children [that] means I am an educator too."[2] It was a generous introduction of Bersin, *qua* educator, to the community. It is typical for news organizations to offer up such soft-focus profiles of a new superintendent. What usually follows is a honeymoon during which the press and school board give the superintendent time to get to know the district and develop a plan of action.

But if Bersin, who was already well known in San Diego as a tough, results-oriented U.S. attorney, had a honeymoon as superintendent, it was breathtakingly brief. Even while his appointment was only rumored, suspicions were expressed in the alternative media about what his real agenda might be. In an editorial, *La Prensa San Diego*, the local weekly newspaper aimed at Latinos, attacked the integrity of the school board for choosing someone who had increased security at the border.[3] *Voice & Viewpoint*, the weekly catering to African Americans, dismissed Bersin as a pawn of the local chamber of commerce. Matt Potter, a self-styled muckraker for the *San Diego Reader*, the largest local alternative weekly, would cynically interpret as self-dealing Bersin's effectiveness as U.S. attorney in reducing violence, drug trafficking, and illegal immigration along the Mexican border, and facilitating trade. He posited that Bersin had worked so hard at calming things down in order to increase the value of real estate near the border in which Bersin and his wife owned a small share. The story was headlined "Border Fixer."[4]

Potter recounted Bersin's brief history in San Diego, described his political connections, and implied, without offering any evidence, that something corrupt accounted for his prominence and success. That a highly accomplished corporate attorney educated at Harvard, Oxford, and Yale who had also been active in Democratic Party politics and had helped President Bill Clinton get elected might have been fully qualified to be a U.S. attorney or a superintendent was not considered. (Potter would write an 8,300-word diatribe, even more outlandish than the first, in November 2009, after President Obama nominated Bersin for U.S. Commissioner of Customs and Border Protection.)[5]

A reporter for the *Union-Tribune*, the main source of news coverage of Bersin's time as superintendent, was dubious as well. In an early article headlined "Bersin Has Friends, and Foes, in High Places," the writer totted up criticisms from former employees of the U.S. prosecutor's office. The writer acknowledged that "many of Bersin's doubters have been converted," that predicted problems did not arise, and that the office's productivity, effectiveness, and stature had grown considerably. Even so, the writer pursued her thesis and, in a tortured sentence, noted that while Bersin "has said he is interested in education because of children," some critics "contend Bersin would use the position of schools superintendent as a stepping stone to something else."[6]

That Bersin had not come up through the ranks as an educator was one source of the skepticism. But the angry, confrontational reaction of educators also indicated that they believed his previous career, and his financial success and connections, meant he could not possibly understand their lot. His success in other fields, they seemed to be saying, ought to disqualify him from working in public education. It was as if they could not believe he could be acting out of altruism. He must have had some angle that he was playing that would bring him financial or political rewards. It didn't matter to them that he didn't need the money.

The alternative media, especially, picked up on the unfounded and unsupported allegations of teacher union leaders and school board critics that Bersin was part of a business-led conspiracy to turn the school district into both a profit center and training operation for local corporate interests. There was no doubt that he was supported by San Diego's business leaders, who were concerned that the district seemed to be adrift. But there was no evidence that he and his backers were interested in anything but improving the quality of education being provided.

Journalists, who in many cases earn significantly less than teachers, also fight, reflexively, against power and wealth, even as they stand in awe of it. To many journalists, the phrase "afflict the comfortable, comfort the afflicted," coined by nineteenth-century Chicago journalist Finley Peter Dunne, is a watchword. In this case, it was Bersin who was comfortable. But what few journalists realize is that Dunne meant the phrase to be an ironic comment on newspapers' tendency to inflate their importance.

The obsession of the media, and his critics, with Bersin as an individual with a distinctive background that did not match the usual career path of a superintendent, had implications for the coverage. Reporters and columnists focused more on his style and the personality that they imagined him to have, which distracted them from paying serious attention to the reforms he was bringing to the school district. Political journalism has long focused on the personalities of the candidates and the horse race of the campaign, noting who is ahead at any minute. Much of the reporting on Bersin struck similar themes.

The media loved to quote teacher union chiefs Marc Knapp or Terry Pesta saying that, with Bersin, it was "my way or the highway." They were never asked to cite examples. Reporters and commentators simply accepted their characterizations, and it soon became common wisdom. In stories Bersin was described as "bold" and "visionary" or, from another perspective, "autocratic" and "abrasive." "Dictator or diplomat?" was the question asked in a May 2005 story in the *Christian Science Monitor* when California Governor Arnold Schwarzenegger appointed Bersin state education secretary after he'd left his San Diego post.[7]

While there's no doubt that Bersin is competitive and willing to fight for his positions on issues—he was, after all, a scrappy all-East, all–New England, and all–Ivy League guard in football and a highly successful litigator—none of his opponents ever cited examples of him being unpleasant or indecorous.

Bersin did come across on television and in public meetings as tough and unbending. He was so serious, so committed, that he appeared to be stern, even gruff, and ready to fend off attacks. The media emphasized the pugnaciousness and almost never mentioned that it arose from his unrelenting pursuit of the goal of providing an equal education for all students.

"When the stories about reform focus on individuals, and when it becomes about personalities, the coverage tends to be superficial and this always favors the status quo," Bersin said. "The media rightly deemed me a public figure in San Diego but then accepted attacks on me by opponents as newsworthy events in and of themselves. There was never much effort by the reporters to assess independently the bona fides of the sources or even the validity of their criticism. They simply took down the quotes, and repeated them. To this extent, reporters became complicit, intentionally or not, with those who wanted to make school reform about the superintendent instead of about the condition of teaching and learning in San Diego."

The reaction to Bersin was more sustained, bitter, and scurrilous than even the dirtiest political campaigns. "Social change, by definition, is going to produce conflict," he said. "The question is whether the changes are leading to progress. The San Diego media for the most part didn't even ask that question, let alone try to answer it. So the message and impression that the public received is that we were just fighting, without any understanding of why the conflict was occurring or what it meant."

It is not the job of the media to root for the superintendent, the school board, or the unions. Reporters are not advocates. But reporters should be able to describe, in a way that is understandable to a general news audience, the issues the school district is facing and the strategy and resources that a school district is bringing to bear on the problem. In addition, reporters need to do on-the-ground reporting to understand the effects of the changes that are being implemented—for good or ill. This is challenging, time-consuming work and, even back then, when mainstream news outlets were relatively healthy economically, few had the capacity to meet that standard.

John Gilmore, a *Union-Tribune* editor who supervised much of the coverage, defended the newspaper's work. But he also said it was difficult for one reporter to cover all that was going on in the district. "It was a very intense time," he said. "We didn't have a lot of time to explore the issues like we would have liked. We're imperfect."[8]

Whatever the cause, it is clear from an examination of all of the newspaper and magazine articles about Bersin's tenure that the real story of reform did not get either the attention or healthy scrutiny that it deserved. Bersin and his team became better at telling their story the longer he was in office. But they lost control of the reform message in the first year or two and were, from then on, defending themselves against untruths and distortions that had become accepted by the media as common wisdom.

San Diego writer Jonathan Freedman wrote that the San Diego reform effort amounted to "the most comprehensive, combative, and closely watched test of standards-based school reforms in America."[9] The boldness of what Bersin and Alvarado were doing drew an unusual volume of national coverage, with stories in the *New York Times, Wall Street Journal, USA Today, Education Week*, and a number of professional publications. Had San Diego readers had access to *Education Week*, for example, they would have understood how the reforms were viewed nationally and how they compared to what was occurring in other cities. The San Diego reforms also were being watched and analyzed by think tanks, researchers, foundations, and policy makers across the country. Graduate students in education were studying San Diego as a case history of comprehensive urban school reform.

But that's not the story San Diegans read about in the news pages of the daily or weekly newspapers, listened to on local talk radio, or saw play out on television. The coverage of the San Diego schools suggests that conventional journalism may not be up to the task of helping communities understand fundamental educational change.

MISSING THE BIG PICTURE

Americans ascribe to schooling lofty goals: opportunity, the development of potential, and the capacity to bear the mantle of citizenship in a democratic republic. But very little news reporting examines schooling in light of such fundamental purposes. Nor does most reporting illuminate the core activity of schooling: a teacher and students interacting around important concepts in the context of expectations. Most commonly, journalists cover public schools as if they were just another government agency shaped by political activity. So, the staples of the education beat in most newsrooms are school board meetings and elections, test scores, budgets, school closings, and the hiring of a new superintendent or the dismissal of a sitting one. To be sure, these are all newsworthy events and dynamics. They may affect property tax rates, foretell changes in educational philosophy or pedagogy, determine how far one's child has to walk to school, or reveal trends in performance.

But these events are, while not unimportant, ancillary to the main activity of the enterprise. If sports reporters covered baseball the way education reporters cover education, they'd pay close attention to the standings, attend the meetings of the owners, spend a lot of time with a team's general manager, write a lot of stories about players' salaries, and report on the cleanliness of the team locker rooms and stadium bathrooms. They'd almost never watch a game, and when they did it would be to look for color to round out a profile of a player, not to report on the game itself.

If education reporters are to go beyond covering the politics and operations of schools, they have to know more than many do about education. They have to be willing to work hard to understand education policy and implementation. They have to find ways to interest often-skeptical editors in explaining education—the challenges, the triumphs, the barriers to improvement—to a general news audience. It is not enough to just cover a superintendent's announcement about a new approach to literacy. Reporters have to ask about how the superintendent is going to make sure the approach succeeds. What training and professional development is going to be offered? How much will it cost? How will the superintendent and the school board define success? How do they plan to measure their progress?

Most importantly, in order to see how policies are being implemented, reporters need to get out into the schools and classrooms to see changes for themselves and hear from parents, students, teachers, and principals. "If our theory of action was right—that the main action was going on in the classroom, among teachers and students in the instructional core—they missed it," Bersin said. "And, as a consequence of that—whether it was laziness or a lack of understanding—the education reform part of the story never went out to the community through the main newspaper in town. And since the electronic media invariably took their lead from print journalism, and was even more comfortable with sound-bite reporting of disputes, only the battle was presented week after week in living color, absent the substance of education reform."

He acknowledged that he did not provide reporters with the access to schools they might have wanted. On the other hand, reporters did not ask.

SAN DIEGO'S MEDIA LANDSCAPE

As in many cities, a single daily newspaper dominated the San Diego media landscape between 1998 and 2005. The *San Diego Union-Tribune* in 2000 was the twenty-first largest in the country and the third largest in California, with a circulation of about three hundred seventy-five thousand.[10] San Diego is the nation's twenty-eighth largest broadcast media market with the usual complement of network, independent, and cable television stations, along with a half-dozen Spanish language channels.[11] Radio and TV news reports generally offered brief stories about only the most noteworthy and often sensational school issues, following the stories that were printed in the *Union-Tribune*. (Local television news reports did break the story of the removal of fifteen principals at the end of Bersin's first year on the job, running their names and schools across the bottom of the screen.)

The city also has a lively alternative weekly newspaper scene, led by the *San Diego Reader* (circulation 173,125) and the smaller *San Diego CityBeat* (50,000).[12] *La Prensa San Diego* is a weekly, bilingual free newspaper (press run 35,000) that "views the news and events through a Hispanic/Chicano perspective," according to its Web site. The San Diego *Voice & Viewpoint* (circulation 25,000) is the African American alternative newspaper. The community also was served by a business-related weekly, a weekly for the Jewish community and others, as well as several magazines.[13]

The roots of alternative weeklies are in 1960s antiauthoritarianism. Today, the stock in trade of many of these publications is to attack politicians, government officials, business leaders, and celebrities—in short, anyone who is rich or has power. Few weeklies are staffed by professional journalists, and they often rely on freelancers who substitute attitude for reporting. Another trope of weekly newspapers is to attack the coverage of the mainstream news organizations as weak and fawning. It's as if only the alternative press has the courage and insight to tell the truth.

PROPAGANDISTS

In San Diego, most of these weekly newspapers functioned as the propaganda arm of the nonstop campaign waged by dissident school board members and the teacher union to drive Bersin out of the district. Many in the district suspected that Frances Zimmerman regularly fed the *Reader's* Potter privileged information about confidential, closed sessions of the school board. "The facts never mattered to Potter," said Peri Lynn Turnbull, who headed up communications in the later years of Bersin's tenure. "It was a constant barrage of gossipy columns that we watched for every week and usually yelled about because they were so ridiculous and outrageous. But talking with him, submitting letters to the editor, nothing changed his style, approach, or coverage."[14]

This was how Potter described Bersin in 2000, at the start of complicated, innuendo-filled story regarding school district real estate: "Subject of endless rounds of favorable coverage in the *Union-Tribune* and the darling of its editorial board, son-in-law of one of the city's most influential land owners, backed by millions of dollars from San Diego's political and business establishment, Bersin, an old college friend of President Bill Clinton's, gets his way on almost every issue that comes before the board of education."[15] Potter went to great lengths to connect Bersin, his judge-wife, or her family to scandal, even if it was only through contorted, six-degrees-of-separation efforts.

Bersin recognized that Potter had a perverse skill set: "Potter was the best I've seen at wordsmithing innuendo and negative implication about his subjects without any foundation in the truth at all. He practiced character assassination by stringing words together semicoherently in such a way as to avoid formal defamation."

Two other constant critics were Ernie McCray, a disgruntled former principal, and Mike McCarthy, a writer and another friend of Zimmerman who tried to get Bersin to hire him and, when Bersin did not, turned on him. McCarthy showed up regularly at school board meetings to criticize and allege wrongdoing in starkly false terms. He and McCray published frequent columns in the three weeklies, attacking Bersin in vicious and hateful ways. In one column McCarthy compared Bersin to Saddam Hussein. McCray was so frustrated by Bersin's continued prominence in public life that five years after Bersin left the district, he was still spewing venom about him in little-read blogs around town.

In April 2002, an editorial in *La Prensa* started this way: "The guerrilla war that has been taking place on the San Diego Unified School District battleground has come to an unsatisfactory conclusion. The well-financed forces, led by (General) Superintendent Alan D. Bersin and consisting of Storm Trooper Board Trustees Ron Ottinger, Sue Braun, and Ed Lopez, have defeated the forces of Righteousness, led by Trustees Frances O'Neill Zimmerman and John de Beck."[16]

When the many errors and falsehoods in one of Mike McCarthy's columns were pointed out to Daniel Muñoz, the editor of *La Prensa*, Muñoz sent an apologetic email to the head of district communications. Muñoz's email provided some evidence that the weeklies were pressured to be part of an anti-Bersin campaign. "For the last couple months I have had to defend my position for backing off and not continuing the attack/stories on Bersin and the Blueprint," he wrote in the 2003 email. "There is a determined segment of the community that would love to see Mr. Bersin leave and the Blueprint shitcanned and they saw/used *La Prensa* as an outlet."[17]

La Prensa was a low-circulation, weekly publication. The damage it and other alternative outlets did was that they "provided a regular forum for scurrilous attack that was quoted and cited around the district," Bersin said. "The constant repetition lent a patina of legitimacy to extreme statements about the reform effort and those leading it that could not have made their way into conventional, even ineffective journalism. But it was repeated because it had appeared 'in print.'"

As a result, he said, "the standard for public comment dropped precipitously and eroded the value of civility as an obligation in civic discourse on the subject of school reform."

THE SAN DIEGO UNION-TRIBUNE

The *Union-Tribune* did more substantive reporting, by far, than any other media outlet in the community. But a review of every article published by the *Union-Tribune* (as well as the major weeklies) found that the coverage was dominated by reports on school board meetings, disputes both between school board members and with Bersin, and Bersin's relationship with the teacher union. A significant amount of space was devoted to the school board elections in 2000, 2002, and 2004, each of which was framed as a referendum on Bersin's policies. But there was hardly any reporting on the effects of reforms on schools and classrooms. Very little effort was made by any journalists in San Diego to talk to teachers, principals, or students. Almost the only depictions of classrooms and schools came in light features; no serious attempt was made to describe the instructional infrastructure Bersin and Alvarado had created, explain the process of coaching, or detail how the teaching of literacy, math, or science had changed.

Although a centerpiece of the Blueprint's reforms was longer classes for those students needing extra help, no reporter ever sat in those classes, talked to the teachers who taught them, or asked students about their perceptions of them. Instead, the reporters relied on the opinions of partisans, and their comments mostly addressed whether they liked the reforms or not and whether Bersin had consulted them before introducing changes.

During most of Bersin's time, the education beat reporter for the *Union-Tribune* was Maureen Magee. Already a veteran of the education beat when Bersin was hired, Magee was still covering schools for the much-shrunken *Union-Tribune* in 2012. Throughout her career she has been a productive reporter, often churning out several stories a week. She was without doubt the most important reporter for Bersin to have in his camp.

Bersin met regularly with Magee after he became superintendent. As Magee would later note, "he invited reporters along while he delivered high school lectures. He alerted the media when he served as guest varsity football coach. He secured a spot on a local TV station."[18]

"It seemed everyone in San Diego was talking about public education and Bersin," she wrote. "The curiosity about this unconventional superintendent and his plans for the schools was almost palpable."

but the vast majority of her stories dealt with school board decisions, complaints by school board members, comments made at school board meetings, and whatever appeared in the teacher union newsletter. She showed little "enterprise," which is the newsroom term for stories that reporters pursue on their own, rather than simply covering events. One exception was the attention she paid to the district's efforts to reduce social promotion of students who were not ready academically. She wrote several articles about the district's emphasis on the professional development of teachers. She wrote about the district's budget problems and building plans. But, in Bersin's view, her work lacked any sense of context and it would have been difficult for even the most regular reader of the *Union-Tribune* to figure out how all of these stories fit together.

An early example of just that was a front-page article on the first day of school in 1998, less than six weeks after Bersin was officially on the job. In the article, Knapp criticized Bersin for undermining the morale of teachers.[19] Ostensibly, the article was about the district's new literacy thrust and how class time would be devoted to phonics, reading aloud, writing, and discussing books. But the article quickly turned a corner. "Nothing will work without teacher buy-in," Knapp told Magee.[20] "Teachers will be here long after the administrators, long after the students, and long after the school board and administration." Already, he said, "there are some unhappy teachers."[21]

Two-thirds of the article was about teachers' opposition to something they weren't even doing yet. No teachers were quoted in the article. Knapp was presumed by Magee to be the authoritative voice for his members.

The article did not seek out experts to explain how the new literacy approach that was being introduced to San Diego differed from others. It did not discuss the research base or the results that had been seen elsewhere. Nor did it address how the ideas about the balanced literacy instruction that Tony Alvarado brought from New York conflicted with the phonics-dominant methods called for in California state policy. What Magee's article highlighted was opposition. The story quoted those easiest to reach—the superintendent, the head of the union, and the president of the board of education—as if the reporter were on a tight deadline on a breaking story. But this was not a deadline story. It was pegged to the opening of school, and the reporter no doubt would have had at the very least several days to gather information.

In short, the story showed a lack of curiosity and represented a missed opportunity for the newspaper to help parents, teachers, principals, and taxpayers understand the big changes in teaching coming to San Diego classrooms. It was about the union getting out front of a reform to shield its members from the need to make any changes in their practice. At that point Knapp had been complaining to Bersin and Alvarado for several weeks that they were moving too fast, in his opinion, and that they had not gotten the union to agree to curricular changes. He wanted the changes delayed until the following spring, and this article was a way for him to try to win public support. Bersin and Alvarado were not willing to wait. So, Knapp had set up a conflict and Magee legitimized it.

In the fall of 1998, when Bersin was campaigning in favor of the construction bond, the teacher union and the school board minority held their fire, not wanting to jeopardize passage. But days after the election, Knapp blasted Bersin in a column in the union newsletter. The *Union-Tribune* fanned the flames with a story across the top of the paper's metropolitan section that quoted heavily from the column. "Morale is as low as I've ever seen it," Magee wrote, quoting Knapp's newsletter screed. "It is sad but true that we are not viewed as the skilled professionals we are."[22] According to Knapp, "If we treated our students like we are being treated we would be fired and deservedly so."

Magee did not cite any examples of how the teachers were being mistreated, nor did she locate teachers to provide specifics. If the anger were so widespread, that should not have been difficult. She let the school district respond after the jump. School board president Ron Ottinger acknowledged some mistakes had been made. Bersin tried to put the complaints in context. "There is a certain amount of anxiety that is associated with change," he said. But he also took responsibility. "The remedy to anxiety is communication, communication, communication."

A few months later, Magee again gave Knapp's anti-Bersin views prominent display in the newspaper.[23] She cited another column in the union's newsletter in which Knapp again claimed that morale was low. She also reported in the third paragraph of the story Knapp's claim that Bersin was trying to "privatize education by infiltrating the district with noneducators and consultants."

Knapp was angry because the Institute for Learning had been bringing in literacy experts to help train teachers and principals. Knapp made the nonsensical claim that turning to outside experts was the equivalent of privatization. School districts buy goods and services from private, for-profit vendors all the time; they could not operate without doing so. But Magee did not question Knapp's claim. She did not explain privatization or place it in context for her readers. She also did not question Knapp's further charge that Bersin wanted to use the superintendent's post as a springboard to higher office, despite Bersin's repeated denials. She simply reported claims, charges, and allegations.

Bersin's response was measured. "I think Mr. Knapp is wrong and I hope he is not deliberately misrepresenting (me)," the article said. "This shows that I have either been misunderstood or misperceived and I will have to make improved efforts at communication."

At the end of Bersin's first year in office, Magee wrote a long retrospective that, on the surface at least, was balanced, in that she mentioned the major initiatives of the first year and quoted both supporters and detractors. Only three of the article's seventy-five paragraphs described changes in classrooms. Most of the article was a rehash in which Knapp and school board members repeated criticisms that had become stock phrases. Frances Zimmerman was quoted making a claim that the superintendency was just a stopover for Bersin on his way to higher office. Zimmerman was not asked to produce any new evidence that this was true. Knapp repeated his mantra-like criticism of what he called "top-down" management without being asked to define what that meant or give any example. Change always requires a mix of top-down leadership and bottom-up engagement in reform, in Bersin's view. He noted, "They were always hammering home that message. When did anyone stop and ask, 'What does this mean?'"

So news audiences were left in the dark, with a vague sense that Bersin was too powerful.

Magee's coverage of the Blueprint also focused on comments from those who were in favor and those who were opposed. It wasn't that all of the reporting was negative. Magee's early stories were generous and comprehensive in describing the scope of the reform plan. But no reporter stepped back and tried to understand the plan's redistribution of resources. Was it a smart plan? What did research say about the effectiveness of double periods of intensive remediation? How would the plan work in high schools? No journalists tried to answer those questions through independent reporting. In fact, no local journalists even recognized that those were legitimate questions to ask. Instead, once the Blueprint became controversial due to opposition from the teacher union and from Zimmerman and de Beck, journalists focused mostly on the controversy rather than the substance.

ELECTION COVERAGE

The weakness of the news media's efforts to explain and analyze Bersin's reforms was clearest in the coverage of the three elections during his tenure. Each of the elections was framed, by Bersin's opponents and by the media, as a referendum on his leadership.

The first important story on the 2000 school board election was published in December 1999, when Magee reported on the formation of an informal advisory committee to give Bersin advice on what to do with the district's substantial excess real estate holdings.[24] Among those Bersin named to the ad hoc committee was his father-in-law, Stan Foster, who was a San Diego businessman and real estate investor. Bersin defended the decision. "The notion that there could be any conflict [with this done entirely in the open] . . . is part and parcel of the kind of poison that infects public life and makes someone throw up their arms and say, 'Why should I step up and get involved?'"

Zimmerman, who would later be fighting for her political life against Julie Dubick, seized on the story and made it a centerpiece of her campaign. Magee gave her an assist when, just three days before the election, she wrote a story that clearly favored Zimmerman. In a campaign appearance, Zimmerman said Bersin was a front man for "'downtown power brokers' looking to control schools and put district real estate up for sale throughout the city."[25]

"According to Zimmerman's theory," Magee continued, "Bersin is teaming up with San Diego's wealthiest financiers to sell schools, chip away at the curriculum and fatten the wallets of businessmen."

"'All of this is tied to the superintendent's interest in selling off school property,' Zimmerman said. 'And you need four or five votes to sell off property, and he currently has only three votes.'"

Readers must have been left confused—and worried. How exactly are selling real estate and "chipping away" at the curriculum, whatever that means, related? Might not selling unused property earn money for the district? Was Zimmerman referring to a specific real estate deal that was in the works? The readers would never know. Such spurious allegations were made, and printed, repeatedly as part of her reelection campaign, and the media did not check them out.

Oddly, Magee gave the campaign, which was one of the most expensive in the nation's history, little attention. She wrote only a few stories describing the donations from leading San Diego business figures and was seemingly uncurious about more than $100,000 in support that came from two East Coast foundations.

The real estate controversy disappeared from the media as soon as the election was over. In 2002, during another election, Potter returned to the question of real estate, even though nothing new had occurred in the interim. As he often did, he inferred something nefarious was underfoot. But nothing ever came of it, and no other media in San Diego found it necessary to determine whether there was any support at all for Zimmerman's allegations.

Potter worked especially hard to defeat a pro-Bersin candidate, Katherine Nakamura. If Nakamura lost and incumbent John de Beck won, Bersin would lose his majority on the board. It was Potter who wrote the story about what he alleged to be improper school district payments to Nakamura's husband, an architect whose firm had done some design work for the district. Not only were the charges false, but also Kotaro Nakamura and his firm had agreed to give up considerable potential income by vowing not to do business with the school district if his wife were elected.[26] That backfired on Potter because his charges turned out to be untrue.

In one of her last stories before the November 2002 vote, Magee added little to the record and again repeated every cliché that been printed repeatedly over the previous four years: with Bersin it was "[his] way or the highway." Curriculum had been "shoved down our throats," according to a teacher. The reforms impose a "heavy dose of literacy."

Magee quoted one teacher who said the reforms had strengthened the profession. But, she said, the "job has gotten harder . . . When you're looking at each kid and trying to reach out to their individual needs, that is time consuming and very difficult—and that's what we are being asked to do."[27]

The only independent reporting that was done to try to assess the effectiveness of the school reforms came from the *Union-Tribune*'s Perspective section from an editorial writer. In a major overview a week before the election, the paper excerpted findings from an independent review that student achievement was rising overall, achievement gaps were closing, and a set of persistently low performing "focus" schools that were receiving additional resources were improving faster than the rest of the district. The section laid out data from the state, which also showed improvement. High school performance was less positive.

"Ironically, if not incredibly, the greatest threat to San Diego's school reform effort comes just when the latest test scores show growing success for the Blueprint," the piece by editorial writer Robert Caldwell said.[28]

But the newspaper report did not just cite statistics. Caldwell had spent time in two very different schools in the district and profiled them, taking readers into classrooms to see how they had changed. It was the kind of independent, enterprise journalism that was sorely lacking through most of Bersin's time in office.

Gilmore said Magee "reported it like it was. She had no personal animosity toward Bersin. As far as I'm concerned, she was fair. She dug. She was a tough reporter." Fair or not, she'd done little to inform her readers of what was most important.

After the 2002 election, Bersin met with the editors at the *Union-Tribune* and asked that Magee be taken off the beat. Gilmore said the paper did not buckle. But another reporter was assigned to the beat when Magee was out on leave and, when she returned, the two shared the beat for a while.

Gilmore met Bersin only once. But, no doubt informed by his reporters, he said that Bersin was a skilled leader. "He was passionate; he was very forceful. His attitude raised questions, though. He came in like the great savior. The man does have an ego."

On the other hand, Gilmore said, "it was great fun covering him. He was a change agent."

The coverage of the 2004 school board election once again described it as a referendum on the reforms. This time, Bersin's candidates lost. Potter exulted in the *San Diego Reader* with a piece headlined "We Won!" Potter's self-congratulatory piece revisited his articles that had examined how each of the school board races had been funded and, once again, implied wrongdoing without spelling out what it might be.[29]

Within days, the teacher union began running advertisements calling for Bersin to be fired. In February, Bersin and the school board agreed he would depart at the end of the school year.

In a story assessing Bersin's legacy a few months later, Magee raised an ironic question. "How does one man accrue so much praise nationwide, yet foster such animosity in his own backyard?" she said. "And what's the recipe for this cocktail of circumstance, politics and personality that thrust Bersin into the forefront of San Diego's civic awareness?"[30]

Perhaps the local media had something to do with it.

SUPPORT ON THE EDITORIAL PAGE

Until it was sold in 2009, the *Union-Tribune* was owned by the Copley family, which had long been involved in conservative Republican politics.[31] The newspaper endorsed George W. Bush in 2000 and 2004. Although a lifelong Democrat, Bersin had the consistent, although not unswerving, support of the newspaper's editorial page. He also was afforded many opportunities to publish op-eds that expressed his views.

"Clearly we recognized the need for reform," said Robert Kittle, the editorial page editor at the time. "It was very encouraging to find someone who came in with a very broad and deep reform agenda, and his ideas seemed solid."

The news pages were independent of the editorial page, and some suspected that reporters went out of their way to counterbalance the paper's support of Bersin with tough coverage.

The contrast was clear in an editorial published in August 1998, shortly after Magee's piece about the literacy plan and opposition to it. The editorial opened by describing a scene of a first-grade teacher whose lesson, it said, illustrated the school district's "determination to improve reading skills."

"In the space of an hour," the editorial continued, the teacher "read a story . . . peppered the students with questions about the story and themselves; conducted a clever spelling exercise—complete with chant—involving each one of the children; had them interview [another] student; and, when it came time for recess, lined them up by name, using phonics."

The editorial noted that while some teachers were miffed by the changes asked of them when they returned to school, "most of the teachers—particularly the good ones—responded in a positive manner." In eleven paragraphs, the editorial gave a more complete picture of the literacy program than would almost any news article published over the next seven years.

Kittle said the editorial page "supported the top-down approach" but with caveats. "I think you have to strike a balance between the top-down approach and collaboration. And Alan never seemed to get the knack of that."

On the other hand, Kittle said, Marc Knapp was "an exceedingly combative figure who was unwilling to listen." The editorial page supported Bersin in the conflict with de Beck and Zimmerman. Kittle said the two were "often mean-spirited and irrational" in their opposition.

"We were a voice on Alan's side," Kittle said. Bersin himself frequently used the op-ed pages to share his perspective. Kittle said the paper also published many letters and op-ed pieces that disagreed with the editorials and with Bersin. "But we also provided our own strong voice, and to the extent that that maybe drew the battle lines, I guess I would plead guilty," Kittle said.

TELLING THE STORY

Whatever the shortcomings of the media, and there were many, the school district under Bersin did a terrible job of helping him tell his story effectively. The changes he wrought affected everything from how teachers taught to how money was allocated, and the district did not come up with a compelling narrative for why the changes were needed, how they fit together, or why they had to be done quickly. Bersin had recognized even before he was on the job officially that the district's strategic communications efforts were weak and reactive. The district's Web site was poorly designed and difficult to use. The communications office was used to churning out press notices and answering queries from reporters, and thus was unequipped to put together a strategy for rolling out a multifaceted reform effort quickly. In the beginning, Bersin was line-editing all of his own press releases, even with the start of the school year that would bring momentous changes only a few weeks away. The district's inability to communicate a reform message would plague Bersin throughout his superintendency. In seven years, five different people would be in charge of the district's communications.

"The opposition beat our brains out most of the time in the communications battle," Bersin said. "Theirs was a well-orchestrated campaign. They were constantly there, hammering home their message. They worked the press. We were getting damaged from the start in the first year, which was so critical, when so many changes were being introduced."

Turnbull, whom Bersin hired as his communications chief in 2002 and who would later go on to serve in that capacity in Fresno, agreed that the union, in particular, outgunned the district from the beginning. "The myths started very early on and they had their own lives, and we were unable to get rid of most of them," she said.

Regarding the media, former Pittsburgh superintendent Richard Wallace has written that "you have to initiate, not respond, and you have to be as willing to accept criticism and share bad news as you are to issue press releases about awards or glowing reports on student achievement. You will find that reporters will respect you if you respect their intelligence and don't try to pretend there are no problems."[32] Even when talking to reporters, superintendents need to remember that, first and foremost, they are educators. They must lay out their reform strategies clearly, and repeatedly, to both internal and external audiences.

Joel Klein and Michelle Rhee also struggled with the challenge of telling their story effectively to the local media. Klein told the Web site BigThink.com that he did not think he had worked hard enough to personally tell the story of the reforms. "It's a lesson," he said, "that I wish I'd learned sooner."[33]

"We let other people characterize the changes in ways that were both inaccurate and harmful," Klein said. "These things are controversial, and you're running up against people who have very sophisticated media machines . . . who can be counted on to mount an effective defense." To be sure, Klein had his own sophisticated media operation. Reporters who cover the district say the communications staff did all it could to control the flow of information from the district and made it difficult to do independent reporting on the reforms under Klein. But blocking reporters is not the same as communicating important ideas.

Rhee made enemies right away for seeking to close twenty-three schools and then battling the teacher union over performance pay and tenure rights. She cultivated a ruthless image, appearing on the cover of *Time* magazine, jaw set, dressed in black, holding a broom, suggesting she was ready to sweep aside all who stood in her way. She also fell into a rocky relationship with the main beat reporter at the *Washington Post*, and for a while refused to talk to him. Rhee came to regret these choices: they assisted those who wanted attention to be shifted away from the desperate need for change.

No matter what districts and superintendents do to try to bring the media along, they cannot completely control the message. Journalists are always looking for stories, and they will never limit themselves to those that a superintendent wants to be told. But, if district leaders can effectively communicate their broad approach to reform, unpleasant news will at least occur against that backdrop. Efforts also must be made to make sure that teachers, principals, and parents all understand the rationale behind the reforms and have many chances to get their questions answered.

COMMUNICATIONS CHALLENGES

Turnbull later reflected on the communications challenges San Diego faced.

One was in regard to the district's use of consultants to help teachers and principals learn the new approach to literacy instruction. Union leaders repeatedly claimed to be insulted that outside experts, rather than local teachers, were hired for that job. Turnbull said the district tried, unsuccessfully, to argue that the consultants were not only highly regarded educators but that they had also had success working in other urban districts. Moreover, they had used the approach to literacy that Alvarado favored. Those inside the district had not.[34]

Another union message was that the district was top-heavy with administrators who were micromanaging reform. In fact, Bersin had eliminated millions of dollars from the central office budget. The union counted as administrators all nonclassroom teachers, including the peer coaches, even though they were union members. Related to that was the inaccurate, but oft-repeated, claim that the communications department had a staff of twenty-two. Regardless of what the district said, and what the budget numbers showed, this myth was repeated so often it was assumed to be true. "It was dishonest, but it sells," Turnbull said.

On instruction, the goal was to create a system in which the curriculum, standards, training, and evaluations were aligned, with "differentiated instruction focusing on each student's needs." That sounds benign, even rational. But, to the union and other critics, this was a one-size-fits-all approach to teaching. (Oddly, critics and the media often said the approach to teaching was "back to basics," as if teachers were expected to drill kids on facts and basic skills. In fact, teachers were being asked to implement a sophisticated, discussion-oriented approach to teaching that some criticized for lacking sufficient emphasis on basic skills.)

The union and other critics also claimed that everything was being eliminated from the curriculum except literacy and math and that art and athletics had been sacrificed. Never mind that the district under Bersin increased its spending on arts and athletics and that no area of the curriculum was ordered eliminated or reduced. But the media did not even try to test the legitimacy of this or any of these other claims.

There also was much misinformation spread about student performance under the Blueprint and before. The union and others claimed student achievement had been rising before Bersin and fell after him. That was not the case. Overall performance, under the Blueprint, was going up and achievement gaps were closing, Turnbull said, although the district acknowledged that high school achievement was not responding to the reforms.

Many opponents of the Blueprint complained that hundreds of millions of dollars were being spent on untried strategies. "What I could never understand was that those funds were already being spent and the results they were achieving were not anywhere near as good as achieved under the Blueprint," she said. "So our messages were clear about this. But, somehow, people thought we were spending additional funds."

The negative images of Bersin himself could not be eradicated. "It was akin to a public brainwashing," Bersin said. "Said over and over again, the characterization becomes taken as true."

Turnbull, like her predecessors, did not believe the district should respond to every misstatement. But she also did not think the district should allow untruths to remain unchallenged.

So, she worked with other district leaders to start what they called a "rapid response team." Every time false information was presented in a newspaper article, union newsletter, or informational flier, Turnbull analyzed the situation and then recommended whether to respond or not. If she recommended a response, she would work with the appropriate person to prepare one. The district's responses began appearing in the *Reader*, *La Prensa*, and elsewhere. But she said the effectiveness of those responses was limited. "We couldn't get any traction because the message was already out there." It had had six years to take hold.

COMMUNICATIONS FAILURES

Bersin considers his inability to get across the substance of the changes he and Alvarado were trying to make to teaching and learning to be one of his biggest failures. Even his allies raised questions. "Eli Broad called me once and told me that I needed to work on my bedside manner," Bersin later said with a rueful smile, referring to the often-brusque Los Angeles philanthropist who was an early backer of Bersin and Alvarado and their ideas for reform.

Given Bersin's previous experience communicating with the media, it is surprising that he wasn't more successful. As he made the transition from U.S. attorney to superintendent, the *Los Angeles Times* wrote that he possessed "considerable public relations acumen," that he knew the power of the "bully pulpit" afforded him by the office, and that he was "savvy about the media."[35]

Yet he never developed an easy rapport with reporters. He approached the media as a lawyer, wanting to articulate his case in a way most favorable to the interests of his client, his agency, and his larger goals. He did not seek media attention to burnish his own reputation or image. He acted much of the time as though the media were an extension of the courtroom:

> Because of my training and experience as a litigator, I mistook what I saw happening with the school board and the union as something I had experienced before. Parties in litigation sometimes would take positions that were not responsible, not based on facts, and not based on law. I would sit for months and

months with irresponsible litigants and their lawyers and listen to or read non-sense or worse in their depositions or briefs. But I learned patience and from experience remained confident that Judgment Day was coming. There would come a time when the truth would out and, whether by a judge or jury, competing perspectives would be evaluated, credibility would be assessed, and nonsense and falsehood would be revealed readily as such.

I believed in the "court of public opinion." I thought that if we could make our case, the community would be able to make the proper judgment about what was the right view.

But, he said, "this outcome depends upon a full record, deliberately and accurately presented. This was almost entirely lacking in the public school context by reason of the ineffective coverage but also because of our own communication failures. There simply was no framework for analysis by or on behalf of the public."

IMPROVING COMMUNICATIONS

In an attempt to improve communications, Bersin in 1999 promoted Norma Trost, a veteran media specialist in the district, to the top job. Trost worked hard to improve the communications among Bersin, the teachers, and the community. But, privately, she was dubious. Years later, in an interview, she said the rapid pace of reform made communications more difficult and did not comport with the district's culture of collaboration and accommodation. With the Blueprint, she said, "there was a sense among teachers and principals that they were being lectured at . . . Despite attempts to get a two-way dialogue going, it was not successful. The Blueprint was imposed from the top down."

She said she and Bersin also disagreed over what to do about inaccurate reporting. Bersin wanted to respond. "The second time—let alone the ninety-seventh time—I was referred to as a dictator, you'd think we would say something in response," he said. But Trost advised against that because "if someone didn't read the story the first time, and they read it the second time, it sometimes stirs up more trouble than it's worth."[36]

Bersin also pushed Trost's successor, Tom Mitchell, to be more aggressive and strategic in communicating the district's reform story, while also quickly countering the many errors and exaggerations made in the press. Mitchell, a savvy former television news editor, was recruited to the district from the outside and was key to the successful Proposition MM bond campaign in 1998. But he agreed with Trost on this issue. Bersin subsequently replaced Mitchell as director and assigned him to "public outreach" where he was valuable in skillfully organizing public meetings around controversial subjects.

But the communications problems went well beyond failing to respond to misinformation. The district did not prepare communications plans to support specific initiatives. Messages were inconsistent. There was no established way of communicating important information internally or externally. The lack of a broader communications policy, and how to tell the district's story, was a nagging and debilitating problem.

OUTSIDE HELP TO TELL ITS STORY

In the fall of 2001, the district tried another way to tell its story. An East Coast consultant who specialized in helping school districts develop communications strategies to build community engagement recommended that the district send out a postcard that trumpeted "Steady Progress" or, in Spanish, "Progreso Constante." The postcard, which on the front was a collage-like graphic rendered in sunny, southwestern yellows, blues, and deep reds, boasted that thousands more San Diego students every year were scoring above the fiftieth percentile on a state test.

As often happens when school districts hire such consultants, the move was quickly criticized. "In a public relations move," the *Union-Tribune*'s story began, "the San Diego school district is spending about $60,000 to send home a mailer touting its students' 'steady progress' on recent state exams."

But the message itself was an overreach. Even the normally supportive *Union-Tribune*'s editorial page said the Blueprint was "far too new to be evaluated conclusively." Inside and outside the district, the postcard was criticized for presenting the data selectively, masking a slight, second-year performance slump.

The district's chief spokesman defended the decision. "'People say this is spin,'" he said. "'What is spin? We are trying to tell our story. We are trying to communicate the best we can.'"[37]

This shows the bind school districts find themselves in. Teacher unions have sophisticated media operations that, during contract negotiations or other conflicts with the district, pump out criticisms of the superintendent, school board members not on their side, and, if the press does not feature their complaints or the editorial page disagrees with them, the news media. Unions stage public rallies, pack school board meetings, and can mobilize their members and their money to support school board members they think will benefit their interests. If the local union is too small to have its own media operation, it can call on the state operation to help out with press releases, spokespersons, advertisements, and outreach to local reporters. If the district does beef up its communications capacity and hire professionals at a professional salary, the teacher union typically responds by saying money should be spent in classrooms, not to polish up the district's reputation.

The district's communications effort was going so badly by that point that Eli Broad helped recruit John Spelich, a veteran communications consultant who had been working for a large public relations firm, to help out.

"[We're] in trouble," Spelich recalls Bersin telling him when he joined the district. Spelich said Bersin made some of his own problems. "If you elect to get into a nuclear war with the teachers union and its leadership, and you do it when you have some easy ways to exploit vulnerabilities, you've made a conscious decision to not care about what people think," he said. "They were on their bad foot from Day 1."[38]

CHANGING THE NARRATIVE

To try to remedy the situation, Spelich began working on a series of brief reports explaining the reforms. He also wanted to try to show what he called "the real Alan Bersin" to the community and to parents. He greatly admired Bersin and his passion for improving education.

But showing Bersin's human side was met with opposition. "In there was true altruism, but we could never get anyone to see that," Spelich said. When Bersin was invited to speak to public town hall meetings, Spelich said, it was "a total setup." Wherever Bersin went, the teacher union sent pickets to march in protest and to dominate the session with attacks and nasty anti-Bersin signs.

"They had money and . . . and they had the media," Spelich said of the teacher union.

In 2002, at Spelich's urging, Bersin gave a "state of the district" speech in which he acknowledged to an auditorium packed with teachers, principals, union officials, and parents that he and his colleagues, in moving fast, had "inevitably stepped on toes, bruised egos, and made mistakes, some very serious mistakes. This is as regrettable as it may have been unavoidable in a process of large-scale change."

He said that, in order to change the tone of the debate in the community, he would empower principals to speak directly to parents and community leaders about the reforms. Teacher focus groups would be established to provide feedback. A new Parent Congress would be created. District leaders would make themselves more available to speak about what they were doing. And community leaders would be invited into the schools to see the changes in instruction and the positive effect they were having.

"We, I, need to do a better job of communicating—of making sure that everyone in the system understands the educational strategies that have been put in place. And we need, I need, to do a much better job of listening—of gathering feedback from the professionals in our schools to improve the reform."[39]

At the end of his remarks, Bersin approached Marc Knapp and shook his hand in a conciliatory gesture. Bersin also had invited a principal who was one of his most vocal critics and gave him time to share his viewpoint. Sue Braun, one of his supporters on the board, called the speech "brilliant."

But it appeared to be too late for speeches or conciliatory gestures. The opposition had hardened, and there was likely nothing Bersin could have said that would have caused them to give him another chance. As he spoke, one hundred fifty teachers and parents demonstrated and protested the district's reform initiatives, with some of the teachers carrying signs calling Bersin a Nazi.[40]

Zimmerman would not give him an inch. As she exited the auditorium, she said to Spelich, "You had a good night, Dr. Goebbels." She was referring to Joseph Goebbels, the Nazi minister of propaganda. "I have not seen any real sign of relenting from the programs he set up," she told a reporter. "It's an iron hand."

The coverage in the *Union-Tribune* the next day showed that the newspaper's reporters weren't backing off either. The shorthand narrative for the Bersin administration had been established, and the newspaper wasn't going to alter it. The article said Bersin was defending his "strict" reforms, which echoed the constant union charge that he had imposed a one-size-fits-all regime of teaching. The article noted the presence of the protesters carrying signs saying "Heil Führer Bersin" and, after quoting Zimmerman, closed with a quote from a teacher. The teacher said the intent of Bersin's speech was to make him look good. But, the newspaper quoted her, "we all know otherwise."[41]

The article did not offer any reason the teacher felt that way. So, readers would have no way of knowing the basis of her complaint. She was not asked to give any specifics.

This speech came at an important turning point in Bersin's tenure. The school board was just about to vote on a four-year contract extension. But, rather than treat the speech seriously and use it as a news hook to assess Bersin's record independently, the reporters contributed little more than stenography.

The story quoted Knapp as saying that most of the district's eight thousand teachers shared the anti-Bersin views of those who were picketing. In response, a letter writer who was a teacher criticized both Knapp and the article. "This comment was not supported by any data," she wrote. "In fact, what should have been reported along with that comment is that fewer than 20 percent of the district's teachers even voted in the recent SDEA election."[42]

Late in Bersin's leadership, Turnbull created an eighteen-page plan, which was designed not only to strengthen the district office's ability to get its message across but also to help principals in talking to their teachers, parents, and communities. The reforms were taking hold, and most principals and teachers had become supporters. But the opponents were becoming angrier and angrier, and the anti-Bersin drumbeat in the media grew louder. Rather than take on the media, the district began to communicate more directly with parents.

"I became convinced that it was not the public affairs office's communications that were critical, it was communication directly by principals to parents," Bersin said. "The typical way that school reform is stymied is by the failure to communicate with parents. The only way around it was to build up the strong principals who would communicate with teachers and then with parents. It was part and parcel of the work. It was not just PR. The really critical communications are not at the center but at the school site."

But Turnbull said she didn't get as much support for her efforts as she would have liked from others in the administration. Information, she said, is power and there were many managers in the central office who wanted to hold on to it. "There was real nervousness about sharing information," she said. On the other hand, she said, she did not hold any workshops on the communications plan or provide training to the district's leaders or principals.

EDUCATING THE MEDIA

Working to educate the media about school reform is even more important today than it was just five years ago. The ongoing economic turmoil in print and broadcast media, and the newsroom downsizing that has occurred as a result, has reduced the number of reporters covering education exclusively. Reporters who are taking over the beat know little about education policy, practice, or research. They also are being pressed to do more stories and turn them around more quickly, so they fall back on what they know.

Today, school reporters are writing blogs, they are producing videos, they are writing for the Web edition as well as the print edition, and they're regularly sending out "tweets" on Twitter. Some reporters provide real-time, ongoing coverage of school board meetings on Twitter. This could be a good thing. Getting facts and tidbits out quickly could allow more time to be devoted to in-depth stories. Some reporters today, such as Ann Doss Helms at the *Charlotte Observer*, are doing a terrific job of reporting on the adoption of Common Core standards and other stories in traditional print mediums. In more and more towns, nonprofit online news sites are providing in-depth coverage that can no longer be found in the print newspapers. But the media, like the coverage, is very much in flux.

The media landscape in San Diego is much different today, just as it is in most communities. The *Union-Tribune* was sold in 2009 to Beverly Hills–based investors who eliminated hundreds of jobs, including those of the editorial page editor and commentary editor and dozens of reporters and other editors. The newsroom was downsized even further in the summer of 2010. The paper was sold again in January 2012. Another source of news, the prize-winning San Diego online nonprofit venture called *Voice of San Diego*, which has gotten a lot of national attention, is now far more influential in San Diego.

The *Voice of San Diego* offers an authoritative, well-reported alternative to the he-said/she-said coverage that dominated the *Union-Tribune*. The site's reporting staff is small and doesn't try to be comprehensive. Rather, when it covers a story it does so in-depth, providing explanation and state and national context, when appropriate. For several years, education coverage was handled by Emily Alpert, who dug deeply into matters of education policy and managed to turn them into compelling and important stories. One can only speculate as to how Bersin and the Blueprint and other reforms would have fared if Alpert and her news organization had been around to scrutinize and explain what he was trying to do. In the spring of 2009, she had stories on the site about a plan by local charter schools to lower the price they were paying to provide special education services by contracting with a distant county; the challenge of getting teacher and parent input into the district's plan for spending new federal stimulus money given tight deadlines; and a new school district effort to reduce student suspensions while improving student conduct. In each case, readers would learn vital information about schools and the challenges and dilemmas they face. None of them were puff pieces for the district. Rather, the stories explained the issues in a way that helped readers understand the complexities.

CHAPTER NINE

High Schools

"We Have Acted . . . As Though High School Doesn't Matter"

High schools emerged in the late nineteenth century during a time of heavy immigration and were designed to create broader access to higher education. At the time, few but the children of the wealthy went to college and few stayed in school long enough to graduate from high school. Over the next century, of course, high school attendance became universal and they had to serve the needs of all students. The increase in high school graduation made the U.S. the best-educated country in the world. But high schools struggled to fulfill all of the expectations placed on them. Americans wanted their high schools to turn out well-rounded graduates who were ready for the factory floor, clerical jobs, the crafts, the family, or college. Until the 1980s, high schools tracked students based on their previous academic performance as well as their personal preferences. But then, beginning in the 1990s, high schools were expected to educate all of their students to a higher level than previously. As superintendent, Alan Bersin recognized that the high schools had to address their students' weak literacy skills if they were to be able to access the subject matter content necessary for success after high school. But he also came to realize that no one strategy would have the desired effect of simultaneously increasing graduation rates and raising academic standards in all of the district's high schools. Instead, San Diego worked to improve the quality of instruction in some of its large high schools and broke others up into smaller schools designed to foster improved teaching and increased student engagement.

When high schools were created in the nineteenth century, they had a singular purpose: prepare talented male students for college. Almost ever since, as it became expected that everyone would get a diploma, high schools have been assigned a longer and changing list of missions. Some students were to be prepared to go to college, but most were not. Today, however, we expect high schools to ready all of their students to succeed in postsecondary vocational or career training or in traditional two- or four-year colleges. We expect this outcome no matter how well students can read or do math or speak and write English when they enter the ninth grade. But even as their mission has changed, American high schools continue to operate for the most part as they did fifty years ago, and about 30 percent of students do not graduate on time. The proportion of those who go right into college after completing high school has never been higher. In 1995, national figures showed, about 30 percent of college freshmen were taking remedial classes in reading, writing, or math, revisiting material they should have learned in high school. The percentage is similar today, and over 50 percent among those who go to community colleges. Bersin knew these problems were acute in San Diego and committed himself to addressing them. But, just as reforming this iconic institution has proven difficult nationally, Bersin accomplished far less than he had hoped to.

By 2002, the fourth year Bersin was in office, test scores of San Diego elementary and middle school students were rising overall and gaps between demographic groups were narrowing. Across all ethnic and language groups, the percentage of students in the lowest performance category was going down. The number of schools performing at the very bottom was shrinking, according to state measures.

But the large, comprehensive high schools in San Diego, just like those nationally, seemed impervious to the instructional reforms and the bolstering of student supports that were succeeding in elementary schools. Almost two-thirds of the district's high school students scored below the national median on standardized tests of reading. Only two-thirds of the ninth graders earned a diploma four years later. Only two in five graduates had passed the courses they needed to be eligible for either the state's University of California, which by design serves the top 12.5 percent of students in terms of achievement, or California State University (CSU), which serves the top third.[1] Of the one in ten San Diego graduates who enrolled in the CSU system, about half had to take remedial English and remedial math.[2] When all students were included, it was estimated that two-thirds of San Diego's graduates who enrolled in college had to take remedial classes in reading or math.

According to Bersin:

> Every year I was superintendent, I would go to high school graduations and ask the students one by one where they were going. Eighty percent replied they were going to college, and three-quarters of these would say Mesa Community College or City College. And what I learned every year was that most of our graduates would get to community college in the fall and drop out by the spring. If

academic achievement was the standard by which we judged our high schools—and this was the standard we insisted on—then our high schools were not working for the large majority of our students. And these were the ones who were graduating, succeeding according to the existing order of things. What about the 35 percent of our young people who were leaving high school between the ninth and eleventh grades? I grasped the gravity of the situation very early on. It was the starkest, most frightening indicator to me of a failing system.

In focus groups conducted in 2001 by San Diego Dialogue, a research group at the University of California, San Diego, high school students said they wanted to be "inspired by teachers and to feel like they were connected to the adults in their schools."[3] Instead, they said that high school was pointless, boring, and "not really intellectually stimulating."[4]

The problems with San Diego's high schools were hardly unique: 40–50 percent of the high schools in the nation's thirty-five largest cities graduate only half their students within four years. Researcher Robert Balfanz calls schools that graduate less than 60 percent of their students "dropout factories," because the way they operate turns out dropouts as predictably as a factory produces cars. The Obama administration has picked up on that language and has targeted several billion dollars toward either turning those schools around or shutting them down.

In focus groups conducted by the National Commission on the High School Senior Year, students said that "what they learned in high school left them unprepared for college, work and the adult world."[5]

But what is both striking and deeply troubling about American high schools is the vast differences between those that serve large numbers of poor and minority students and those that serve largely middle- and upper-middle-class students. These differences were particularly stark in sprawling San Diego, which, unlike many large cities, still enrolled many middle-class students from affluent neighborhoods.

The schools in the northern part of the district, which included the then nationally recognized La Jolla High School as well as several others that sent most of their students on to successful college careers, enrolled relatively large numbers of these students. Those to the south—among them, Lincoln High, once a football powerhouse, and San Diego High, the district's oldest—mostly served low-income black and Hispanic students, many of whom were recent immigrants.

"Interstate 8 is the Mason-Dixon line, and in the high schools north of 8 families are mostly satisfied." Bersin said. "Kids are graduating and going to college. Whether most are getting a superior education is not clear."

The state had intervened ineffectively at San Diego High in an attempt to remedy chronic academic weakness; Lincoln had such a bad reputation that it had become a last-chance school for those who had been turned away from or kicked out elsewhere; and Gompers High, another school in the south, had only a few hundred students left. Some of the students in those and other low performing, predominantly low-income schools on the south side were bused to the north through the district's voluntary integration busing program. On average, the bused students did better than did those who attended schools in their neighborhood. Nonetheless, the quality of the education they received was not equal to that received by students from La Jolla and other affluent neighborhoods who they passed every day in the hallways. The schools in the north were largely segregated academically, with the neighborhood students taking far more demanding classes. The transfer students, whose academic skills were weaker, were relegated to classes that did little to help them catch up.

Initially, Bersin thought it made sense to defer dealing with the problems and inequities of San Diego's high schools. "I thought we would get a better return focusing on our future high school students," he said, because he wasn't confident that the high schools, as they currently operated, could help those who were three or four or more years behind catch up in the span of four years.

But he abandoned that idea. "First of all, we can't, just like that, give up on young people. Because San Diego is what it is and where it is, we'd always have large numbers of immigrant students who were poor and who were twelve, thirteen, fourteen years old coming into the system speaking a second language. That is a real issue. We also wanted to make sure that by the time the younger students reached high school, we would have in place the supports they would need through the high school years. So, we had to improve the quality of teaching in high schools to make sure students would learn the academic language and concepts required to succeed today."

Tony Alvarado wanted high schools to spend as much time on literacy as did the elementary and middle schools. "Differentiating between high schools, on the one hand, and elementary and middle schools, on the other, as well as among the high schools themselves, creates tensions for a reform effort like ours, particularly at the outset," Bersin said. "We sought to build a K–12 system focused coherently on improving instruction. If you respond to differences in circumstance before a firm common ground is established, you risk accelerating the big centrifugal forces at work in public education politics and culture. These revolve around a competition for resources and over status, and the attendant frictions that traditionally have divided grade levels and schools."[6]

So, the district insisted that high school teachers attend professional development sessions, meet regularly with principals, accept the help of peer coaches, and follow the recommendations of the districts' instructional leaders. High school teachers were required to learn some of the same pedagogical approaches for literacy instruction as their colleagues in elementary and middle schools.[7]

LITERACY IN HIGH SCHOOLS

Educators who have analyzed the reasons so many students have to take remedial courses when they enroll in college say the most significant is that they don't have the knowledge of vocabulary or the comprehension skills to extract meaning from expository texts. Low achieving students come to high school three or four years behind in their reading skills. Many have never read a book for pleasure. Anyone who has spent any time at all in a low performing American high school understands how profoundly this reality affects instruction. Teachers in such schools often complain that they can't teach the subject matter that they're required to because the students either can't or won't read or do any writing.

This leads some teachers to substitute an exercise known as "giving notes" for actual teaching. In this empty exercise, teachers write on the board detailed notes on the day's lesson and tell the student to copy the notes and then study them. In this way, the teacher can communicate the content the students are supposed to learn without addressing their serious gaps in skills. The method has the added benefit of keeping students busy for much of a class period. Teachers also assign fill-in-the-blank work sheets that give students hints as to where to find the answer ("first paragraph, second sentence, third word").

It is easy to understand why teachers resort to such techniques. Most high school teachers are trained in their disciplines: history, science, English, and so on. They are not trained in how to teach adolescents how to read well. Moreover, they know that high school students have to be exposed to the content they'll need to know to pass high school exit exams, let alone make it into college. So the schools in San Diego had to offer the college prep classes required for admission to the California State University and University of California systems or else they would be held responsible for denying their students opportunities. But there is a big difference between offering the classes and preparing students for college. So teachers and schools are pulled in two directions: teach unprepared students the skills they need in order to access high school content, or focus on higher performing students and teach them the skills and knowledge they need to succeed in postsecondary education or the job market. Put another way, should high school be accommodating or demanding? Is there a core of knowledge and skills that all students should learn? Or is it better to adjust to the fact that students come in with different levels of preparation and to assume that they likely have different educational goals and so shouldn't be expected to master that common core? This is the question that has bedeviled high school reformers for more than one hundred years.

It is of particular relevance today, given the current intense focus on the Common Core standards that are geared to career and college readiness. High schools will have a very difficult time being true to those standards if the students who come to them are such poor readers that they cannot access the meaning of the texts that are assigned.

In San Diego, most of the high schools were doing little or nothing to improve students' reading skills. One person who had taken on the problem was Shirley Peterson, who would serve as one of the instructional leaders under Bersin. Prior to that position, she had been the principal of Morse High School. When she started there, a third or more of the students were two or more grade levels behind in reading. She worked with experts in adolescent literacy to develop a rigorous reading program that tailored instruction to the needs and reading tastes of students. She believed the techniques were appropriate for all students, not just those who lagged behind. "The expectations were that even students in Advanced Placement classes would be challenged to a higher level than they were," she said.[8] Bersin and Alvarado picked up on what Peterson did at Morse as a model for the district.

In Bersin's second year, he and Alvarado introduced a new, two-hour high school class called Genre Students aimed at helping ninth graders who were far behind. The goal of Genre Studies was the same as what teachers were trying to accomplish in the reading and writing workshops that had been put in place in elementary and middle schools: use books at students' reading level to teach them to engage more deeply in the texts they read so that they gained deeper understanding. Students who also were behind in math were enrolled in a two-hour class called Algebra Explorations.[9]

Teachers in the Genre Studies classes were supposed to demonstrate certain reading skills and talk to students about them. Then, the students were expected to use those skills in their own reading, according to Peterson. For example, a teacher would display a passage on an overhead projector. "The teacher would begin reading [and] think aloud, having students see what the teacher is doing, maybe taking notes, they may talk about the text, the teacher will ask questions."

This is what Bersin and Alvarado wanted to see in all high school classes. But Peterson worried that few high school teachers knew how to teach this way and that they were more likely to fall back on what they had always done—lecturing and then assigning homework. "We knew going in that we were constrained by a lack of trained reading teachers at the secondary level, and in that sense some looked upon it as more of an elementary model."

Pat Crowder was appointed by Bersin in 2002 as principal of Patrick Henry High School. She was greeted with hostility because Bersin had appointed her. "There was a lot of backlash," she said. Most high school teachers, focused exclusively on traditional subject matter content, believed those who adopted the recommended pedagogical changes were "going over to the dark side."[10]

But she was determined to implement the district literacy framework and invigorate the Genre Studies classes. She said that before those classes were introduced, high schools had had no organized literacy program for students who were weak readers. "The kids just went into regular high school English classes and got lost," she said.

Previously, Crowder had been principal of Lewis Middle School and had instituted Genre Studies classes there. Like Peterson, she had brought in experts in adolescent literacy to demonstrate to the Lewis teachers how to teach those classes. The school's state Academic Performance Index rose sharply.

Crowder said middle school teachers typically received more literacy training in college and on the job than did high school teachers. Also, she said, middle school faculties are generally smaller, more cohesive, and less attached to their disciplines. "I had some real stars as teachers," she said, some of whom followed her to Patrick Henry. At Patrick Henry, she assigned her more skilled teachers to the ninth and tenth grades and emphasized writing. It took a year or two for teachers to master the techniques, she said.

Eventually, however, she was able to get most of her teachers on board by proving to them the classes worked and that instead of undermining the acquisition of high-level content, literacy instruction actually supported it. As with all changes in instruction, leadership matters. "Changing the culture was the hardest part," she said.

PUSHBACK FROM PARENTS, TEACHERS, AND PRINCIPALS

While the focus on literacy was necessary, it gave critics another issue to use to attack Bersin, because it required significant changes in teaching and high school operations. Some of the "pushback came from parents of kids who had the three-hour literacy block because they were segregated," said Peterson.[11] But some parents of students not in the classes also were unhappy. They argued that the relatively small number of students per teacher in the literacy classes forced schools to eliminate some enrichment classes because there weren't enough teaching positions to cover both. John de Beck derided the literacy methods for not providing explicit instruction in basic skills. The district argued back that, properly done, the literacy blocks shouldn't be restricted to just lessons in reading. Well-trained teachers could teach reading using lessons in history, science, and other subjects. But that argument did not ease concerns. Frances Zimmerman mocked the longer periods of instruction as prisons that destroyed students' interest in school and would cause more students to drop out.

Bersin argued the opposite point of view. "This was the first time any school system acted on the recognition that dealing with the dropout problem meant you had to deal with adolescent illiteracy. We made that a centerpiece of our approach to high schools." Some principals rejected the criticism and said they had been addressing their students' needs for literacy instruction all along. But, if they were, there was little evidence that they were succeeding.

Dana Shelburne, the principal of La Jolla High School and one of Bersin's most strident critics, said the students in the Genre Studies classes "didn't ever learn to read deeply. They didn't learn to defend ideas. They didn't learn to work collectively on anything."[12] Shelburne and other critics often claimed that the classes stole from students the option of attending college.

But Bersin was not persuaded by that argument. "It was ridiculous. These students couldn't read; they couldn't access content. They weren't headed to college. But we could help them learn to read better, pass the high school exit exam, and be prepared for postsecondary education and training and the workplace."

What was playing out in San Diego—essentially a debate as to whether high schools should focus more on teaching students the skills they'd failed to learn earlier or teach them high school–level content—echoes throughout the history of the American high school.

AN INSTITUTION WITH MANY MISSIONS

The first American public high school, the English Classical School, opened in Boston in 1821. Fifty years later the United States had only five hundred public high schools serving well under fifty thousand students. In 1874, the Michigan State Supreme Court ruled that taxes could be levied to support public schools that extended beyond the eighth grade. The number of high schools grew rapidly. The curriculum of early high schools consisted entirely of strictly academic rather than applied courses.

This began to change in the late nineteenth century when, amid rising immigration, high schools dropped their entrance exams and opened their doors to girls and working-class youths. Many of the girls who enrolled wanted to become teachers, and the immigrants studied skilled trades. Vocational training became the central purpose of many high schools.

Concerned about the marginalization of academics, the National Education Association, an administrators' association that would later evolve into the nation's largest teacher union, convened the presidents of ten elite colleges to study the issue. The panel, known as the Committee of Ten, issued a report in 1893 that identified academic subjects that its members thought all high school students should master: Greek, Latin, mathematics, literature, history, geography, civics, and political economy.[13] The committee asserted that a broad, liberal arts education was valuable for all—those going to work as well as those going on to college.

After the turn of the century, as immigration continued to soar, urban schools began serving more students who were new to the country. In 1908, 71.5 percent of children in the New York City public schools had foreign-born fathers, as did 67.3 percent of the children in Chicago, 63.5 percent in Boston, and nearly 60 percent in Cleveland, Providence, Newark, and San Francisco.[14] Progressive educators began to argue that it was elitist and inappropriate to make children who were unlikely to attend college master an academic curriculum. Rather than expecting children to grow intellectually, they contended, schools should give each child the education that was most appropriate for him or her, based on what was likely to be the child's station in life.

A report issued in 1918 expressing that view, "The Cardinal Principles of Secondary Education," held that the primary purposes of high school were "health, citizenship and worthy home-membership and, only secondarily, command of fundamental processes."[15] This document laid the foundation for modern American high schools and provided the theory behind tracking of students based on their test scores into a college-bound track, a vocational track or, for a majority of students, a general studies track. As historian Jeff Mirel has persuasively documented, this philosophy dominated American thinking on high schools for most of the twentieth century.[16]

Fast-forward to the 1950s and 60s, when the launch of *Sputnik* caused panic among American leaders and, in response, the federal government invested in programs to make high schools more academic—but only for the top 20 percent or so of students who were expected to help the nation regain its technological superiority. The 1954 *Brown v. Board of Education* decision eventually resulted in greater racial integration. But the decision did not change the assumptions about how high schools should operate. Tracking continued, and black and Hispanic students attending integrated schools were mostly assigned to lower-level classes. Many white families left the cities, shrinking the tax base in most urban areas and resegregating the schools. James B. Conant, the president of Harvard, said that rather than try to prepare African American students in the cities to attend college, the schools should provide them with vocational training that would help them get jobs in factories or in the trades. "The educational experiences of youth should fit their subsequent employment," he wrote.[17]

Standards and expectations were relaxed even more during the social upheaval of the 1960s and 1970s. The core curriculum was neglected as students were offered hundreds of narrowly focused electives. Social promotion became standard practice. The high school diploma was devalued.

The *A Nation at Risk* report published in 1983, eighty-nine years after the Committee of Ten issued its call for all students to study an academic curriculum, said that the standards of U.S. high schools had grown so lax that they threatened national security. The report rejected the idea of a differentiated curriculum. "All regardless of race or class or economic status are entitled to a fair chance to . . . [develop] their individual powers and minds and spirits to the utmost," the report said.[18] In response to the report, many states immediately began requiring students to take more math, science, English, and history in order to graduate. But little was done to make sure those courses were rigorous, and overall test scores rose little and the racial achievement gaps remained large. That led, in the late 1980s and 1990s, to requirements that all states adopt academic standards to try to ensure classes were rigorous. But most high schools were not structured to help students who had the greatest academic needs, and the teachers, though most were knowledgeable about their disciplines, did not know how to best teach them.

"We have been reforming high schools since they were created," wrote Paul Houston, executive director of the American Association of School Administrators in Washington, D.C. And educators are still at work because "we haven't reached a consensus on what high schools are supposed to do." Not altogether facetiously, he wrote that "Western society has created a waiting room for young people called 'adolescence,' which is a purgatory between childhood and adulthood, and high schools are where we put them until they ripen."[19]

High schools are sometimes said to be sorting machines that funnel students toward different pathways—toward four-year colleges, technical training, the military, menial jobs, or the street and prison. The history of the institution supports that contention. The standards movement was supposed to disable that machine and push all students toward greater possibilities. But standards and the tests and accountability systems that accompanied them did not lead to the creation of curricula and use of methods that would help all students meet those expectations. Rather than address those fundamental issues, it was easier to pretend that all students were the same.

Students who came to high school unable to read, Bersin said, "did not participate in class, did not do homework, could not pass tests, and were marginalized in all ways in the classroom." Students who had been promoted even though they lacked academic skills in ninth grade failed their high school classes and became more likely to drop out. "They were basically illiterate," he said.

"Because of the civil rights movement and the focus on equal educational opportunity we did away with formal tracking but, because we had promoted students to high school even though they could barely read and do math, we ended up tracking them out of the system altogether," Bersin said.

Now, with forty-six states attempting to implement the Common Core, that history haunts. What will high schools do this time? According to Bersin:

> We now say that all students should be prepared to go to college, but we know we are fooling ourselves because we really don't have the system it would take to furnish the academic support needed, and we don't yet have the political support necessary to create that system.
>
> In order to be politically correct then, we have acted, in effect, as though high school doesn't matter, in and of itself; only college does. We've lowered the standards of high school to accommodate mass attendance, and in doing so we've devalued high school altogether. A high school education doesn't get you much now, even if you do graduate.

PHYSICS FOR ALL

This tension between challenging academics and serving all students' needs played out explicitly in San Diego in a sometimes-ugly battle over a decision to give more students the opportunity to take physics.

California and its public universities had begun requiring all students to take two years of science, including one laboratory science, for graduation and admission to college, regardless of how well they were performing in other classes.[20] At the time, only 10 percent of San Diego students were taking physics, compared with 20 percent nationally.[21]

The district's solution was to reverse the traditional sequence of science courses so that physics came first followed by chemistry and biology—a change that science educators had long advocated. The district also wanted to mandate that all schools begin using a curriculum called Active Physics.

Typically, physics is taken by science-oriented, college-bound students who have mastered the advanced mathematics required to manipulate the equations that express physical relationships. The Active Physics curriculum required far less mathematical knowledge and instead used drawings and hands-on activities to help get across key concepts such as force, acceleration, and the different types of energy. This "learner-centered, inquiry-based approach" was consistent with Alvarado's constructivist view of how all subjects and all grades should be taught.[22] Developed with the support of the National Science Foundation by "leading physicists, physics teachers and science educators," Active Physics was designed around seven thematic content areas—communication, home, medicine, predictions, sports, transportation, and light, according to the program creators.[23] For example, one lesson challenged students to develop a sport that could be played "in the meager gravity of the moon's environment."[24] "We thought we would focus on the teaching as well as the content," Bersin said.

The San Diego school board in June 2001 approved the purchase of Active Physics instructional materials for $1.8 million. Before making the decision, the district consulted Nobel Prize–winning scientists, who helped convince them to adopt the program.[25]

Not incidentally, Bersin also thought that the redesign of the science curriculum might serve as a starting point for changing the culture of high schools so that more students got a good education. The proposal quickly became the fuse that ignited an upper-class uproar that was heard most loudly at La Jolla High School. La Jolla teachers joined forces with the community's parents, who were powerful, well connected, media-savvy, and furious. Many of them also were scientists. Opponents derisively referred to the new thin textbooks as comic books, replete as they were with colorful illustrations and simplistic diagrams. Shelburne, the La Jolla principal, asked his physics department to review the materials "and they said, 'There's no physics here.'" He organized a community meeting at which 375 people showed up, many of them intent on grilling Bersin, Alvarado, and the district's science supervisor about the program.

"I knew it was going to get ugly," Shelburne said. "I handed the microphone off to the first questioner, and that microphone never got back to me. People were grabbing at it, and the place went chaotic . . . I had teachers on the stage yelling. The parents were screaming at Alan."[26]

Bersin attributed the resistance to a desire to maintain physics as an advanced class available only to those headed to college. "The elite science faculty could not stomach the notion that we would democratize the curriculum. Part of the resistance was due to the reallocation of resources that would occur, but most of it was generated by a perceived loss of status by physics teachers, even though their professional lives would not be affected one whit."

"A TERRIBLE MISTAKE"

One principal said the decision "came as a surprise to everyone. Not one science teacher knew that a discussion was on about how science was implemented in San Diego City Schools . . . One day it's the way it's always been for the last 50 years, and the next day they said, 'Okay, we're going to reverse this. The 9th grade is going to do this; the 10th graders are going to do this. This class is out. Change this name.'"[27]

Bersin quickly agreed that the way the policy was introduced was "a terrible mistake" and that the district should have moved more slowly. He said he never intended to force all students to take the same course. And, as soon as he heard of the proposed requirement, the policy was changed to give students a choice of physics classes. An honors class was developed and the Advanced Placement physics class was retained. The science requirement was imposed starting the following year. "They took advanced physics if they were identified as students at that level, or they were in Active Physics," Peterson said. "There were no waivers."[28] All students, not just 10 percent of them, began taking physics in the fall of 2003.

Scientist and community activist Miyo Reff, who organized press conferences in opposition to the new curriculum, claimed the opposition wasn't elitist. "It's a desire for a certain type of education," she said, noting that many lower-income immigrant families also opposed the requirement. "The Blueprint did reallocate resources to the kids who needed the most help. I don't want to be one of those Alan bashers. But I thought he missed the mark on high school reform."[29]

The Blueprint "was not supportive of an academic high school," Reff said.[30] Many others agreed with Reff's assessment, including Leslie Fausset, the former top state education official who later became Bersin's deputy superintendent: "There probably wasn't sufficient attention paid [in the Blueprint implementation] to making sure that college-bound, academically competitive students were adequately challenged and that their needs were accommodated."[31]

The physics controversy exposed all of those tensions and quickly escalated into a broader protest movement. It provoked the La Jolla opponents to declare their intention to become a charter school that would operate independently of the school district. Bersin said La Jolla was the "flagship of a tin-can fleet" of high schools because the data showed that many students there were not receiving a good education. But he also recognized that if the district's highest performing high school were allowed to break free, it would seriously threaten his reform plan and probably his superintendency.

Bersin turned to Jack McGrory, a former San Diego city manager, for help. The two men worked out a compromise that gave La Jolla academic autonomy, meaning that the school did not have to follow the district's curriculum. But it remained a district school. This was a serious blow, but Bersin learned from it. Perhaps the most important lesson was that every high school has different needs. "People in middle-class neighborhoods are happy with their schools and will fight to prevent them from changing," Bersin said.

A NEW APPROACH NEEDED

In 2000, San Diego won a $250,000 grant from the Carnegie Corporation of New York that was to be used to come up with a new districtwide strategy to improve literacy, math, and science in its high schools. The district would then compete for a much larger grant to carry out the plan. A year later, San Diego was awarded $8 million from Carnegie and the Bill & Melinda Gates Foundation, which had joined Carnegie's "Schools for a New Society" initiative. The goal was to "transform . . . high schools from an 'obsolete, factory model' into places where all students can learn at high levels."[32] The San Diego grant was part of a $60 million effort to improve high schools in seven urban districts nationally.

"This grant will permit our principals and teachers to begin thinking about a new way to provide a high school education," Bersin said at the time.[33] One goal of the grants was to find ways to engage students more deeply in high schools by breaking down large institutions where it was easy for them to be anonymous into smaller, more personalized learning communities. The eighteen San Diego high schools that were written into the grant were to start that process by asking students for their ideas and by creating opportunities for teachers to build stronger relationships with their students. The district also agreed to eliminate meaningless high school courses, establish districtwide end-of-course exams, and expand training programs for teachers and principals.[34] Entering ninth graders identified as needing extra help would be able to attend a summer "bridge" program where they could work on their literacy and mathematics skills.

A week earlier a national blue-ribbon panel organized by former Secretary of Education Richard W. Riley had called on high schools to do more to keep seniors engaged and to provide every student with a college prep education. Just as San Diego was turning its attention to its high schools, the rest of the nation was as well.

San Diego had a long way to go. As the work under that grant began, student achievement in San Diego's high schools was getting worse, not better. The strategies to improve teaching and learning employed in the earlier grades were not working. When it came to high schools, Bersin said bluntly, the Blueprint strategies "were a failure."[35]

Leslie Fausset said the focus on literacy and the Genre Studies classes did not solve the problem of teaching both content and skills. "[By] focusing only on literacy in isolation, you don't get the connections to content that you need," she said.[36]

The lack of progress was frustrating. At his 2002 "state of the district" speech Bersin unveiled a new, differentiated approach to high school reform—one that recognized finally that high schools were not the same as elementary schools.

Bersin laid out a set of ambitious "stretch" goals for San Diego's high schools. By 2006, he said, he expected all San Diego high school students to pass the state's high school exit exam, a long way from the 42 percent who were passing at the time. He also wanted to double the percentage of graduates who had passed all of the college prep classes required for admission to the state's public universities. Those students, he vowed, would not have to take remedial classes in college.

Perhaps even more important than the specific goals, Bersin announced a critical course correction—no longer would all high schools be treated the same. Schools succeeding would be given "flexibility in how they get the job done, so long as the rate of achievement continues to rise. This will . . . allow the district to sharpen its focus on making dramatic achievement in schools that have further to go."

It was a promise to loosen the district's tight reins on schools, which critics had been railing against for more than three years.

REMAKING SAN DIEGO'S HIGH SCHOOLS

To take on the job of reforming high schools, Bersin hired John DeVore, a veteran principal who had achieved significant success in a nearby district. DeVore's task was to systematically improve instruction in the district's high schools. "John and his colleagues started to build . . . systems around professional growth, systems around accountability, systems around instruction," said Fausset.[37]

"One of the big needs I saw was that instruction was not rigorous," DeVore later wrote. "The second thing we saw was that every teacher had a different approach."[38]

DeVore worked on developing common instructional practices in English, math, and science in grades nine and ten so that more students passed the state high school exit exam and the California Standards Tests, which were one factor in how the State rated schools. In the upper grades, he brought in the highly regarded Advancement Via Individual Determination (AVID) program to help middling students get on track toward college and pushed schools to enroll more students in honors and Advanced Placement classes. He also wanted to make sure the academic standards and instruction for students enrolled in career and technical training were as rigorous as for those who were on the college prep track, something that had never been done in American high schools.[39] Getting "teachers out of isolation" and giving them opportunities to build professional learning communities with their fellow teachers were key tactics.[40] In addition to improving instruction, he worked to increase student engagement by focusing on ninth graders.

A few months after DeVore was hired, Chief Academic Officer Mary Hopper laid out the district's new plan for high schools. Significantly, the report did not present one approach, but five.

A set of generally successful high schools, called "challenge schools," would work on doing a better job of serving their low-income and minority students. The district's alternative high schools were to work on becoming more focused and rigorous academically and on trying new models. A larger group of schools, "community engagement schools," would strive to become a more attractive choice to students who lived in the neighborhood. Those schools also were to add the AVID program. Four of the district's lowest performing high schools were going to be closed and broken up into smaller schools. And, finally, new, small high schools were going to be created to provide more alternatives for students.

All of the schools were expected to adhere to four principles: high expectations, meaning that students were to be enrolled in "an ambitious and rigorous course of study"; personalization, which would be achieved by redesigning schools so that students had a close relationship with at least one adult and a personal learning plan; promotion to the next grade based on performance to bring an end to social promotion; and collaboration, so that teachers would have time to work together to help one another get better.

"Why shouldn't we stop refusing to accept the notion that there are different circumstances that call out for different approaches?" Bersin said. In the "challenge schools" in La Jolla, San Carlos, Point Loma, and University City, most of the students were succeeding. But others, most of them bused in, were not. "Our efforts to persuade the teachers, parents, and students in these communities that complacency was not warranted largely fell on ears deaf to the proposition," Bersin said. Rather than trying to change those schools entirely, the district would provide them with resources and incentives to focus on their less successful students. "That's a different problem than the one we faced at other high schools south of I-8 like Crawford or San Diego High, where 80 percent to 90 percent of the students were not succeeding by any reasonable standard."[41]

In November 2003 the Gates Foundation awarded the district $11 million to support the reorganization of three failing high schools into eighteen small, self-contained high schools. "This grant will help move us toward a diverse portfolio of high-quality schools for all San Diego students," Bersin said at the time.

That didn't mean, however, that he thought instruction was any less important. "We needed to improve the teaching, to deliver skills and knowledge, and to engage our students to educate themselves. But none of that was possible in certain schools within the existing framework. We had to change the structure and process to create the conditions for better instruction by teachers and more engagement by students."

Mary Hopper said the benefits of small schools included better attendance, stronger academic achievement (especially for low-income students and students of color), lower dropout rates, higher grades, fewer failed classes, greater participation, less vandalism, and fewer behavioral incidents.[42] Bersin said there was little evidence as yet that small schools increased learning, but "the status quo was so unsatisfactory that I was prepared to proceed."

"These schools could hardly be worse for the students," he said.

SMALL SCHOOLS

Someone needed to be in charge of that part of the plan. So, in December, right after receiving the Gates grant, Bersin hired Matt Malone, an aggressive, thirty-four-year-old ex-Marine who had successfully reorganized an inner-city high school in Boston. He was put in charge of all of the high schools south of Interstate 8, with a goal of replacing three of them with fourteen smaller schools. The schools had not yet been designed, there was no funding formula in place, and the school board had not yet given its go-ahead. "They didn't have any work done before I got there," said Malone. "We moved absolute mountains."[43]

"Basically, Alan set up two competing strategies or tactics to see who could get the best results," Malone said. "That was the artistry in this. When I say Alan's brilliant in what he did, most people don't understand that."[44]

Indeed, others thought the two-pronged strategy, with DeVore and Malone in competition, was divisive. Among them was Libia Gil, a senior fellow with the American Institutes for Research who was given the responsibility of helping the district implement its Gates grant. Malone stepped on eggs, she said. And, "as I said to Alan, someone has to make an omelet out of this mess."[45]

"I'm going to describe some friction there," DeVore said, cautiously. "The reason Alan was doing this, I think, is because he didn't believe one size fits all. But where I was coming from always was that the instructional part of this ought to be the same, although there would be some differences in how we organized structurally. But there was not harmony, and we didn't really cross over and work in any way together, and that was frustrating."[46]

"My agenda was . . . to do innovation, saying the hell with everything," said Malone, who described DeVore's work as the continuation of Alvarado's theories.[47]

Gil said Malone was intensely focused on "advocating and protecting the small schools as if they were the only ones that mattered in the district . . . It created tremendous backlash and resentment from all of the other schools and everybody else in the central office. The feeling was they were getting preferential treatment."[48]

"San Diego's a nice-guy place; they don't like guys like me," said Malone, who talked about "the level of dismay and disorder" he caused in the central office. "I would have strategy meetings that my team called 'moving the boulders,' and we would . . . say, 'Whose butt do we have to kick in this department to get what we need for our people?' And we'd strategize and go do it."

"Disrupting the system," he said, was exactly what Bersin wanted him to do. "He said, 'Step on as many toes as you [have to] because I want [these high schools] shaken up . . . He threw out the Blueprint and the book on what San Diego City Schools was all about, to support what we were doing in the small schools."[49]

Significantly, Malone reported directly to Bersin while DeVore reported to Hopper. It was one of the conditions Malone had set for taking the job. "If I don't have your protection, we're never going to get this thing off the ground," Malone recalls telling Bersin.[50] Bersin agreed.

WORKING WITH TEACHERS AND PARENTS

Malone worked with teachers and parents to design the schools. The teachers chose the leaders of the committees, which were tasked with the job of creating a school culture that valued academics, strategies for supporting students academically as well as socially, and instructional methods that valued inquiry and student engagement in their learning. The leaders "generated momentum and . . . they went out to sell it to parents," Malone said. When the time came to get the school board's approval, "we showed up with an army. We had rappers, we had dancers, we brought in buses of people from the neighborhoods."[51] Even the teacher union was on board, according to Malone, who said his efforts in Boston to convert a high school from the top down resulted in a political war. "This was one of the most successful teacher-led movements in high school history," he said. "In San Diego, it was bottom-up with top-down support. The teachers at each site voted to do this and they convinced the union not to mess this up."[52]

The schools opened in the fall of 2004 with themes that included construction technology, the performing arts, business, law, digital media, science and technology, health, and others.

Despite her concerns about competition and internal turmoil, Gil said San Diego was one of the few districts that managed the process of breaking large high schools into smaller ones with no complaints. She attributed the smoothness of the process both to the community work led by Malone as well as to the work of the central office to support the effort. "It was very unusual to not have a single objection . . . given the speed at which it all occurred," she said.

Bersin observed that what appeared to be an extraordinary shift in philosophy—from bringing about change centrally to allowing teachers to not only choose their leaders but also design all other aspects of their schools—really was only a tactical change. Whether change should be led from the top or arise from the ranks, he said, "has always been situational for me."

With the high schools, he saw that the top-down approach was not accelerating learning. But, he said, the Blueprint had actually set the stage for change, by establishing that the focus of all the schools had to be on increasing achievement, closing achievement gaps, and improving instruction. Once that was established, he could allow greater variety in curriculum and instruction.

MIXED RESULTS

The performance of the new, smaller schools was mixed in their first few years. The strongest schools academically focused on international studies, international business, performing arts, digital media, and science. The weakest performers included schools emphasizing invention and design, law and business, visual arts, and a school focusing on communications, where three out of four students were English language learners.

The School of International Studies, which featured a rigorous International Baccalaureate program, became one of the best urban high schools in the state, replacing La Jolla on *Newsweek*'s list of the highest performing high schools in America. The school offered the AVID program, which, according to the school's principal, allows her to "provide academically challenging instruction and strong encouragement for a diverse student population."[53] As of August 2008, 90 percent or more of the seniors had passed the California high school exit exam at nine of the fourteen schools. At two of the highest performing small schools half of the students were poor, while at several of the weakest ones 90 percent or more of the students were. At two of the highest performing schools, less than 10 percent of the students were English language learners. The correlation between the percentages of poor students and English language learners on the one hand and student achievement on the other remained strong, regardless of school size.

Despite the variations, Gil, who has studied the small-school model nationally, noted that other measurements besides increased test scores are valid assessments of success. A 2009 survey by the University of California, San Diego, of students attending the small schools concluded that "the schools continue to perform, as a group, exceedingly well on many measures." Almost 75 percent of four thousand one hundred student respondents agreed that their teachers believe all students can learn.[54] About the same percentage said they are getting the college-related information they need. And 70 percent reported doing class projects to demonstrate what they have learned.

"The schools with few exceptions are not performing at the level that we would want them all to perform," said Gil. "We know there is a lot more work to be done."[55]

Lincoln High School, which had been razed in 2002, reopened as four schools on a new $129 million campus in the fall of 2007. All entering ninth graders enrolled in the Center for Social Justice, where they would take ninety minutes each of geometry and English to improve their basic skills. In the tenth grade, the students could enroll in one of three other schools with different themes—the arts, public safety, or science and engineering. All Lincoln students were required to take college prep courses of study. They had access to both Advanced Placement and vocational classes. Whereas few parents wanted their children to attend the old Lincoln High, there was a long waiting list when it reopened.[56] In a sense, the new Lincoln High was designed to solve the dilemma that is at the core of high school reform: how can a school that serves students with different levels of skills, talents, and ambitions ensure that each one graduates with both the skill set and knowledge they need to succeed as adults without watering down the offerings in order to prevent low achieving students from dropping out?

With its new facilities, new staff, and new students, Lincoln is considered a startup, which research has shown often has greater success at accelerating learning than a conversion school. But Bersin cautioned that changing a school's structure alone without altering teaching and learning practices is insufficient. "Small schools mean nothing unless they improve the conditions for instruction," he said. "The jury remains out on the new Lincoln." But he said he had no regrets about shutting down the old Lincoln.

Gil worried about sustainability for San Diego's small schools without stable leadership at the district. "This is our fourth year, and we're now going on our fourth superintendent," she said several years ago.[57] After she was interviewed, San Diego lost another superintendent and a new one was hired. UC San Diego's Bud Mehan, whose organization is working with the schools on the Lincoln campus, said the performance of those schools is uneven. He was not a fan of the centralization that Bersin brought to the district in the early part of his administration, but he also praised Bersin's strong focus on teaching and curriculum. He said the district has lacked that leadership since Bersin's departure and that, in some quarters, there is a nostalgia for Bersin's strong hand on the tiller heading in a consistent direction.

Bersin finds it ironic that, while he is still known in San Diego for centralizing the power of the district, he also wound up presiding over a high school reform plan that produced a portfolio of very different schools. And he thinks that while the work on high schools in San Diego led to improvements, it also was incomplete when he left in 2005 and remains so today. "High schools continue to pose the central challenge to American public education." As schools throughout the country attempt to implement new Common Core academic standards, this challenge will become more intense.

Bersin was invited to deliver the Cubberley Lecture in 2006 at the Stanford Graduate School of Education. In his remarks, he focused on high schools. He said it is important to reduce the high school dropout rate. But he said schools must not do that by lowering their standards, because that will fail students who want to go on to college, which hearkens back to high schools' original purpose. Bersin believes the high school curriculum must be both academic and applied, and that career and technical education should be emphasized much more.

> For me, when we talk about high school, we should be discussing an experience that is dedicated to high-level literacy and mathematics, critical thinking, clear communication, character development and connection to the adult world for every young person. Or at least to offer that to every teenager and make sure that everybody who graduates from high school does so with those skills, qualities and experiences. And then we might be a lot less oriented to high school as a preparation phase . . . We say we prepare our students for college and the work-place. I think part of what we want to do with high school is to reinvent high schools to make them a very meaningful experience for academic and intellectual growth and social development on their own terms.[58]

He said radical changes are needed. As much as 75 percent of the academic curriculum could be offered online. Students could move through the curriculum quickly and then begin taking college classes. High school should focus on character development and help students make real life choices. Students need to learn basic skills, and some will need direct instruction to acquire them. But students also need to work on projects and to be given opportunities for service learning.

Although he thinks high school reform in San Diego fell short, Bersin also believes the effort made a contribution and focused on the right issues at a time of uncertainty: "We really are in a period, since erosion of the progressive theory of high schools, where we don't know anywhere near precisely what the right answer is for secondary education in urban America. But our contribution remains that we asked the right questions and didn't shy away from rejecting the worst answers that history had produced for students and teachers alike and seeking to invent better ones."

"His heart was with the kids that needed the most support," said Malone, who left San Diego in June 2005 to become superintendent of the Swampscott and then Brockton school districts in Massachusetts. "That's where [Bersin's] greatest commitment is and has always been. His commitment to social justice is from such a deep intellectual level."[59]

"Alan's very brilliant," DeVore said. "He's multiple years ahead of all of us. We were just players in his [plan]. He probably knew what he was doing the whole time, but it was going to take a lot longer than he probably thought."[60]

Although critical of some of his methods, Katherine Nakamura, who remained on the school board and became its conscience after Bersin left, grew wistful at the recollection of the high school reform era under Bersin. "It was like Camelot," she said. "It was a very exciting time. People were willing to take risks. Alan tried to make it better on so many levels."[61]

CHAPTER TEN

Choice and Charters

"People Have the Right to Pick Their Own Lawyers and Doctors, so Why Shouldn't They Have the Right to Pick Their Own Schools?"

Charter schools offer an alternative to low performing public schools that, in some cases, can address problems that otherwise seem impossible to fix. This was the case in San Diego. After seven years of building a cohesive school district that operated within a framework of instructional expectations and support, accountability, and clear goals, Alan Bersin recognized that the schools that continued to fail needed a different approach. Using the process for dealing with low performing schools laid out in the No Child Left Behind Act of 2001 (NCLB), Bersin became one of the first leaders in the country to put the lowest performing schools out to bid for groups that wanted to run them as charter schools. As it turned out, there were few takers. But the parents, teachers, and principals of two middle schools and an elementary school seized the opportunity. Working together, they were able to change the culture of the schools and turn them around. The experiences of these schools and their leaders can inform current turnaround efforts.

Thirty African American and Hispanic seventh graders wearing navy blue pants or skirts and white Oxford shirts and ties stand in parallel lines in the outdoor corridor of Gompers Charter Middle School, located in San Diego's Chollas View neighborhood, one of the city's poorest. Seventy percent of the students' families live on incomes of less than $21,000 a year. The seventh graders are silent, waiting for the young teacher to direct them to enter the classroom. The teacher takes a step back, nods her head, and, as the students file past her, shakes each one's hand. Each student looks her in the eye. The teacher momentarily focuses her gaze on each face, a gesture of respect as well as greeting.

Inside, students move purposefully to their seats. For the next ninety minutes, they will study math, with the goal of being prepared to succeed in algebra as eighth graders so that they are on track to pass the high school math they'll need to get into college. They copy the homework assignment from the whiteboard as the teacher explains that the focus of the day's lesson will be on learning to graph equations. After the class works independently for a few minutes, a student named Michelle is asked how she can tell whether an equation represents a line or not. "Walk me through your thinking," the teacher asks.

Michelle stands, poised and confident, and points to parts of a graph drawn on a flipchart as she explains. The teacher poses another question and asks Michelle to choose three classmates to offer their own conjectures. The teacher facilitates the discussion so that it keeps moving forward and covers key concepts.

In other classes here at Gompers, students are equally engaged. In an English as a Second Language class, the students warm up by quickly writing a few sentences to describe a family celebration tradition. They talk with the members of their small group and then to the whole class about their answers. In another class, music plays quietly as the students work in groups to explain a mathematical pattern.

During a spring 2009 visit, every aspect of the Gompers campus bespoke a school culture dedicated not just to order, but also to academics, high expectations, and common purpose. The school's mission is to "accelerate academic achievement for ALL students through a college preparatory culture and curriculum."[1] Students study math and English for one-hundred-minute blocks each morning, and those who are behind receive additional instruction in the afternoon. The school day, which is longer than most to accommodate an independent reading period and a homework help study hall, lasts until 4 p.m. and is followed by activities including extra tutoring and sports until 6 p.m. Students are expected to attend, and teachers are required to teach, Saturday Academy morning classes that provide extra tutoring and instruction in study habits—as well as free snacks and lunch.

The school's motto—*Respect. Enthusiasm. Achievement. Commitment. Hard Work*, or REACH—is on display everywhere. The school has a chant, a cheer, and a song that the students and teachers are expected to know and participate in on the spot. Academic achievements are celebrated. Parents, teachers, and students all must sign a document that commits them to work hard to further academics and "a culture of learning." Those who fail to do the work risk suspension, expulsion, or, in the case of teachers, dismissal. Teachers are expected to share and act on the belief that all students can learn if they conduct themselves appropriately and are properly taught.

Eighty-five percent of Gompers's students enter the school two to four grade levels behind, just under half of them speak English as a second language, and 18 percent are classified as having special education needs. "We know where we're coming from and we know where we're going," said the school's gifted young director, Vince Riveroll. "One hundred percent of our graduating students will have the right to choose to go to college."

The contrast to what this campus looked and felt like five years earlier is startling. Then, a good day at Gompers was one in which there were no fights that injured students. The school had been a social and academic failure for many years, and the reforms introduced under Bersin's leadership that were making a difference in most of the district's schools had failed to improve conditions there. The turnaround started when the school was shut down and then reopened as a charter school in September 2005. The new school had a new leadership team, mostly new teachers, renewed optimism, and a strong focus on academics.

TRANSFORMATION

Although Bersin had always thought that choice and competition—in the form of charter schools as well as a variety of types of regular public schools—should be as much a part of education as any other area of American life, he initially did not push to convert San Diego's worst schools into charter schools as a way to fix them. He wanted to reform the district, not expend energies fixing schools one at a time. But Gompers and eight other San Diego schools had been failing so badly for so many years that, finally, he decided to add a new tool to his toolbox for education reform.

Today, Gompers offers one image of what a school turnaround, which is the term used by today's education reformers and the Obama administration, can look like. Back then, the school looked and felt to parents and teachers like a prison, with the walkways fenced in and gated so that the eleven security guards and city police officers who patrolled the campus each day could lock down an area to contain fights so that they didn't spread and involve other students. More than one thousand students were suspended each year. The chaos drove students and teachers away. Now, the covered walkways that connect this California-style campus are litter-free and landscaped. The atmosphere is calm, orderly, and academic.

A SOCIAL AND ACADEMIC FAILURE

In 2003, Gompers was a high school with a fast-dwindling enrollment, though it stood to get an influx of transfer students when the nearby Lincoln High School was razed. Students who wanted to learn, and whose parents were able to figure out how to access the district's open enrollment system, attended high schools elsewhere. That year, in response to community leaders who wanted the district to do something to make sure students were better prepared for high school, the district opened a middle school in an unused part of the lightly attended campus.

Tracy Johnson was a committed, passionate young teacher assigned to the new middle school's literacy team. When she started there, she quickly realized that most days she could teach only during the first two periods. After that, she'd have to spend most of her time calming down students who had become too agitated and hostile. "They'd been in classes where kids were jumping onto tables, throwing chairs, talking back to teachers, and most of their teachers did as little as they possibly could," she said.[2]

Allison Kenda was the school's literacy coordinator. Instead of helping teachers become more effective, she had to help them cope with violence. She recalled the time she went to a science class where a fight between two girls had left blood splattered on the walls. On her first day at Gompers, she was confronted by a high school teacher from across the campus who was angry because he understood that the motivated, focused educators sent by the district were a threat to others' settled existence. When Kenda filed a complaint against the teacher, she was told by a Gompers administrator that she needed to "slow down."

"There was such a culture of dysfunction that no amount of money, no amount of support, could change that. We used to say that this place needs to be shut down. It wasn't fixable. It was the teachers, the students, the parents, the community. It just was so very, very sick."[3]

Alan Bersin likes to tell the story of the transformation of Gompers. The tale is dramatic and involves individuals he refers to as "remarkable, ordinary people" who discovered strength and talents they had not known they had. But he also likes to tell the story because of what it taught him about the possibilities of and the requirements for school turnaround—lessons that are among the most powerful he learned as superintendent.

PARENTS AND TEACHERS KEY TO EDUCATION REFORM

School district leadership and strong effective governance are vital to successful public education. Bersin's first priority as superintendent had been to set up an instructional infrastructure that would improve teaching. But he came to realize that while a school district could create the conditions for success, the principals, teachers, and, importantly, the parents had to make it happen. Community and parental support had to be a pillar of reform. He had always talked about the "democratization" of public education. In the least advantaged neighborhoods, not only would parents have to support change, but they'd have to demand it.

That was what happened at Gompers and the nearby Keiller Middle School. A small group of teacher leaders and the principals of the two schools worked with parents—largely low-income and minority—and, with the help and encouragement of the district, took back control of their schools. What the schools did with their autonomy was create the kind of professional learning communities that Bersin would have liked to have left as his legacy throughout San Diego's impoverished neighborhoods. One reason he did not succeed in creating such an environment in most of the "south of 8" schools, he believed, was that he and his team did not do as well rallying parents to the cause as they needed to do. "Overcoming the inertia of everyday life for parents and the false confidence generated by the status quo," he says in a deliberately massive under-statement, "is not easy."

> The story of Gompers in some ways is a microcosm of our entire effort. It illus-trates how the San Diego reform effort was calculated, in terms of the politics, the sequencing of specific policies and approaches, the issues of how to achieve and sustain the change and how to maintain a board majority and a parent com-munity in support of change. Throughout the time Tony [Alvarado] and I col-laborated, it was a calculated struggle, inside and outside, that was gripping and compelling. To obtain charter approval for Gompers and Keiller, in the face of determined school board and union opposition, required a six-month, three-dimensional strategy that was challenging to play out and even more dramatic in its outcome. And best of all, success came from efforts exploding from the bot-tom up in the wake of previous tumultuous change from the top down. Once the authentic voices of parents and teachers were joined, they formed a river whose current just would not be denied. The wave of change found a way around every obstacle thrown in its way. We saw how the force of belief and passion and hard work could overwhelm a stubborn status quo and the usual suspects who defended it.

SCHOOL CHOICE TO INCREASE EDUCATIONAL EQUITY IN SAN DIEGO

Gompers was built after World War II amid a tract of basic ranch homes that sprung up to accommodate San Diego's growing population. Over time, the neighborhood would change due to immigration, suburbanization, and the de-cline of local manufacturing.

In 1977, more than twenty years after the U.S. Supreme Court ruling in the *Brown v. Board of Education* case, a state court ruled in *Carlin v. Board of Education* that San Diego had to reduce segregation at twenty-three of its schools and better serve its disadvantaged students. Most of those schools, including Gompers, would be identified as persistent failures in 2004, nearly three decades later.

As part of the remedy, the court ordered the district to develop a voluntary busing program and to create high-quality magnet schools. The court's decision was typical of that judicial era, after the Supreme Court had ordered the end to mandatory busing as a means to racial integration of the nation's schools.

In response to the ruling, San Diego created the Voluntary Ethnic Enrollment Program (VEEP), which bused black and Latino students from their home neighborhoods on the south side of the district to largely white schools on the north side. The intent of the magnet school program, which became one of the largest and best known in the United States, was the reverse. Magnet programs and schools were located mostly in the south and were intended to entice white students to enroll in specialty programs in math, science, art, music, and languages. A math, science, and computer technology magnet program established at Gompers attracted students who won national honors. However, the magnet did not achieve the desired integration. Most of the students in the magnet program were white, while nonwhite neighborhood students mostly attended regular classes. The entire school was designated as a magnet school in 1989 and white parents began sending their students elsewhere. The school's performance began to slide.[4] The magnet was shut down altogether in the 1990s at the insistence of an African American school board member who complained that the mostly black and Latino students in the school were not benefitting from the magnet programs. Integration no longer mattered to her or to her supporters.

TWO TYPES OF SCHOOL CHOICE

San Diego offered two other types of school choice. A 1990s California law permitted all students to transfer to schools outside their neighborhood if they could be accommodated in the school they wanted to attend. In 2002, as required by NCLB, the district also began offering transfers to students enrolled in schools that had failed to meet the law's Adequate Yearly Progress goals.

The district's choice programs are popular with parents. A 2006 study by the Public Policy Institute of California (PPIC) found that 28 percent of San Diego students attended charter schools or took advantage of one of the other school choice programs.[5] But there was only a limited number of seats in the most desirable schools, so there were long waiting lists.

Despite the popularity of these programs, Bersin was dubious for good reason. According to a study of the results of school choice programs from 2001 through 2004, only a handful of choice schools enhanced student achievement.[6]

Predominately white schools welcomed the nonwhite students because, had they not come, the schools would have been too small and expensive to operate. The district also needed the programs to continue because, otherwise, there would not be enough space in many schools in the southern part of the district. And many families of color wanted their children to attend better schools "out of the ghetto" in neighborhoods perceived to be safer.

In 2002, the San Diego school district conducted a comprehensive review of its magnet schools and programs. Those that weren't improving student achievement were shut down.[7] That freed up some of the money that could be spent on the Blueprint. "It was clear," Bersin said, "where choice and magnet programs had produced neither integration nor academic achievement, that the allocation of resources was unproductive and required deployment elsewhere."

AN EARLY EMBRACE OF CHARTER SCHOOLS

San Diego, like California as a whole, embraced charter schools early on. By 1997, seven of the state's one hundred charter schools were in San Diego. But the charter schools, five of which were converted district schools, mostly were academic failures. The substantial autonomy they enjoyed had not produced results. All of the teachers were unionized and all of the schools seemed captured by the school leaders, teachers, and sometimes parents who had converted them, Bersin said. There was little support for them within the district, and Bersin eventually closed several of them down.[8]

Though unimpressed with the results of those schools, he supported competition and accountability, principles that he emphasized undergirded American political and economic theory. He recognized that successful charter schools competed with traditional district schools for resources and students. But he did not think the school district should stand in the way.

"The values of competition and choice were attractive to me intellectually and viscerally from other contexts. People have the right, if not always the power, to pick their own lawyers and doctors, so why shouldn't they have the right and the power to choose their own school and why shouldn't the district be willing to compete?"

As long as the rules of engagement are fair, bad schools are shut down, and unwarranted barriers to the entry of newcomers are brought down, he said, then the competitive tension should be welcomed. "By the same token, when charter groups complain that their districts are not collaborating with them, they ought be reminded to stop complaining and start competing. After all, this is about improving student achievement in all schools and not about winning an ideological battle."

Soon after he started, Bersin learned that the district, which in California is the charter school authorizer of choice, was dragging its feet on approving two applications. If a district blocks the way, charter school operators can seek authorization from the state.

So, he set about clearing a path for them. One of the applications came from High Tech High School, founded by Larry Rosenstock, a strong proponent of project-based learning and independent study. High Tech had strong support from foundations and the Jacobs Family, founders of the wireless giant Qualcomm in San Diego.

Another stalled application had been submitted by Robert Dynes, then chancellor of the University of California, San Diego. In 1996, Californians had voted for Proposition 209, a constitutional amendment that prohibited using race as a factor in college admissions and other governmental decisions. Peter Preuss, then a university Regent, along with his wife, Peggy, and Cecil Lytle, a music professor, wanted to provide low-income African American and Latino students with a higher-quality education that would better prepare them for college.

With a push on their behalf by Bersin, both charter schools opened up in the fall of 1999 and would go on to become national models, considered among the best middle and high schools in America.

A third application seeking autonomy, but not in charter form, came from San Diego businessman and philanthropist Sol Price. Price led a group that included the San Diego Education Association (SDEA) to operate an elementary school, a middle school, and a high school in the district's City Heights neighborhood. The schools would serve as a teaching laboratory for San Diego State University. This idea also had been blocked, but Bersin's support got it moving and the schools opened in 1999.

The Preuss School at UCSD and High Tech High wanted to operate without unionized teachers. At that point, Bersin did not think that mattered. But, because he was agnostic on that point, when Bob Chase, then the visionary and reformist head of the National Education Association (NEA), sought a site for a union-sponsored charter school, Bersin was enthusiastic. He obtained school board approval for offering the NEA an available school in east San Diego, assisted the SDEA in establishing its Kwachiyoa Charter School on the site, invited Chase to the district, and joined him and Marc Knapp at the formal announcement of the school in 1999.[9]

In 2001, at Bersin's urging, the district convened a conference of charter school experts to help it craft a cutting-edge charter school policy, a first in California. It established clear guidelines for approval and renewal, included provisions for facilities and fiscal accounting, and outlined a fair but rigorous accountability system. The policy, approved by the school board, became a model for relationships between charters and school districts statewide. The board also declared that the district "actively supports the development of district-authorized charter schools that provide high quality learning opportunities to the students of San Diego."[10]

ADDING CHARTERS TO THE REFORM MIX

All of this laid the groundwork for Bersin to push for more charter schools. But for five years, he did not do so. The main reason was that Tony Alvarado, like many public school educators, was uncomfortable with them. Bersin found that odd because one of Alvarado's claims to fame was that, as a superintendent in East Harlem, New York, he had enabled renowned small-school advocate Deborah Meier in 1974 to create Central Park East Elementary School. The school served mostly low-income children and was designed around a progressive curriculum that Meier asserted mirrored what was offered in New York City's finest prep schools. The creation of Central Park East had launched the small-schools movement in the United States. Eventually, fifty small, autonomous schools of choice would open in New York based on Meier's work.

"Yet," Bersin said, "for Tony, charter schools, even though they were public schools, seemed like the school system itself: few schools are excellent, most are second-rate, and many of them are horrible. And perhaps most telling for Tony, charter school autonomy detracted from the K–12 systemic reform he had designed and we were then implementing districtwide."

Even without Bersin's backing, however, more charter schools were opening in San Diego. State education officials believed the district was not doing enough to oversee them. In response, San Diego district officials proposed creating what Bersin called a "mini-bureaucracy" to regulate them. "I thought it was oxymoronic," he said. "Charter schools are meant to be self-regulating within a framework of standards and accountability. That calls for a system of compliance and enforcement which differs from the standard operating procedures of school districts."

Instead, Bersin set out to invent a new relationship between the district and charter schools based on the charter school policy adopted previously. He created the Office of School Choice and recruited Brian Bennett to run it. Bennett, a celebrated former principal of a Catholic school in the San Diego diocese, had run a statewide political campaign, supported by John Walton and others, to promote choice in California through vouchers. With Bersin's complete support, he cultivated the role of the Office of School Choice as actively supporting charter schools, while holding them accountable, and assisting entrepreneurs who wanted to start new ones.

Bersin said he and Bennett, to some an unlikely pair, developed a deep and mutually admiring professional relationship. After Bersin left the district in 2005, Bennett became a national figure in the charter school movement, joining the National Association of Charter School Authorizers. Shortly afterward, Bennett was diagnosed with amyotrophic lateral sclerosis (Lou Gehrig's disease), and he died in 2009. Bersin wrote this eulogy: "The grail for Brian Bennett was student learning and success; he was resolute in supporting charter schools that served children well and worked fairly to close those which failed that standard. Brian was a giant in the struggle for quality education for all children, a warrior in the battle against obstacles to that end, and a gentle, thoughtful human being. He was the strongest, most selfless and courageous individual I have been privileged to walk beside in the education sector or otherwise."[11]

IN NEED OF A TURNAROUND

Bersin had long been aware of the problems at Gompers. It is located at 47th and Hilltop Streets in a neighborhood that at the time was home to as many as fifty rival and notoriously violent gangs. It is adjacent to a small park that for years was ruled by drug dealers. As U.S. attorney, Bersin had encouraged the city to cut down many of the park's trees, which the dealers used to keep their drug business hidden from police and nearby residents. His office supported the prosecution of any dealers who were arrested. "City police had it cleaned up from the openly law-less and morbidly violent atmosphere that existed. But it was beyond the power of law enforcement to clean up Gompers."

Not surprisingly, the school was an academic disaster as well as a social one. For a number of years, Gompers had been on a statewide list of unsuccessful schools even under the less stringent rules in place prior to NCLB. The Preuss charter school that had opened on the UCSD campus, near La Jolla, attracted many of its students from the Gompers neighborhood. Those who stayed behind weren't learning much. In 2003, fewer than 8 percent of Gompers seventh graders were proficient in English, and only 6 percent in mathematics.

As superintendent, Bersin had done much to try to help the school. After creating the middle school on the Gompers campus, he assigned two peer coaches and two content administrators to help the school's teachers. Students who were behind in reading got help in a double-period class of only twenty. The math classes in grades six through nine were smaller, too. Summer school was offered. Some students attended afterschool programs to receive extra help. Teachers could visit a district-run laboratory school to observe model lessons. The teachers and the school's principal attended district-offered professional development sessions.

But nothing worked. The school's chaotic environment did not allow for much teaching or learning.

Not surprisingly, in January 2004 Gompers, and the nearby Keiller, were both on a list of nine schools that had failed for four years in a row to meet the state's definition of Adequate Yearly Progress under NCLB. That meant the district had to intervene. Many educators considered NCLB to be a threat to their independence. But Bersin, who had supported the Bush administration in promulgating the law, saw NCLB as an opportunity to disrupt the pattern of persistent educational failure that continued to plague these schools. The law—which is still on the books, though much of it has been gutted by Obama administration waivers—required that such schools be restructured in one of several ways. The district could turn the school over to the state to run; replace the principal and have all the teachers reapply for their jobs; reconfigure the school into smaller units; overhaul the curriculum; or authorize the school to operate independently under a district-granted charter. The vast majority of U.S. school districts, faced with the question of how to deal with persistently failing schools, would choose the least disruptive option—making some changes in curriculum. Up to that point, no school district in the country had chosen to close a school down and reopen it as a charter school.

"We had provided all of the Blueprint interventions, all of the professional development, all of the books and materials. Each of these schools had been assigned an excellent principal. But we recognized that we had not broken the losing streak in these schools and fostered the conditions for them to succeed," Bersin said.

To bring in new approaches, Bersin recommended that the district put out a "request for proposals" from private entities—churches, nonprofits, advocacy groups, unions, and charter management organizations—to take over a number of schools and bring in fresh ideas and a renewed sense of commitment.

The idea of turning the schools over to others met fierce resistance from his staff. Bersin understood their concern that charter schools took money away from the school district. But he didn't accept it. "They did not really internalize that charter schools are public schools," he said. Bersin only rarely disregarded the advice given him by his executive team. But, in this case, he did. "I was absolutely convinced that this was something we had to pursue. We had to break the monopoly and make clear that charter schools are part of the system."

The three school board members in Bersin's camp endorsed the strategy at an emotionally charged meeting in September 2004. That was the meeting at which Frances Zimmerman compared Bersin to those Jews who had helped the Nazis in the Holocaust. Bersin sloughed Zimmerman's opposition off but then, to avoid being at the center of a public fight over the issue, he moved Tom Mitchell, the district's outreach director, and Brian Bennett to the forefront of the process, just as he had earlier positioned Matt Malone in the struggle over small high schools.

As soon as the "request for proposals" was issued, Bersin contacted Caprice Young, then head of the California Charter School Association (CCSA), the organization that advocates on behalf of and provides technical assistance to the state's now more than eight hundred charter schools.[12] CCSA and Bersin solicited bids from charter school operators and tried to convince ASPIRE, a Northern California–based charter management organization founded by Don Shalvey, who later joined the Gates Foundation, to expand its operation to Southern California. The Urban League of San Diego, a Latino community organization, local churches, and the San Diego Padres baseball team all were asked to consider taking on the responsibility.[13]

Mitchell suggested that each school form a working group of teachers, parents, union leaders, and community members to examine the various restructuring strategies. Although Bersin was convinced that the schools should become charters, he knew that option would stir up external as well as internal opposition and that the union and the school board would try to stand in the way if parents and teachers were not on board. "There was no way," Bersin knew, "we could do this on a cram-down basis. It had to be a bottom-up decision supported discretely from the top." The state charter school law also would require the support of the teachers and parents.

Unfortunately, no bidders emerged. As Joe Williams and Tom Toch observed in a report for the Washington-based policy think tank Education Sector, potential operators were reluctant to take over schools where failure was engrained in the culture and they perceived a "lack of commitment to reform." There also was concern about entering an unstable political environment. Several candidates in the school board campaign then under way had vowed to do away with anything that Bersin had supported.[14]

Bersin turned the question back to the working groups. In the end, five of the nine groups rejected the idea of becoming charter schools and came up with their own restructuring proposals. One of the remaining schools, Memorial, was a charter middle school that had been operating for several years with little success. In Bersin's view, the school had used its charter as a shield to block implementation of the Blueprint and avoid accountability. The principal and teachers who controlled the school decided to seek a new charter, which would be granted in the spring of 2005. That left Gompers and Keiller.[15]

PUSHING THE CHARTER SCHOOL OPTION

In the fall of 2004, Bersin, Mitchell, and John DeVore went to see Vince Riveroll at Gompers and Patricia Ladd, the principal at Keiller. Riveroll had impressed

Bersin when he was a teacher at Keiller. As with Ladd, Bersin had suggested that Riveroll enroll in the district's Educational Leadership Development Academy and then promoted him to the principalship of Keiller. Riveroll made remarkable progress at that school and, while there, mentored Ladd. Then, with Gompers falling apart, Bersin moved Riveroll there to take over that leadership challenge. Ladd succeeded him as Keiller's principal. "I wanted Vince and Patty seriously to consider organizing their schools as charter schools because, unless they did so, they'd have difficulty creating and sustaining a new school culture and building and retaining a quality faculty," Bersin explained.

But the working groups at the two schools were not immediately inclined to quit the district. "We started by asking ourselves, 'What is the business we are in?'" Riveroll said. "We asked: 'What is our mission? What are our core beliefs?' We started with building an academic culture because we believe it is the single most important component in raising student achievement."[16]

SEEKING A STABLE, COMMITTED FACULTY

The leaders of the schools' working groups realized that they would not be able to make much progress if they were unable to build a stable, committed faculty. But as is often the case in low performing schools, many teachers spent as little time there as possible. Once they'd gained enough seniority to "bump" a teacher in a more desirable school, they would leave. Half of Gompers's teachers left every year. That churn made it impossible to establish and maintain academic momentum. But the school was prevented by the district policy and the union contract from recruiting teachers on its own. Riveroll tells the story of a teacher the district sent him who did not want to teach at Gompers and whom Riveroll did not want to hire. But the teacher was assigned there anyway, and Riveroll only found out at the staff meeting that started the 2004–2005 school year. At the time, he had eighteen vacancies for teachers so he had little choice. The school would still have six vacancies the following spring.

Nonetheless, Riveroll said he and his team were wary of breaking away from the school district. "What we were really looking for was a waiver from the seniority and compensation provisions of the teachers union contract," Riveroll said. A waiver would let the school "hire our own teachers and create a team that was going to be here awhile."[17]

In a September 2004 meeting with the union's president and executive director, Bersin proposed work rule changes that would make it easier for the failing schools to recruit and hold on to good teachers. The union officials walked out of the meeting, according to Williams and Toch.[18] Camille Zombro, then the SDEA's president, told them that the union was willing to discuss waivers but that the district had not first collected the teacher signatures required under the contract. Once again, rather than solve the underlying problem, the union declared that a failure to follow procedural rules made compromise impossible. Two months later, Gompers and Keiller formally requested a waiver with the required signatures. Again, the union's leaders rejected the request, saying the schools had failed to obtain the approval of two-thirds of their teachers by a secret ballot.

With the prospect of waivers off the table, the work groups decided to submit an application for a charter. But time was running out. As part of putting together a charter application, the work group had only until early January to gather signatures from supportive parents.

GETTING THE SUPPORT OF PARENTS

Michelle Evans, a parent of a Gompers student, attended a meeting in September at which it was announced that the school would be closed down for poor performance. Evans, who is African American, was already frustrated with the school as well as with the Blueprint and Bersin. Her own schooling had not gone well. She hated taking a bus out of the neighborhood to predominantly white schools where she felt looked down on. She'd not made much of an effort, and she didn't learn to read until she was almost eighteen years old and was attending an alternative school.

By then, she had given birth to her first child, a daughter, and later had two sons. She didn't want her children to repeat her errors, so she tried to do all she could to ensure that they would get a good education. They, too, were bused to distant schools. But by the time her older son was entering middle school she wanted him to go Gompers because it was close. Her two brothers had attended the math and science magnet school at Gompers, and she was under the impression that it was a good school.

She'd been badly disappointed. Her son had been an honors student in elementary school. But, after his first day of school at Gompers in September of that year, he "came home and told me they'd put him in slow learner classes. I couldn't believe that and told him just to be patient." At the end of the first week she called the counselor and was told, "Don't worry; it will be fixed." At the end of the second week the school began calling, saying her son was acting out.[19]

"I'd done had it," Evans said. Her son had never had behavior problems before. He told her he was bored and that teachers told the students in his classes that they were stupid.

"When I came to the school it looked like a prison and I said to myself, 'What did I do to my kid?' I was raising my kids to go to college, not to Attica. But at the school I got the runaround. My twin brothers came to the school. We were angry. In the English class, my son was being asked to read books that my other kids had read in fourth or fifth grade." She pulled her son out of school right there and began putting him on a bus to a school ten miles away. "You're putting my kid on the fast track to jail," she told the school's counselors.

Still, Evans didn't think closing Gompers was the answer. "That still did not deal with the poor quality of education the kids were getting. Sending the kids somewhere else wasn't going to help. How about firing all the teachers?"

Tom Mitchell went to Evans and told her, "I need you to be my friend." Evans was then invited to another meeting to figure out what to do. Evans says that at that meeting, the lawyers for the district were speaking in a language that none of the parents understood. Evans threatened to walk out, but Mitchell persuaded her to stay. At that point, Evans says, she realized that the parents had to fight to get the education they wanted for their children. She agreed to be a parent leader in the work group.

The California Charter School Association worked with the teams at Gompers and Keiller to help them prepare their applications. The association paid for translators so that Spanish-speaking parents could participate in the meetings. The organization gave Riveroll and Ladd a crash course on governance, teacher recruitment, charter school law, and other topics. It also set up key partnerships with a private company that provided back-office services to charter schools. Bersin helped Gompers establish a partnership with UCSD, which agreed to help the school replicate the school created on that campus. Cecil Lytle, the guiding force behind Preuss, and Hugh "Bud" Mehan, who directed a campus education research center, joined Gompers' board of directors. Bersin brokered a similar partnership between Keiller and the private University of San Diego. Paula Cordeiro, dean of the USD School of Leadership and Education Sciences, became president of the Keiller board of directors.[20]

PARENT SIGNATURES NEEDED

Under California's charter school law, the work groups had to gather signatures from a majority of the parents. The school district supplied them with lists of names and addresses. Though they had little time, the group persevered and volunteers went door-to-door during the 2004 Christmas holiday, a winter that was particularly cold and wet, to drum up the necessary support.

The volunteers encountered many parents who were afraid to send their children to Gompers and Keiller because they feared for their safety. Even so, the schools collected signatures from more than 70 percent of the parents. Denise

DeVall, a Keiller parent, told the *San Diego Union-Tribune* that she was willing to take a chance on the school operating as a charter. "They haven't been paying attention to us until now," she said.[21]

However, when the Gompers and Keiller groups presented the signatures and their petition in January 2005, the newly elected school board imposed a new requirement: the teams also needed more than half the schools' current teachers to sign on or else the charter schools would not be able to stay on their campuses. That would be hard, of course, because many of the teachers would not be rehired by the newly constituted charter schools.

The board obtained a legal opinion saying that the schools were not closing down and reopening. Rather, they were *converting* a public school to a charter school. In such cases, the teachers at the school had to agree. The board had changed the rules to thwart the move and, indirectly, to slap down Bersin.

PARENT PROTESTS AND ANOTHER CHANCE

Parents shouted and threatened to launch a recall as the board members discussed the issue.[22] Shelia Jackson, a former elementary school teacher who left the district's employ shortly before running for the school board, led opposition to the charters. She proposed that a committee of retired principals, administrators, and former board members decide the schools' fate. Instead, the schools were given more time to gain the teachers' support. The decision threatened to derail the whole charter process because the union was advising its members to oppose it. Teacher union president Terry Pesta told a reporter that the union was not opposed to the schools becoming charter schools; he just wanted the teachers at the schools to know they'd lose the protections of their contract if the charters went through.

Brian Bennett worked with Riveroll and Ladd and the local union representatives to get the teachers' endorsement. In the end, many of the teachers who voted for the charters had no intention of remaining at the schools and, instead, used their seniority rights to relocate to a different school. Bennett persuaded them that they could do right for the children and well for themselves at the same time by voting in favor of the charter, though they'd not be subject to it. Bersin said, "Both to their credit and their benefit, they did."

ANOTHER HURDLE

A month later the school board tried another tactic to block the charter school effort. Led by Jackson, the school board ordered Bersin to reassign Riveroll. Not only had Riveroll been leading the charter effort, he also had already done a lot to clean up the troubled middle school campus. But Jackson, who represented the

Gompers neighborhood, didn't want to lose control of the school or the teacher union's support.

According to a nine-page memo Riveroll submitted to the San Diego School Administrators' Association, Jackson had attended meetings of the working group at Gompers and had crudely berated him and belittled teachers in front of their colleagues and the parents.[23] Bersin said she came to him and told him that "Riveroll wasn't up to the job and that he was weak and had broken down" and that she wanted him transferred. Bersin confronted her. "I told her, 'Ms. Jackson, you're way off-base. You can't stop this by firing Riveroll. He's the only real leader Gompers has had in years.'"

But the board forced Bersin to move him. Riveroll recalled the day Bersin told him the news: "The silence in the superintendent's office at 6 p.m. was deafening. He told me I had to stand there like a leader and take it. He told me that in time I would know why this was happening and that I had to have faith that it would work out."[24]

Bersin couldn't tell Riveroll all that he knew because he understood that unless the decision were reversed, Riveroll would likely have a strong legal claim against the district. Having done what he knew was wrong, Bersin had to go into a board meeting and act as if nothing had happened. By that point, Bersin had already agreed to resign at the end of the school year. But he was still committed to making sure the process he had started gave the nine schools, especially Gompers, Keiller, and King Middle School (another perennially low-achieving Southside school), a fresh start.

Riveroll's removal hit Gompers hard. Students, teachers, and counselors cried and hugged and protested what they understood was an attempt to prevent Gompers from breaking away from the district's control.[25] A math teacher at the school said, "Vince has inspired us to stand up for these kids. He has done so much for this school." Another teacher said, "I have never taught for a man this good. It's political and I will resign. This board doesn't know how to put kids first."

The district sent counselors, and extra security, to prevent the angry reaction of teachers, parents, and students from boiling out of control. But rather than derail the movement, Riveroll's sudden removal strengthened it. "It sealed the charter decision," he said, "because it made it so clear that it was only by going charter that they would get to choose their own leader."

Several hundred parents from Gompers, Keiller, King, and Memorial (another struggling middle school) showed up six weeks later to press the board to approve the charter applications. But, still, Shelia Jackson tried to stand in the way. She proposed that the schools operate under an autonomy arrangement like the one the board had given La Jolla High School. The schools would still be subject to the contract provisions regarding teacher hiring and transfers but would have the freedom to choose their own curriculum. No one was fooled. The motion failed for lack of a second.

THE CASE FOR INDEPENDENCE

Parents, teachers, and community leaders then laid out the case on behalf of Gompers. The team had the support of 734 community members, more than 75 percent of the parents and, surprisingly, 58 percent of the teachers. "Even when you changed the rules, they came back and they brought you what should have been impossible, the teachers' signatures," said Edith Smith, a resident who had been part of the working group. "Some of you promised that if we got the teachers' signatures you'd give us the charter. And I expect that to happen here tonight."[26]

"We have an opportunity we've never had before, to work with UCSD," said Gloria Cooper, a community organizer and a Gompers alumna. "This is your opportunity for you to say you trust the teachers, the parents, and the community to do what's right for our children."[27]

Finally, the school board voted 5–0 in favor of the charters for all four schools. The audience members rose out of their seats as one, exploding, according to Bersin, "with the joy of hard fought and unexpected total victory. The place went wild as David beat Goliath."

Bersin said it was the most dramatic school board vote in the seven years he was superintendent. "It demonstrated how eminently possible it is to organize parents to push hard for and get change if you can help them truly understand the reasons their children's schools are failing. The union and school board naysayers were completely silenced as parents and principals and teachers stepped forward to take control and restructure their schools as charters to go forward," he said. "And the rest is history."

"It may be hard for many to see and grasp, and it will take years before it is plainly visible, but what happened that March night is that monopoly control over the school system in San Diego was broken." Bersin believed the end of the district monopoly was not only good, it was permanent.

CHARTER SCHOOLS AND EDUCATION REFORM NATIONALLY

Charter schools were part of Secretary of Education Arne Duncan's strategy for turning around failing schools when he was superintendent in Chicago. He has said numerous times that as many as five thousand failing U.S. schools need to be closed or restructured over the next five years. One of the strategies allowed by both the administration's Race to the Top program and its $3.5 billion School Improvement Grant (SIG) program is to shut down failing schools and reopen them as charter schools. But, of the schools that received SIG grants in 2010, only 4 percent have chosen to go this route.[28]

The experience in San Diego shows that it takes a lot of support from school districts, teachers, school board members, parents, community members, and outside organizations to get charter schools off the ground. Writing the charter, gathering signatures, getting it approved, hiring new teachers, and everything else that goes into creating a new school and building a cohesive team of teachers and camaraderie all takes time and extraordinary effort. Sustaining the momentum and the intensity of effort presents a never-ending challenge.

No matter what it took, and continues to take, the outcome at Gompers has been dramatic. Bersin said he felt close to those at Gompers and Keiller because he identified with their struggle and their commitment to change. So he visited regularly when he was in town. One day in 2007, he dropped by the Gompers Saturday Academy and spent some time tutoring a young boy named Carlos who had just come to the United States from Mexico. As he helped the middle schooler read a picture book, Bersin was reminded of how much help students like Carlos require to develop the English vocabulary they need to succeed academically. Carlos was getting that support at Gompers.

The school's test scores have gone up steadily. So has attendance. The number of suspensions fell 90 percent in a single year.

Most impressively, the school firmly established an academic culture. Before it became a charter school, one teacher said, the faculty was just trying to make sure they got through the day safely. Now, they work together on improving their instruction and figuring out ways to better serve students. Students seek to transfer out of Gompers not because it's unsafe, but because they think school will be easier academically elsewhere. The traditional public schools in the area have begun marketing themselves to parents to compete with Gompers. In the fall of 2009, the school expanded to become Gompers Preparatory Academy, a school for grades six through twelve. And in 2012, the school's first graduating class won their diplomas.

"We've been working since seventh grade for this moment to graduate all together," Isaac Ramos, a graduating senior, said. "It's really not only for us as seniors but for the community to show we've been working hard and, thanks to their support and belief in us, we're going to make it." All of the Academy's first class of graduates will enroll in two- or four-year colleges.[29]

Bersin attended the graduation. "This shows what it takes for a turnaround. It doesn't happen without struggle, and if we want opportunities for all of our children in America, we must continue to move forward on a long-term plan to change conditions for teachers and students." He could have said the same thing for urban education more generally.

CHARTER SCHOOLS NOT ALWAYS THE ANSWER

Despite his enthusiasm about Gompers and charter schools generally, Bersin is not a charter school advocate. He has been a fierce defender of the rights of charter schools but also a harsh critic of their failures.

"Charters have not lived up to their original promise," Bersin said. "Charter schools were inspired by the obvious benefits competition had brought to consumers of virtually all other goods and services in America. Charters were supposed to serve as a prod to school districts for continuous improvement. They also were to constitute laboratories in whose crucibles of experience best practices would be generated for application in the district at large. To date, neither objective has been met."

In 2004, there were three thousand two hundred charter schools nationally, more than five hundred of which were in California. By 2011, there were about five thousand six hundred charter schools in forty-one states, serving over 2 million students or about 4.2 percent of U.S. public schools enrollment. In California, 982 charter schools served about 10 percent of the state's students. New York City was home to 156 charter schools that served 56,600 students in 2012. New York Mayor Michael Bloomberg said after he was elected to a third term in 2009 that he would push the state legislature to let him add as many as one hundred more charter schools over the next four years.[30] Thirty-eight of the sixty-eight schools in the "recovery district" set up in New Orleans after Hurricane Katrina are charter schools.

Despite the growth, charter schools have not reached a "tipping point" from a market perspective. According to Bersin: "Districts have increasingly considered charters as competition but have not perceived them as powerful enough in their effect to adopt any of their best practices. Instead, charters have been atomized and isolated from the districts that have authorized them. Districts have utilized their authority over facilities to block charter expansion rather than to take their example for purposes of replication. Charters are deemed as 'threats' rather than as citadels of promising practice."

But Bersin also recognizes that many charters are anything but models to be emulated. In 2009, the Center for Research on Education Outcomes at Stanford University found wide variance in performance, with only 17 percent of charter schools reporting academic gains significantly better than traditional public schools. About 37 percent of the schools studied turned in worse performance. And the rest were indistinguishable in performance from the traditional schools.[31]

Even so, as the example of Gompers and Keiller demonstrate, sometimes they are the only answer.

CHAPTER ELEVEN

The Lessons of San Diego for Urban Education Reform

As soon as the votes were counted on election night in November 2004, it was clear that Alan Bersin's time in the district was drawing to a close. The new majority was committed to dismantling much of what he'd put in place. In January, the board voted to buy out the last year of his contract. That same month, the board halted the use of math and literacy consultants who had been working with teachers for seven years to help them with the district curriculum. The next month, the board eliminated the peer coaches that were another critical element of the instructional infrastructure. In his first year on the job, Bersin had pushed for full-day kindergarten to better prepare children for first grade. The new board thought the expectations for them were too high and that they shouldn't necessarily be reading until the first grade. It also severed the relationship between the district and the Education Leadership Development Academy—despite the many principals who testified that the training they received there had been critical to their success.

A few days after he'd announced that he would be leaving, Bersin attended the monthly meeting of San Diego's principals, as he usually did. Leslie Fausset, who became Bersin's deputy late in his tenure, introduced Bersin using imagery from *The Wizard of Oz*. She said Bersin was like "the wizard, with a brain that sometimes works overtime, courage that's absolutely fearless." He also, she said, "always leads with his heart."[1]

The crowd of three hundred fifty principals and assistant principals gave Bersin a loud, thirty-five-second standing ovation. He walked to the podium, smiling broadly and clapping his hands, returning the appreciation. The *San Diego Union-Tribune* reported the next day that Bersin was "showered with adulation" and that there were "tears, hugs, applause, handshakes" as the school leaders expressed a "determination to carry on Bersin's work."[2]

Bersin took note of the progress that had been made. In 1999, when the reforms began, one in five San Diego schools was ranked academically in the lowest two deciles of schools statewide in California. He reported to the principals that

that number had been reduced to twelve, or 7 percent, of the schools. The number of schools scoring above that 800 mark had grown by 42 percent, from 75 to 107. That rate of improvement, Bersin said, far exceeded both the statewide and county averages.

"This is a celebration of the difference principals make," Bersin said, giving them and their teachers the credit for the gains.

With a poster-size reproduction of the iconic Norman Rockwell painting of Ruby Bridges entitled *The Problem We All Live With* as a backdrop, he reported that achievement gaps between whites and blacks and Latino students had narrowed. To Bersin, Rockwell's depiction of the African American girl escorted through hatred and ignorance to a previously all-white school in New Orleans by faceless federal marshals captured the essence of what he'd been trying to accomplish in San Diego. That image had been prominently on display in the eighty monthly instructional conferences held during Bersin's tenure as well as many other meetings and public appearances. It was such an important image for Bersin that his wife, Lisa, would later obtain for him an original signed by Rockwell that continues to grace their home.

Beyond the test scores, Bersin underlined the cultural change that he asserted had made the gains possible—and sustainable. "Individually and together, this leadership team has developed the habits of mind, the courage, and conviction to focus on learning issues, to identify problems and solve them, and to take responsibility for results, both positive and negative," he said. "That is the essence of the change you have led in two hundred schools."

He told the principals at the meeting that they had the knowledge, confidence, and results to be able to stand up and offer their professional judgment about what was working well in the district and what still needed to be fixed in its classrooms. Without being explicit, he was rejecting the criticism that all that had happened during his tenure had been forced on educators from the top. He was arguing that his reforms had increased the capacity of the system by strengthening not just teaching, but also school-level instructional leadership. More than 80 percent of the district's principals had been hired while he was superintendent, they had been well trained, and now they were intrinsically motivated to continue the journey they had begun.

Bersin left his position at the end of June. The next day he began serving California Governor Arnold Schwarzenegger as his secretary of education and also as a member of the state board of education. He left for his successor a frank discussion of the strengths and weaknesses of the district.

He was proud of the intense focus on improving student achievement that had been a product of the Blueprint. "All parties," he wrote, embraced "a shared responsibility for supporting student achievement."[3] The idea that the educators, the adults, had to hold themselves accountable for whether students were learning or not, rather than blaming the kids and their circumstances, had been firmly implanted. He also reported that he saw "clear evidence of coherent instructional programs and purposeful teaching and learning aligned with state content standards, especially at the elementary and middle schools." He took note of a state compliance review team that found "support for the educational needs of students and families" and "a culture of learning and purposeful instruction."

He reported that in 2004, San Diego met all of its Adequate Yearly Progress targets under No Child Left Behind. Its ranking on the state's Academic Performance Index was second highest among large districts. The achievement gap between white students and students of color had narrowed substantially, especially in language arts. Overall student achievement was up as well, especially in elementary school.

He was proud, too, that the district had learned how to carry on through major shifts in policy and had gotten better both at recognizing successful schools and identifying those that were struggling and helping them improve. In addition, parent involvement had increased on his watch.

But he was not self-congratulatory. He also cited ten weaknesses. First, Bersin's team acknowledged that its focus on teaching and learning had diverted attention from important operational issues. Staff had not been adequately trained in basics such as scheduling classes, testing, and course selection and student placement, nor had their performance been closely monitored. These shortcomings had "caused a number of serious consequences for students and district/school staff."[4]

The academic performance of San Diego's high school students was another serious shortcoming. Although the school board had declared that students had to take more advanced courses in math and science to graduate, many students were failing to pass them. One in four students was failing chemistry; one in five, physics; and one in eight, biology. Failure rates in algebra, geometry, and intermediate algebra were higher still. Many of San Diego's high school students had as of that point failed to pass the state's high school graduation test, meaning they were in danger of not earning a diploma.

Achievement gaps also remained large among high school students. While nearly two-thirds of white and Asian students were proficient in language arts, only about 20 percent of African American and Hispanic students had reached that level.

Another disappointment was that a large percentage of students still learning English was not making sufficient progress toward fluency, as measured by state tests. The high school dropout rate, which had motivated Bersin and his team to create the Blueprint in the first place, was still stubbornly high. Over two thousand students dropped out during the 2003–2004 school year, and half of them were Hispanic and four hundred were African American. Also noted as a weakness was that not enough was being done to help low performing schools before they had to be targeted with sanctions laid out in NCLB. Finally, the document reported that internal communications were still ineffective and often left staff members working at cross-purposes.

But, of course, the full effect of the Bersin-era policies had not yet been seen. Even though much of what he'd brought to the district was eliminated soon after he left, the skills and knowledge that teachers and principals had gained due to the district's massive investment in training did not evaporate and continued to influence student achievement. As one principal told the new school board, the training under Bersin's leadership had helped him develop "the ability to analyze teaching and learning through the eyes of the students. I now understand what children can and cannot do, based on the teaching practices of the adults."[5]

The percentage of San Diego students proficient in English language arts rose every year between 2003 and 2012; the percentage proficient in mathematics did as well. The district's gains on the National Assessment of Educational Progress in mathematics were even bigger. In 2003, one in five San Diego fourth graders and eighth graders were proficient or advanced in mathematics. By 2009, two out of five fourth graders and one-third of eighth graders hit that mark.

Even more positive was a report by Julian R. Betts and colleagues at the Public Policy Institute of California (PPIC). Betts had begun studying Bersin and his work in San Diego in the late 1990s. As noted earlier, in 2005 he said that the Bersin-Alvarado approach to early literacy instruction merited emulation nationally. He put another report out in the fall of 2010 that measured the long-term impact of the Blueprint on student achievement. Betts found that the longer sessions in reading for middle school students and a longer school year for low performing elementary schools were particularly helpful.[6] Struggling high school students who attended triple-length literacy sessions were more likely to be promoted to the next grade. Fears that such an intensive focus on literacy would bore students and cause them to drop out or burn out were unfounded. Betts said these and other ambitious reforms that were part of the Blueprint could be implemented elsewhere if states and the federal government made policy changes to let school districts use funds more flexibly.

A "key aspect of San Diego's reform program was that it was comprehensive and coherent," Betts found, and "professional development was delivered uniformly, with a single focused goal, to teachers throughout the district." This was precisely what the teacher union and its supporters on the board had complained about the most. Whether that strategy was worth the turmoil and resentment it caused is a matter of judgment and philosophy, rather than statistics.

Perhaps the most important lesson, the report concluded, was that "many of the reforms took several years to bear fruit. Most notably, the peer coaching system for teachers did not result in gains in the first year or two at most schools, but did appear to do so by the later years. An obvious lesson here is that school district leaders everywhere, when they implement reforms, must show considerable patience in their quest for improved student literacy."

LEADERSHIP TURNOVER

After driving Bersin out, the school board conducted a national search for his replacement. What they were looking for more than anything was someone who was not Alan Bersin. In October 2005, the board hired Carl Cohn, who had retired from the Long Beach Unified School District as the longest-serving urban superintendent in the country. Cohn was brought on to make peace with the teacher union and the school board and to reduce the influence of the central office over curriculum, teaching, and professional development. Those decisions were to be left up to principals and their teachers. As was explained in chapter 6, these policies did not establish a strong, working relationship with the teacher union and left Cohn frustrated.

Cohn also was frustrated with continuing divisions on the school board. Most matters resulted in a 3–2 vote, just as in the Bersin administration. "The problem with a 3–2 split [on the board] is that it encourages the forces of the status quo," Cohn told the *Union-Tribune* soon after he started on the job.[7] "They think, 'All we have to do is pick off one person in the next election and we can change this.'" Bersin had made the exact same observation when he was superintendent. Cohn lasted two years before the school board's micromanaging and his inability to get the teacher union to be more cooperative drove him away.

In January 2008, the school board hired Terry Grier, a veteran superintendent from Guilford County, North Carolina. He arrived in the midst of a severe budget crisis, but his options for dealing with it were limited. He notified teachers that they might be laid off if the budget picture did not improve. That infuriated the leaders of the teacher union, and in the fall of 2008 the union successfully backed school board candidates who pledged not to lay off any teachers to balance the budget. Grier resigned in September 2009 to take a job as superintendent of the Houston Independent School District in Texas. He told an interviewer that one reason that job was attractive was that raising student achievement was the number one goal of the board of education in Houston. In San Diego, he said, adult issues got in the way of serving the needs of students.

"We have 60,000 children in San Diego who read below the level of proficiency . . . and yet we don't have a uniform literacy program in the district and we don't seem to have a desire to do that," he said of San Diego. "We don't want to anger parents. I keep coming—I've said this every day I've been here, it's as if I'm still living with the Alan Bersin ghosts . . . so we don't want to focus on literacy because, well, Alan Bersin focused on literacy . . . When 60,000 children can't read at a proficient level, you have to be willing to embrace literacy as one of your prime goals and objectives."[8]

Grier was eventually replaced by Bill Kowba, a veteran business manager in the district who had previously served in an interim capacity and who acknowledged that he did not have a strong background in instruction. In choosing Kowba, school board members made it clear that they did not want anyone who would attempt to bring about big changes.[9]

In July 2010, the Center for Education Policy and Law at the University of San Diego issued a status report on the San Diego school district that covered the years 2003 to 2009.[10] Based on twenty-six interviews with people associated with the district, the report found that educators were hungry for the kind of intensive professional development opportunities afforded to them by Bersin, though they wanted it to be tailored to their needs, not the same in every school. Teachers and principals wanted the return of the teacher coaches that the school board had eliminated. Those interviewed were concerned that the school district did not seem to have a clear strategy and that discord among the teacher union, the superintendent, and the board of education was diverting attention from the needs of students. "The last time where it seemed like you had some kind of coherence between the board and the superintendent was with Alan Bersin and the three board members who consistently supported him," one of those interviewed for the report said.[11]

In March 2010, San Diego school board president Richard Barrera gave a "state of the district" speech in which he described the Blueprint in a manner that no one who worked in the district while Bersin was superintendent would have recognized. He said it was a "corporate model" reform that was the local version of NCLB and that it developed "easy-to-measure standards to which local schools and classroom teachers are held accountable." Barrera never even mentioned that instruction was at the heart of everything Bersin did. In fact, Barrera never even mentioned teachers or teaching in his speech. But he explicitly rejected what he called "top-down" reforms in favor of "community-based" reforms.[12]

The district announced in September 2010 that a new reform plan would be developed after principals had held seventy-five community meetings to gather input. Essentially, teachers at each school would look at student test scores and other data and work with community leaders to come up with their own, unique plan for reform.

Each building principal would decide on interventions to implement with the school's teachers and parents, and they would share successful programs among themselves informally, through site visits to other schools. Of course, it is impossible to hold schools or teachers accountable for student learning if each school is operating under its own plan and timetable. That was essentially the decentralized approach to school reform the school district negotiated with the teacher union in 1989. The school restructuring reforms that emerged then had no effect at all.

A decade earlier Bersin had been hired to gain control of the district and set goals and steer the district toward it. But that had made the adults in the system— the school board members, union leaders, and teachers—uncomfortable. The cycle from decentralization to centralization and back to decentralization had now been completed.

LARGER LESSONS

Bersin left his position in the Schwarzenegger administration after eighteen months but continued to serve on the state board of education until 2010. He remained involved in education in other ways as well. He served on the board of a nonpartisan education policy think tank based in Washington, D.C., which involved him in work related to union-district relationships. He served on the board of overseers for Harvard University and on the visiting committee for the Harvard Graduate School of Education, and helped Dean Kathleen McCartney and others establish an innovative program to prepare top leaders.

In 2009, President Obama appointed him to the position of Assistant Secretary for International Affairs in the Department of Homeland Security, which came with special responsibilities for security along the border with Mexico. He was promoted in 2010 to Commissioner of U.S. Customs and Border Protection, where he oversaw fifty-seven thousand employees and administered an $11 billion budget. In 2012, he took another position as Assistant Secretary of International Affairs and Chief Diplomatic Officer under Secretary of Homeland Security Janet Napolitano.

Bersin continued to think about the lessons to be drawn from his time in San Diego and their continuing relevance for education reformers.

One big lesson was to recognize that changes required to improve urban education are "truly staggering" and can only come about if there is a "paradigm shift" as to how change occurs. "The governing paradigm in public education today holds that in urban school systems, changes made around the edges and on the margins will over time produce the dramatically different results we want for all of our children," he wrote in an essay in *Education Week* that also appeared in the local newspaper.[13] What was needed was not incremental improvements, but "enormous gains in productivity." That could occur only if every policy decision was evaluated on the criteria of whether it was likely to improve student achievement. "This notion may seem obvious outside education, but inside the public education community, it is met with resistance."

So, he wrote, "it is not surprising that the tools for achieving productivity common in virtually every other sector in America—flexibility, competition, incentives, efficiency and innovation—are not used systematically in our schools. Instead, they are conspicuously absent."

Bersin's experience in San Diego taught him that achieving that paradigm shift would require building enduring political coalitions. It took him seven years to pull together what he thought was a strong proreform coalition in San Diego that consisted of parents, civil rights activists, principals, some teachers, and religious, business, and political leaders. Even though the San Diego Education Association had become a bitter, relentless enemy, he had strong support among unions representing nonteaching employees in the district as well as public employees outside of education.

His experience also told him that power matters a lot in school reform. It's not enough to have good ideas that make sense. Witness the fact that his opponents on the school board as well as the leaders of the teacher unions approved of the Blueprint strategies, at least initially. But the spending shifts that paid for the Blueprint threatened other interests. The union wanted the school site councils to control the spending of federal Title I dollars. Those who believed in magnet schools, whether they were serving their purpose or not, didn't want to see them go away. Middle-class parents wanted to preserve small class sizes for their children, even if that meant that students struggling academically couldn't get more intensive assistance in smaller groups. So, leaders must clearly understand what interests are threatened by their policy changes. But, sometimes, they have to move ahead despite the fact that their decisions will be opposed. Many observers have criticized Bersin for not building stronger support for his agenda from the teacher union before moving ahead, but he disagrees. Waiting, he argued, would not have brought about agreement. It is naive, he said, to "think a change of heart from entrenched opponents is right around the corner."

On the other hand, he observed that there were other decisions that were unnecessarily antagonistic to important constituencies. The decision to move ahead quickly to implement the Active Physics curriculum was just such a mistake because it angered affluent parents and teachers, and was not central to the larger reform agenda.

Although he thinks public education will ultimately benefit from competition, he has been disappointed in the failure of the charter school movement to police its own effectively. While there are certainly many successful charter schools such as Gompers Preparatory Academy, in general "charter schools have not risen to the challenge and remain unfinished business." In addition, he believes the current push for traditional school districts and charter schools to collaborate closely is misguided and akin to "sheep and lions lying down together."

Despite Bersin's faith in competition and innovation, his experience in San Diego also left him wedded to the idea of instructional and curricular coherence as a framework within which well-performing schools could be given freedom and autonomy. There was no contradiction in his mind, however. Standards, such as the Common Core, and locally defined goals create a context within which innovation could occur.

But he worried that there had not yet developed an agreed-upon body of knowledge about teaching and learning that could serve as the foundation for that autonomy, saying, "We know painfully little about how to diagnose learning issues and respond to them instructionally." As a result, he concluded, noneducators routinely dictate how teachers should teach and how their work should be assessed. He observed that teachers rise in the field based on their ideology about teaching and their longevity, rather than on the quality of their professional judgments, although this may change as states and districts put into place new evaluation systems.

He also worried about what he called "a profound lack of knowledge about how to replicate examples of successful schools with fidelity, or how to build the systems that would routinely produce them."

Bersin considered learning how to create great schools and mustering the political will to do so to be a great national challenge. He came to believe, as did the authors of a 2012 report from the Council on Foreign Relations, that the weakness of American schools posed a threat to national security.[14]

"History is unforgiving to those who, when their society faces a turning point, do not turn, and we are unquestionably at a turning point regarding education," he wrote in a reflective essay.[15] "The consequences of not making the changes required far outweigh the cost of the investments required."

What he accomplished in San Diego required repetition, focus, and leadership. "What it took demonstrates for any superintendent wanting to establish a culture of improvement the scope and range of the resources—money, to be sure, but also talent and time and political skill—they must be willing to commit to the struggle," he wrote.

Bersin sometimes despaired about the prospects for success nationally. He worried about what it would take to put forth new models of school district governance, transform teacher unions into professional associations, and develop the technical knowledge and political momentum to bring about reforms that would benefit all children. He wondered, at times, whether, indeed, education reformers were "tilting quixotically at windmills after all."

Most of the time, however, he believed that meaningful reform and improvement were possible. To him that meant that the nation would some day fulfill the ambitions for social justice and equal education that had been expressed in the U.S. Supreme Court decision on the *Brown v. Board of Education* case and also remain globally competitive economically.

In a speech in the spring of 2005, he said that "I am optimistic today that we shall again draw on the principled wisdom seasoned by common sense that has guided our national jouney and that this quality will enable us to meet this next educational challenge of our genuinely remarkable history."

Commentary

*Making Schools Productive: The Point of Accountability and the Key to Renewal**

A generation ago, Thomas Kuhn in *The Structure of Scientific Revolutions* introduced the concept of "paradigm shift" to characterize transformational changes in ways of seeing and thinking that have produced progress in the history of science. Our central perspective on a matter, he suggested, implies much about how we fill in the remaining details. Ptolemy's "humancentric" view of the universe, which placed Earth at the center of the solar system, influenced the shape of the surrounding culture. When it was replaced by the Copernican concept, which moved the sun to the core and Earth to the periphery, the paradigm shift changed not only the way we viewed ourselves and our world, but also how we conducted our affairs.

The governing paradigm in public education today holds that in urban school systems, changes made around the edges and on the margins will, over time, produce the dramatically different results we all want for our children. Were we to adopt an alternate paradigm, one that centered on maximizing productivity, our view of what ails public education and the prescriptions for improving it would shift dramatically.

Growth in student achievement, reflected in multiple indicators, must be the outcome measure we use to gauge productivity in public education. Of every program in place, and every reform proposed, we must ask: Does it improve student achievement? This notion may seem obvious outside education, but inside the public education community, it is met with resistance. So it is not surprising that the tools for achieving productivity common in virtually every other sector in

---

* Editor's note: This essay by Alan D. Bersin was originally published in the April 20, 2005, edition of *Education Week*. It is reprinted here with permission.

America—flexibility, competition, incentives, efficiency, and innovation—are not used systematically in our schools. Instead, they are conspicuously absent.

By grasping how our system has become immune to harnessing self-interest in support of the common good, we gain an understanding of why there has been so little change in public education over the past 40 years in spite of endless and recurring reform.

A fundamental question we have to ask about our large school systems is whether they are primarily sources of employment for adults or education for children. If we are trying to maximize productivity, the answer is clear: Our mission is to educate children. In doing this, we have to take into account the interests of the adults who work in our school systems. They are the crucial "input" in the schooling. But striking the right balance between the needs of students and the interests of teachers is among the central challenges facing public education today.

Because economic benefits in education are perceived to be low compared with other sectors, the negotiated compromises on work rules have been enormous, and the relinquishment of ordinary management prerogatives routine. While I agree wholeheartedly that bashing unions is unwarranted because they are doing their job in terms of asserting employee interests, the long-term health of the educational enterprise requires that their efforts also take into account the question of how to improve student achievement.

A handful of extraordinary labor leaders are embracing this responsibility. But the typical union leader's incapacity or unwillingness to do so—combined with the inability of parents, from inside the system, or political interests, from outside, to balance union power effectively—has contributed to our unacceptable status quo. That is why the power curve in large urban systems is leaning toward mayoral control, as down-ballot, low-interest school board elections and stricter campaign-finance laws combine to produce employee-dominated governance structures.

Existing power relationships, and the fiscal allocations that follow, are absurd from the standpoint of productivity. Consider the peculiarities of teacher assignment. No one would expect a doctor fresh out of medical school to take on the responsibilities a surgeon with years of experience must shoulder. Yet in education, we regularly assign our newest practitioners to our most challenging inner-city classrooms. This is a function of both rigid seniority systems and anachronistic personnel systems. Seniority makes all the sense in the world based on individual choices. Systemically, though, it adds up to educational catastrophe.

With novice teachers regularly assigned to the most intractable classrooms, we end up with what we prescribe: Many children remain significantly untaught, and half of our beginning teachers leave the profession within the first five years of practice. The so-called teacher shortage is much more the result of our incapacity to retain teachers than our inability to recruit them in sufficient numbers.

This is not to denigrate new teachers. On the contrary, if novice law students were assigned to try singlehandedly multimillion-dollar antitrust cases, or recent medical graduates were required to conduct open-heart surgery, attrition rates in those professions would be no better than education's. What marks both of those fields as professions is a continuum of study, mentoring, and experience that prepares practitioners for solving the hardest cases. The absence of this in education is a major handicap.

One consequence of this handicap is the invariable frustration that leads us to believe that the condition of the students, not any lack of professional capacity on the part of adults in the system, is the problem. We point to students' absence of motivation and their low socioeconomic standing or family dysfunction as prime reasons for the system's failure. Cold opposition follows any suggestion that teachers must improve their practice for student achievement to improve, or that substantial changes in teachers' education and training are needed.

This logic produces a central anomaly: In public education, the evaluation of teachers and administrators rarely involves linking their performance to levels of improvement in student achievement. In no other sector is this disconnect in the measurement of productivity so firmly rooted: Teachers don't fail; only their students do. This helps explain why productivity reforms have never taken hold in public education, and why we should not underestimate the political challenges to their implementation today.

In contemporary school reform theory, all of the stakeholders, particularly teachers' unions, must "buy in" for reform to succeed. Because it is so difficult for educators to change, the conventional wisdom says that change must take place incrementally over time. Seven to 10 years may be required before results become apparent.

The difficulty with this analysis is that reformers have been trying to change urban school systems for decades in this country, with only a handful of urban systems ever seeing significantly improved student achievement.

Even in those systems that seem to succeed, the results have been neither dramatic nor sustained. It may well be that the conventional reform view of the change process itself is as flawed as the components of the various programs it continually proposes. Rather than viewing the change process as one calling for "collaborative" strategies to be applied continuously over time, we may come to see (as virtually every other sector has) that the process of change involves cycles that require different strategies for different circumstances. The phases of change must be sequenced, so that follow-up reforms actually draw on strengths produced by changes previously made.

This elementary concept of reform cycles has been resisted, because it suggests that, in the beginning of change, there may be significant conflict, struggle, and tumult as basic power relations that have paralyzed the system are challenged.

Implicit in the collaborative view of reform is the assumption that each major stakeholder retains a pocket veto over any agreement. Thus, if any stakeholder is unwilling to proceed, the status quo is maintained. This is a perversion of the concepts of consultation, collaboration, and cooperation, and it tends to drive agreements to a lowest-common-denominator consensus level. The result has been paralysis and virtual immunity to systemic change—all in the interest of what former General Electric chairman and CEO Jack Welch calls "superficial congeniality." New programs are layered in over the existing structure of programs, practices, and budgetary allocations. The hope is that each succeeding program will prove to be the silver bullet that can energize the entire resource base, both human and fiscal, to accomplish greater gains in student achievement. This cannot happen, and never does.

The causes of our paralysis have come to be routine. It would be so much easier if we could assign blame to any one of the actors. The opposite is true. What we have has been built into the foundation of our governance arrangements, political accommodations, fiscal allocations, and cultural ties. To change it will require a paradigm shift centered on productivity that evaluates everything we do and every change we consider from evidence of its impact on improving the quality of instruction, and hence student achievement.

The situation may be comparable to what faced the U.S. automobile industry after 1975. Business and union leaders developed together a unified response to international competition that preserved the industry in America and the economic infrastructure that rested on it. This was accomplished by ruthlessly focusing on productivity, and productivity alone.

Competition also will be crucial to the reinvention of public education that is necessary for its survival in large urban areas. For every success in the industrial sector comparable to Detroit's, there are 10 examples where management and labor were unable to come together enough to recognize the common danger they faced and the jointly pursued solutions that were possible to overcome them.

We educators should remind one another of this fact: It's the teaching and learning that matters. If our students and teachers don't succeed at greater rates and in greater numbers, the franchise is doomed. We should therefore welcome the competition that charter schools, for example, present to our continued existence. Only when faced with the risk of loss will we summon the urgency to make productivity reforms and accept the terms of accountability key to public education's renewed viability in urban America.

If we do not, over the next generation our case will go to the jury, and the American people will decide. One suspects that, as has generally been true throughout our history, the people will choose ultimately in favor of children and their welfare. Should this result in severing the historic link between public finance and public schools, the implications are profound for both public education and the democratic culture that nurtured it—and then permitted it to decay, beginning in the inner city.

Notes

Introduction

1. Council on Foreign Relations, "U.S. Education Reform and National Security," Independent Task Force Report, 2012, no. 68.
2. National Commission on Excellence in Education, *A Nation at Risk: The Imperative for Educational Reform* (Washington, D.C.: U.S. Department of Education, 1983).
3. National Center on Education Statistics, NAEP 2008 Trends in Academic Progress (2009), figure A, http://nces.ed.gov/nationsreportcard/pdf/main2008/2009479_1.pdf.
4. Ibid.
5. Defined as fiftieth percentile or above, on the California STAR test, an adaptation of a nationally normed standardized achievement test; accessible at http://star.cde.ca.gov/star98/reports/37-68338-0000000.html.
6. Unless otherwise specified, all quotations from Alan D. Bersin in this book are from conversations with the author or notes dictated by Bersin between July 2005 and September 2010.

Chapter 1

1. San Diego Unified School District data. Pupil/Racial Ethnic Census Report 1998–1999, which is archived at http://old.sandi.net
2. Ibid.
3. Mel Katz, interview by Marsha Sutton, February 1, 2007, San Diego.
4. Ibid.
5. Ron Ottinger (board president, San Diego Unified School District), in discussion with the author, December 2007.
6. Council of Great City Schools, "Urban School Superintendents: Characteristics, Tenure, and Salary, Fifth Survey and Report," *Urban Indicator* 8, no. 1 (2006).
7. National School Boards Association, "Tenure of Urban School Superintendents Almost Five Years" (press release), January 29, 2002, www.nsba.org.
8. Chuck Lucier, Eric Spiegel, and Rob Schuyt, "Why CEOs Fall: The Causes and Consequences of Turnovers at the Top," *strategy+business*, July 15, 2002, http://www.strategy-business.com/article/20306?gko=bfb5b.
9. Thomas E. Glass, Lars Bjork, and C. Cryss Brunner, *The Study of the American Superintendency: A Look at the Superintendent in the New Millennium* (Lanham, MD: American Association of School Administrators/R&L Education, 2000).
10. Paul Riede, "The Hard Business of Searching," *The School Administrator* 60, no. 6 (2003), http://www.aasa.org/SchoolAdministratorArticle.aspx?id=9160.
11. Ibid.
12. Ibid.
13. Ron Ottinger, discussion.
14. Rich Collato, interview by Marsha Sutton, February 2007, San Diego.
15. Mel Katz, "The Citizen's Committee Report: The 15 Most Desired Characteristics of the New Superintendent," provided from his personal files.

16. Maureen Magee, "Wanted: Schools Chief Who Can 'Walk on Water,'" *San Diego Union-Tribune,* December 11, 1997.

17. From Paul Vallas's biography on the Web site of the School District of Philadelphia, where Vallas moved in 2002, http://www.phila.k12.pa.us.

18. Vallas has since extended his influence to Illinois and Indiana. He heads the Vallas Group, a consultancy that specializes in turning around schools and districts. The firm has partnered with a for-profit company called Cambium Learning Group to extend its reach nationally. In 2012, the firm won a three-year, $18 million contract to work with schools in Indianapolis.

19. "John Stanford becomes superintendent of Seattle Public Schools on September 1, 1995," HistoryLink.org, *The Free Online Encyclopedia of Washington State History,* http://www.historylink. org/essays/output.cfm?file_id=3347.

20. Valerie Strauss and Sari Horwitz, "A Well-Financed Failure," *Washington Post,* February 16, 1997, http://www.washingtonpost.com/wp-srv/local/longterm/library/dc/schools/schools1.htm.

21. "Resignation letter of General Julius W. Becton as CEO/Superintendent of D.C. Public Schools," April 14, 1998, http://www.dcpswatch.com/dcps/980414.htm.

22. Scott LaFee, "Outside the Ropes: Superintendents from Business and the Military Learn About System Leadership Informally and in Seminars," *School Administrator* 61, no. 10 (2004).

23. http://www.broadacademy.org/.

Chapter 2

1. Bess Keller, "San Diego's New Chief an Unlikely Pick," *Education Week* 27, no. 17 (1998): 1.

2. Ibid.

3. Stefani Mingo, "Superintendent-to-Be Alan Bersin Chats with District A," *La Jolla Village News,* June 18, 1998.

4. Maureen Magee, "Bersin Turns Page to a New Era for San Diego Schools," *San Diego Union-Tribune,* July 2, 1998.

5. Karen Heinrich, telephone interview by Melissa C. Payton, May 1, 2007.

6. Susan Moore Johnson, *Leading to Change: The Challenge of the New Superintendency* (San Francisco: Jossey-Bass, 1996).

7. Larry Cuban, "The Superintendent Contradiction," *Education Week* 18, no. 7 (1998): 56.

8. Larry Lashway, "The Superintendent in an Age of Accountability," *ERIC Clearinghouse on Educational Management* (2002), http://www.ericdigests.org/2003-3/age.htm.

9. Richard F. Elmore and Deanna Burney, *Professional Development and Instructional Improvement in Community School District #2, New York City* (Philadelphia: University of Pennsylvania, Graduate School of Education, Consortium for Policy Research in Education, 1996).

10. Alan D. Bersin, unpublished notes, November 2007.

11. Ibid.

12. Ibid.

13. Maureen Magee, "Bersin Unveils School Reorganization," *San Diego Union-Tribune,* June 16, 1998.

14. http://old.sandi.net/propmm/.

15. Ibid.

16. Magee, July 2, 1998.

Chapter 3

1. Amy M. Hightower and Milbrey W. McLaughlin, "Building and Sustaining an Infrastructure for Learning," in *Urban School Reform: Lessons from San Diego,* ed. Frederick M. Hess (Cambridge, MA: Harvard Education Press, 2005), 74.

2. Alan D. Bersin, unpublished notes dictated to prepare for the *San Diego Review,* September 2004.

3. Ibid.

4. Amy M. Hightower, *San Diego's Big Boom: District Bureaucracy Supports Culture of Learning* (Seattle: Center for the Study of Teaching and Policy, University of Washington, 2002).

5. Lynn J. Stinnette, ed., "Decentralization: Why, How, and Toward What Ends?" *Special Policy Report, No. 1, Policy Briefs Series,* North Central Regional Education Laboratory, Learning Point Associates (1993), http://www.ncrel.org/sdrs/areas/issues/envrnmnt/go/go0dcent.htm#chicago.

6. "2 Leading School Reform Groups Merge," *Los Angeles Times*, February 8, 2000, http://articles.latimes.com/2000/feb/08/local/me-62155.

7. Jeff Archer, "An Edmonton Journey," *Education Week* 24, no. 20 (2005): 33–36.

8. Ibid.

9. Louis Sahagun, "Two Years Later School Reform Report Mostly Disappointing," *Los Angeles Times*, January 28, 1999.

10. Lynn Olson, "In San Diego, Managers Forging 'Service' Role," *Education Week* 8, no. 24 (1989): 1.

11. Ron Ottinger, in discussion with the author, January 2006.

12. David Tyack and Larry Cuban, *Tinkering Toward Utopia: Reflections on a Century of Public School Reform* (Cambridge, MA: Harvard University Press), cited in Lauren B. Resnick and Megan Williams Hall, "Learning Organizations for Sustainable Education Reform," *Daedalus* 127, no. 4 (1998): 89.

13. Richard F. Elmore, "Teaching, Learning, and School Organization," *Educational Administration Quarterly* 31 (1995): 355–374.

14. Linda Darling-Hammond, Amy M. Hightower, Jennifer L. Husbands, Jeannette R. Lafors, Viki M. Young, and Carl Christopher, *Instructional Leadership for Systemic Change: The Story of San Diego's Reform* (Lanham, MD: Rowman & Littlefield Education, 2005).

15. Amy M. Hightower cited in James A. Phills, Linda Darling-Hammond, and Michael Milliken, "Reforming San Diego City Schools: 1998–2002" (case study), Stanford Educational Leadership Institute/Stanford Graduate School of Business, Case SI-53 (2004), 17–19.

16. Carol Pike, interview by the author, July 2007, San Diego.

17. Debbie Beldock, interview by the author, July 2007, San Diego.

18. Pike, interview.

19. Maureen Magee, "Will Literacy Plan Float? Cruise Planned for Kickoff," *San Diego Union-Tribune*, August 8, 1998.

20. Administrators Association of San Diego, "Questions for Leadership Team Meeting" (memo to the Institute for Learning, San Diego City Schools), October 8, 1998.

21. Ibid.

22. Anthony Alvarado, "Questions, Resolutions & Clarifications" (memo to Institute Planning Council), October 8, 1998.

23. Ibid.

24. Ibid.

25. Ann Van Sickle, interview by the author, July 2007, San Diego.

26. Donald R. McAdams, *What School Boards Can Do: Reform Governance for Urban Schools* (New York: Teachers College Press, Columbia University, 2006).

27. Ibid.

28. Ibid.

29. Hightower, *San Diego's Big Boom*, 8.

Chapter 4

1. Angela Bass, interview by the author, March 2007, San Diego.

2. Bernstein v. Lopez, No. 02-55119, D.C. No. CV-99-02714-MLH (9th Cir., Nov. 6, 2002), http://archive.ca9.uscourts.gov/ca9/newopinions.nsf/2A8BED8F1D5D767188256CDE007859CF/$file/0255119.pdf?openelement.

3. Educational Leadership Development Academy Business Plan, University of San Diego.

4. Linda Darling-Hammond, *Preparing School Leadership for a Changing World: Lessons from Exemplary Leadership Programs* (Stanford, CA: Stanford Educational Leadership Institute, Stanford University, Finance Project, 2007), 26.
5. Ibid.
6. "History of the Educational Leadership Development Academy at the University of San Diego," School of Leadership and Education Sciences, http://www.sandiego.edu/soles/centers/elda/about.php.
7. Patricia Ladd, interview by Marsha Sutton, June 2007, San Diego.
8. Ibid.
9. San Diego Unified School District Board of Education videotape, February 2005.
10. Donna Tripi, interview by Marsha Sutton, June 2007, San Diego.
11. Ibid.
12. Carole Osborne, interview by Marsha Sutton, June 2007, San Diego.
13. Debbie Beldock, interview by the author, March 2007, San Diego.
14. Marian Kim Phelps, interview by Marsha Sutton, June 2007, San Diego.
15. Carol Pike, interview by the author, March 2007, San Diego.
16. Patricia Ladd, interview by Marsha Sutton, August 2007, San Diego.
17. Phelps, interview.
18. San Diego Unified School District video of Carol Pike's Learning Community, December 2000.
19. San Diego Unified School District video of Kimiko Fukuda's Learning Community, March 2001.
20. Lauren Resnick, telephone interview by the author, June 2005.
21. Karen Seashore Louis, Kenneth Leithwood, Kyla L. Wahlstrom, Stephen E. Anderson et al., *Learning from Leadership: Investigating the Links to Improved Student Learning* (Minneapolis: Center for Applied Research and Educational Improvement, University of Minnesota; Toronto: Ontario Institute for Studies in Education, University of Toronto, July 2010).
22. Linda Rees, interview by Marsha Sutton, July 2007, San Diego.
23. Transcript of San Diego City Schools video of December 2000 meeting with principals.
24. Dana Shelburne, interview by Marsha Sutton, October 2007, San Diego.
25. Michael Fullan, *Leading in a Culture of Change* (San Francisco: Jossey-Bass, 2001), 61.
26. Ibid.
27. Linda Darling-Hammond, Amy M. Hightower, Jennifer L. Husbands, Jeannette R. LaFors, Viki M. Young, and Carl Christopher, *Building Instructional Quality: "Inside-Out" and "Outside-In" Perspectives on San Diego's School Reform* (Seattle: Center for the Study of Teaching and Policy, University of Washington, 2003).
28. Tripi, interview.
29. San Diego Unified School District principals meeting video, August 2001.
30. Kenneth Leithwood, Karen Seashore Louis, Stephen E. Anderson, and Kyla L. Wahlstrom, *How Leadership Influences Student Learning: Executive Summary* (Minneapolis: Center for Applied Research and Educational Improvement, University of Minnesota; Toronto: Ontario Institute for Education, University of Toronto, 2004), 4.
31. Fullan, *Leading*, 44.

Chapter 5

1. Jere Brophy, "Social Promotion: In Comparison to Grade Retention, Advantages and Disadvantages, Different Perspectives," http://education.stateuniversity.com/pages/2431/Social-Promotion.html.
2. "Survey on Implementation of Current Policy on Social Promotion/Retention for Grade Level 8" (report to the San Diego Board of Education), March 4, 1999.
3. "Preliminary 1997–1998 Retention Tabulations," San Diego district data, October 1999.
4. Hugh Mehan and Scott Grimes, "Measuring the Achievement Gap in San Diego City Schools" (study commissioned by San Diego Dialogue), March 1999. Available in the San Diego City Schools archives or the archives of the San Diego Dialogue, http://www.sandiegodialogue.org/.

5. "Student and Promotion Support Report" (district memo), July 13, 1999.

6. Alan D. Bersin, personal recollections prepared for this volume.

7. Videotape of principals meeting, September 28, 1999.

8. "Social Promotion in Schools," *The NewsHour with Jim Lehrer*, aired March 8, 1999, http://www.pbs.org/newshour/bb/education/jan-june99/retention_3-9.html.

9. Melissa Roderick, Anthony S. Bryk, Brian A. Jacob, John Q. Easton, Elaine Allensworth, "Ending Social Promotion: Results from the First Two Years" (report), *Charting Reform in Chicago, Series 1*, Consortium on Chicago School Research (1999), http://ccsr.uchicago.edu/publications/ending-social-promotion-results-first-two-years.

10. Maureen Magee, "Failing S.D. Students Promoted Despite Ban," *San Diego Union-Tribune*, October 12, 1999.

11. "Shell Game: San Diego Unified Blinks on Social Promotion," *San Diego Union-Tribune*, October 14, 1999.

12. Ibid.

13. Alan D. Bersin, "A New Year, New Directions: Superintendent Aims for Next Level," *San Diego Union-Tribune*, September 5, 1999.

14. Ibid.

15. Maureen Magee, "Major School Overhaul Proposed: S.D. District Aims to Put End to 'Social Promotion,'" *San Diego Union Tribune*, December 14, 1999.

16. Bryan Gottlieb, "Bersin to WTC: Business Must Get Involved in Education," *San Diego Daily Transcript*, February 14, 2000.

17. Maureen Magee, "Battle over the 'Blueprint'; School Overhaul Plan, Up for Vote Today, Splits District," *San Diego Union-Tribune*, March 14, 2000.

18. "City Schools' Reform Plan Sacrifices Classroom Aides," Letters to the Editor, *San Diego Union-Tribune*, March 5, 2000. Supportive letter was from Ron Villa of Lakeside; those opposed from Cynthia Cordero, an instructional assistant from Marshall Elementary School in San Diego, and Sheryl A. Harris of San Diego.

19. Lea Hubbard, Hugh Mehan, and Mary Kay Stein, *Reform as Learning: School Reform, Organizational Culture, and Community Politics in San Diego* (New York: Routledge, 2006), 205.

20. Maureen Magee, "Educators Prepare for Reform Plan; Bersin Plans Meetings with Parents, Teachers," *San Diego Union-Tribune*, March 16, 2000.

21. Maureen Magee, "School Reforms Receive Grant Support," *San Diego Union-Tribune*, November 6, 2001, quoted in Julian R. Betts, Andrew C. Zau, and Kevin King, "From Blueprint to Reality: San Diego's Education Reforms" (report), Public Policy Institute of California (2005), 3, http://www.ppic.org/main/publication.asp?i=408.

22. James A. Phills, Linda Darling-Hammond, and Michael Milliken, "Reforming San Diego City Schools, 1998–2002" (case study), Stanford Educational Leadership Institute/Stanford Graduate School of Business, Case SI-53 (2004).

23. "Evaluation of the Blueprint for Student Success in San Diego City Schools" (executive summary), American Institutes for Research (2003): xiv.

24. Hilda Rodriguez, interview by the author, April 2008, San Diego.

25. "Evaluation of the Blueprint," xiv.

26. Ibid.

27. Julian R. Betts, Andrew C. Zau, and Kevin King, "From Blueprint to Reality: San Diego's Education Reforms" (report), Public Policy Institute of California (2005).

28. Frederick Douglass, "West India Emancipation" (speech), Canandaigua, New York, August 3, 1857.

Chapter 6

1. Duke Helfand and Howard Blume, "Mayor Names Schools Leader," *Los Angeles Times*, February 26, 2008, http://articles.latimes.com/2008/feb/26/local/me-mayor26.

2. "A Q & A with Rod Paige," *San Diego Union-Tribune*, October 27, 2002.

3. Michael Kinsman, "Marc Knapp; Honored Teacher Aimed to Make School Fun; 60," *San Diego Union-Tribune*, January 6, 2007, http://www.utsandiego.com/uniontrib/20070106/news_1m6knapp.html.

4. "MOU Between the SDEA and the SDUSD" (union memo to Alan Bersin), August 4, 1998.

5. Marc Knapp, "President's August Column," *The Advocate*, San Diego Education Association, August 1998.

6. Marc Knapp, "President's January Column," *The Advocate*, San Diego Education Association, January 1999.

7. Alan D. Bersin, "Notes from my conversation with Tony. Issues re: discussion of staff developer" (memo), Bersin personal papers, undated.

8. Richard Lee Colvin and Liz Willen, eds., *From Contracts to Classrooms: Covering Teachers Unions: A Primer for Journalists* (New York: The Hechinger Institute on Education and the Media, Teachers College, Columbia University, 2007).

9. "A Q & A with Marc Knapp, President, San Diego Education Association," *San Diego Union-Tribune*, May 26, 2002.

10. Ibid.

11. Alan D. Bersin and Mary Vixie Sandy, "Professionalizing the Occupation of Teaching in a Time of Transition," in *Measurement Issues and the Assessment of Teacher Quality*, ed. Drew Gitomer (Thousand Oaks, CA: SAGE Publications, Inc., 2009).

12. Marc Knapp, "President's September Column," *The Advocate*, San Diego Education Association, September 2000.

13. Ibid.

14. Marc Knapp and Robin Whitlow, *Little SDEAdvocate* (newsletter), vol. VIII, no. 7, January 5, 1999.

15. Jonathan Freedman, "Shuttle Diplomacy," *San Diego Magazine*, February 2003.

16. Robin Whitlow, SDEA, "Re: Staff Developers," (memo to Mary Hopper, San Diego City Schools), February 2, 1999.

17. Alan D. Bersin, "Quality Assurance Must Be Key Factor in Staff Developer Program," San Diego City Schools press release, undated.

18. Maureen Magee, "Bersin Plans Literacy Mentors Despite Union," *San Diego Union-Tribune*, April 9, 1999.

19. Ibid.

20. Marc Knapp and Robin Whitlow, *Little SDEAdvocate* (newsletter), vol. IX, no. 1, February 16, 2000.

21. Office of the Superintendent, minutes of February 24, 2000 meeting attended by Alan Bersin, Deberie Gomez, Marc Knapp, Terry Smith, and Robin Whitlow.

22. Knapp and Whitlow, *Little SDEAdvocate*, February 16, 2000.

23. Letter from Robin Whitlow, SDEA, to Deberie Gomez, San Diego City Schools, March 20, 2000.

24. Memo from Marc Knapp to SDEA membership regarding implementation of Blueprint, March 2000.

25. Robert Kittle, interview by Marsha Sutton, August 2008, San Diego.

26. Christine Campbell, "San Diego City Schools: Breaking Eggs: Omelet or Scrambled?" (unpublished case study prepared for the Broad Institute for School Boards), 2002.

27. Malin Burnham, "Acrimony 101: Moving Beyond the Personal Hostility," Opinion, *San Diego Union-Tribune*, July 21, 2001.

28. Marc Knapp, "President's June Column," *The Advocate*, San Diego Education Association, June 2002.

29. Joe Williams, "The Labor-Management Showdown," in *Urban School Reform: Lessons from San Diego*, ed. Frederick M. Hess (Cambridge, MA: Harvard Education Press, 2005).

30. Joe Williams, *Cheating Our Kids: How Politics and Greed Ruin Education* (New York: Macmillan, 2005).

31. Larry Cuban, unpublished paper, in response to Joe Williams, "The Labor-Management Show-down," in *Urban School Reform: Lessons from San Diego*, ed. Frederick M. Hess (Cambridge, MA: Harvard Education Press, 2005).

32. Diane Ravitch, *The Death and Life of the Great American School System: How Testing and Choice Are Undermining Education* (New York: Basic Books, 2010).

33. Larry Cuban and Michael Usdan, "Fast and Top-Down: Systemic Reform and Student Achieve-ment in San Diego City Schools," in *Powerful Reforms with Shallow Roots: Improving America's Urban Roots*, eds. Larry Cuban and Michael Usdan (New York: Teachers College Press, 2003), 77.

34. Carol Pike, interview by the author, March 2007, San Diego.

35. Campbell, "San Diego City Schools."

36. Emily Alpert, "From Public Schools to Presidential Politics: Questions for Carl Cohn," *Voice of San Diego*, December 22, 2007, http://www.voiceofsandiego.org/uncategorized/article_2013d6b6-3e73-50d4-8677-673737e0020d.html.

37. Alex Roth, "Bersin Eyes Run with Aguirre," *San Diego Union-Tribune*, January 4, 2008.

38. Alan D. Bersin and Randi Weingarten, interviews prepared by Collaborative Communications Group for the conference "A New Dialogue: Collective Bargaining in Public Education," orga-nized by the National Governors Association, Rhode Island Governor Donald L. Carcieri, and the Rhode Island Foundation, Newport, Rhode Island, December 10–11, 2006, http://www.annenberginstitute.org/CB/pdf/Conference_Report.pdf.

39. Frederick M. Hess and Coby Loup, *The Leadership Limbo: Teacher Labor Agreements in America's 50 Largest School Districts* (Washington, D.C.: Thomas B. Fordham Institute, 2008).

40. Victoria Van Cleef, "Half Empty or Half Full? Challenges and Progress in Hiring Reform," in *Urban School Reform: Lessons From San Diego*, ed. Frederick M. Hess (Cambridge, MA: Harvard Education Press, 2005), 185.

41. Elaine Korry, "Union Contracts Stymie School Hiring Decisions," National Public Radio, November 16, 2005, http://www.npr.org/templates/story/story.php?storyId=5015623.

42. Bersin and Weingarten, interviews.

43. Alan D. Bersin, "Making Schools Productive: The Point of Accountability and the Key to Renewal," *Education Week* 24, no. 32 (2005): 30, 40. This conclusion was amplified in Bersin and Sandy, "Professionalizing the Occupation of Teaching in a Time of Transition."

44. Ibid.

45. Bersin and Weingarten, interviews.

46. Jeremy P. Meyer, "School Wants to Set Own Course," *Denver Post*, December 6, 2007, http://origin.denverpost.com/privacypolicy/ci_7648275.

47. Ibid.

Chapter 7

1. Meeting of the San Diego Board of Education (video recording), San Diego, October 12, 2004.

2. Helen Gao, "Trustees Censure Zimmerman for Remark," *San Diego Union-Tribune*, October 13, 2004. Zimmerman was censured for this remark, which she made at a school board meeting on September 28, 2004. "I am gonna use an analogy that you may not like. But you know that, what Gauleiters are. Gauleiters were the people in the ghetto in Europe who shepherded, they were Jews who worked for the Nazis, and they shepherded their own people onto the trains and that is what we're being asked to do here." In fact, Gauleiters were members of the Nazi Party who were put in charge of a neighborhood or a geographic district.

3. "Resolution of Censure of Board of Trustees Member Frances O'Neill Zimmerman" (San Diego Unified School District Board meeting report), October 12, 2004, http://old.sandi.net/board/reports/2004/1012/index.html.

4. Meeting of the San Diego Board of Education.

5. Robert Kittle, interview by Marsha Sutton, San Diego, August 2008.

6. Maureen Magee, "S.D. Trustees Seek Harmony Through Therapy," *San Diego Union-Tribune*, June 21, 1998.

7. Ibid.

8. Ibid.

9. Arthur L. Vaughan, "Superindentent [*sic*] Clashes with Board Member—Chastises Blacks Who Spoke Before Board," *Voice and Viewpoint*, October 1, 1998.

10. Maureen Magee, "City School Chiefs Draw Union's Fire; Teacher Group's Charge of Privatization Is Denied," *San Diego Union-Tribune*, January 22, 1999.

11. Michael D. Usdan, "Board Governance and External Constituencies," in *Urban School Reform: Lessons from San Diego*, ed. Frederick M. Hess (Cambridge, MA: Harvard Education Press, 2005), 11–32.

12. Ibid.

13. Maureen Magee, "School Board Members Agree to Strict Rules on Behavior," *San Diego Union-Tribune*, September 18, 2008.

14. William Howell, ed., *Besieged: School Boards and the Future of Education Politics* (Washington, D.C.: Brookings Institution Press, 2005), 2.

15. Ibid., 3.

16. Ibid., 4.

17. Terry M. Moe, "Teacher Unions and School Board Elections," in Howell, *Besieged*, chapter 11.

18. Ibid., 255.

19. Jane Elizabeth, "The Disappearing School Board," *Pittsburgh Post-Gazette*, November 30 and December 1, 2003.

20. Christine Campbell, "San Diego City Schools: Breaking Eggs: Omelet or Scrambled?" (unpublished case study prepared for the Broad Institute for School Boards), 2002.

21. Maureen Magee, "Zimmerman Armed with Confidences; Bersin Critic Keeps School Board Seat," *San Diego Union-Tribune*, November 26, 2000.

22. Ibid.

23. Maureen Magee, "Nakamura Edging Lee; de Beck Wins," *San Diego Union-Tribune*, November 6, 2002.

24. Arne Duncan, National Journal Education Experts blog, July 6, 2009, http://education. nationaljournal.com/2009/07/is-mayoral-control-the-answer.php.

Chapter 8

1. Maureen Magee, "Bersin Turns His Attention to Agenda as Schools Chief," *San Diego Union-Tribune*, March 15, 1998.

2. Ibid.

3. "U.S. Attorney Alan D. Bersin Loses Appeal by Accepting a Flawed Selection Process to the Superintendency of the San Diego Unified School District" (editorial), *La Prensa San Diego*, March 12, 1998.

4. Matt Potter, "Border Fixer," *San Diego Reader*, September 24, 1998.

5. Matt Potter, "Obama Taps Alan Bersin to Oversee Border," *San Diego Reader*, November 18, 2009.

6. Valerie Alford, "Bersin Has Friends, and Foes, in High Places," *San Diego Union-Tribune*, March 9, 1998.

7. Randy Dotinga, "A Lightning Rod Takes on California Schools," *Christian Science Monitor*, May 31, 2005, O3.

8. John Gilmore, interview by Marsha Sutton, August 2008, San Diego.

9. Jonathan Freedman, "Shuttle Diplomacy," *San Diego Magazine*, February 2003, http://www.sandiegomagazine.com/San-Diego-Magazine/February-2003/Shuttle-Diplomacy.

10. AdvertisingAge DataCenter, "Newspapers by Circulation for 6 Months Ended 9/30/2000," http://adage.com/datacenter/datapopup.php?article_id=106309.

11. Bill Gorman, "Nielsen Local Television Market Universe Estimates," September 10, 2008, http://tvbythenumbers.zap2it.com/2008/09/10/nielsen-local-television-market-universe-estimates/5037/.

12. Audit Bureau Circulation numbers from publication websites as of 2005 verified audit.

13. The Voice of San Diego, an online news site, began operating in February 2005, only months before Bersin left, and has risen steadily in importance as a local news source as the *San Diego Union-Tribune* has faded and cut staff and news pages.

14. Peri Lynn Turnbull, telephone interview by the author, March 2008.

15. Matt Potter, "Sellout," *San Diego Reader*, April 6, 2000.

16. "Bersin Wins the Battle, but May Lose the War!" (editorial), *La Prensa San Diego*, April 12, 2002.

17. Daniel Muñoz, email message to Peri Lynn Turnbull, related during interview with author, March 2008.

18. Maureen Magee, "Bersin's Legacy a Study in Contradiction: Departing Schools Chief Hailed Nationwide, yet Reviled by Many in San Diego," *San Diego Union-Tribune*, May 1, 2005, A1.

19. Maureen Magee, "Reading: Job One from Day One," *San Diego Union-Tribune*, August 31, 1998.

20. Ibid.

21. Ibid.

22. Maureen Magee, "With Bond Passed, Teachers Air Grievances," *San Diego Union-Tribune*, November 15, 1998.

23. Maureen Magee, "City School Chiefs Draw Union's Fire; Teacher Group's Charge of Privatization Is Denied," *San Diego Union-Tribune*, January 22, 1999.

24. Maureen Magee, "Bersin Put Father-in-Law on Land Panel," December 25, 1999.

25. Maureen Magee, "S.D. School Race Shows No Signs of Easing Up," *San Diego Union-Tribune*, November 4, 2000.

26. Matt Potter, "What the Blueprints Don't Show," *San Diego Reader*, September 12, 2002.

27. Maureen Magee, "Bersin: Leadership Style Grates on Many Teachers," *San Diego Union-Tribune*, October 27, 2002.

28. Robert J. Caldwell, "Reform at Risk," *San Diego Union-Tribune*, October 27, 2002.

29. Matt Potter, "We Won!" *San Diego Reader*, November 18, 2004.

30. Magee, "Bersin's Legacy."

31. The paper was sold again in January 2012. By then it had gone through several rounds of layoffs and its circulation had fallen to about two hundred twenty-five thousand.

32. James Harvey, *The Urban Superintendent: Creating Great Schools While Surviving on the Job* (Washington, D.C.: Council of the Great City Schools, February 2003).

33. Ibid.

34. Personal email to author from Peri Lynn Turnbull, April 2008.

35. Ken Ellingwood, "'Border Czar' Ends a Highly Visible Reign," *Los Angeles Times*, June 28, 1998.

36. Norma Trost, telephone interview by the author, March 2007.

37. Maureen Magee, "School District Mailer Draws Fire," *San Diego Union-Tribune*, September 11, 2001.

38. John Spelich, telephone interview by the author, March 2007.

39. Alan D. Bersin, "State of the District" (speech transcript), April 4, 2002.

40. Jill Spielvogel and David E. Graham, "Bersin Says Schools Well on Their Way to Improvement; First 'State of the District' Speech Fails to Placate Foes," *San Diego Union-Tribune*, April 5, 2002.

41. Jill Spielvogel and David E. Graham, "Bersin Says Schools Well on Their Way to Improvement; First State-of-the-District Speech Fails to Placate Foes," *San Diego Union-Tribune*, April 5, 2002.

42. Letter to the Editor, *San Diego Union-Tribune*, April 7, 2002.

Chapter 9

1. Under the California Master Plan for Higher Education, the ten-campus University of California system serves the top 12.5 percent of the high school graduating class who have taken the required high school classes; California State University has twenty-three campuses and is designed to serve students who take the classes required for admission and graduate in the top third of the state's high school class.

2. Ibid.
3. "Status Report on District High School Reform," San Diego City Schools, September 9, 2003.
4. Ibid.
5. Ibid.
6. Michael Milliken, James A. Phills Jr., and Linda Darling-Hammond, *Reforming San Diego City Schools: 1998–2002* (Cambridge, MA: Harvard Business Publishing, 2003). Quote is from a personal communication with Alan D. Bersin.
7. Christine Campbell, Michael DeArmond, and Sara Taggart, "Toward a Portfolio of Schools: High School Renewal," in *Urban School Reform: Lessons from San Diego*, ed. Frederick M. Hess (Cambridge, MA: Harvard Education Press, 2005), 142.
8. Shirley Peterson, interview by Marsha Sutton, October 2007, San Diego.
9. Ibid.
10. Pat Crowder, interview by Marsha Sutton, January 2008, San Diego.
11. Peterson, interview.
12. Dana Shelburne, interview by Marsha Sutton, October 2007, San Diego.
13. The history in this passage draws on "From There to Here: The Road to Reform of American High Schools," an issue paper prepared for the High School Leadership Summit, U.S. Department of Education.
14. Diane Ravitch, *Left Back: A Century of Battles over School Reforms* (New York: Touchstone, 2000).
15. "From There to Here," 2.
16. David L. Angus and Jeffrey E. Mirel, *The Failed Promise of the American High School, 1890–1995* (New York: Teachers College Press, 1999).
17. Ibid.
18. *National* Commission on Excellence in Education, *A Nation at Risk: The Imperative for Educational Reform* (Washington, D.C.: U.S. Department of Education, 1983).
19. Paul Houston, "Intelligent Redesign: Reframing the Discussion on High School Reform," *Education Week*, June 15, 2005, 40.
20. Linda Darling-Hammond, Amy M. Hightower, Jennifer L. Husbands, Jeannette R. Lafors, Viki M. Young, and Carl Christopher, *Instructional Leadership for Systemic Change: The Story of San Diego's Reform* (Lanham, Maryland: Rowman & Littlefield Education, 2005), 166.
21. Mike Forbes, "Is La Jolla High's Curriculum Going 'Fast Food'?," *La Jolla Light*, April 12, 2001.
22. Darling-Hammond et al., *Instructional Leadership*, 166.
23. http://www.its-about-time.com/htmls/ap.html.
24. http://www.nsf.gov/about/history/nsf0050/education/scienceinstruct.htm.
25. Peterson, interview.
26. Shelburne, interview.
27. Darling-Hammond et al., *Instructional Leadership*, 166.
28. Peterson, interview.
29. Miyo Reff, interview by Marsha Sutton, September 2007, San Diego.
30. Ibid.
31. Leslie Fausset, interview by Marsha Sutton, October 2007, San Diego.
32. Debra Viadero, "City Districts to Change 'Obsolete' High Schools," *Education Week*, October 17, 2001.
33. Maureen Magee, "S.D. Granted $8 Million to Reform High Schools," *San Diego Union-Tribune*, October 12, 2001.
34. Ibid.
35. Collaborative Communications Group, "A Theory of Action for High School Reform: A Conversation with Alan Bersin, California Secretary of Education and Former Superintendent of the San Diego City Schools" (report prepared for the Carnegie Corporation of New York), 2006.
36. Fausset, interview.
37. Ibid.

38. John DeVore, "Tackling Instruction Head-On: The San Diego Strategy," *VUE* magazine, Summer 2005, 29.
39. John DeVore, interview by Marsha Sutton, October 9, 2007, San Diego.
40. Ibid.
41. Collaborative Communications Group, "Theory of Action," 2.
42. Mary Hopper, "Status Report on District High School Reform" (report), September 9, 2003, http://sandi.net/board/reports/2003/0909/e6y_report.pdf.
43. Matthew Malone, interview by Marsha Sutton, October 2007, San Diego.
44. Ibid.
45. Libia Gil, interview by Marsha Sutton, October 2007, San Diego.
46. DeVore, interview.
47. Malone, interview.
48. Gil, interview.
49. Malone, interview.
50. Ibid.
51. Ibid.
52. Ibid.
53. San Diego City Schools, "Newsweek Ranks Fourteen San Diego High Schools Among Best in the U.S." (press release), May 5, 2006.
54. Susan Yonezawa, Larry McClure, and Makeba Jones, "A Report of Results from a Student Survey Regarding the Fifth-Year Implementation of the San Diego Unified School District's New 14 Small High Schools," University of San Diego, California, Center for Research on Educational Equity, Assessment, and Teaching Excellence, May 30, 2009.
55. Gil, interview.
56. Helen Gao, "Rebirth of Lincoln High," *San Diego Union-Tribune*, September 2, 2007, A-1.
57. Gil, interview.
58. Collaborative Communications Group, "Theory of Action," 5.
59. Malone, interview.
60. DeVore, interview.
61. Katherine Wakamura, interview by Marsha Sutton, October 7, 2007.

Chapter 10

1. Gompers Preparatory Academy Web site. http://www.gomperscharter.org/about/mission.jsp.
2. Tracy Johnson, interview by the author, May 2007, San Diego.
3. Alison Kenda, interview by the author, May 2007, San Diego.
4. Helen Gao, "Parents and Teachers Walk Door-to-Door to Fulfill a Dream," *San Diego Union-Tribune*, January 1, 2005.
5. Julian R. Betts, Lorien A. Rice, Andrew C. Zau, Y. Emily Tang, and Cory R. Koedel, "Does School Choice Work? Effects on Student Integration and Achievement," Public Policy Institute of California (August 2006).
6. Ibid.
7. Andrew C. Zau and Julian Betts, "The Evolution of School Choice," in *Urban School Reform: Lessons from San Diego*, ed. Frederick M. Hess (Cambridge, MA: Harvard Education Press, 2005).
8. Catherine Mahoney and Frank Kemerer, "Charter Schools: Opportunities and Challenges," in *Urban School Reform: Lessons from San Diego*, ed. Frederick M. Hess (Cambridge, MA: Harvard Education Press, 2005).
9. The local Kwachiyoa teachers elected not to operate with a school principal but rather a consortium of teacher leaders. The local union leadership, never really supportive of the charter school, took no action as the school slid steadily into academic failure. In 2004, it was closed by the district with the SDEA's concurrence.
10. San Diego Unified School District, Charter School Policy and Guidelines, November 13, 2001 (revised in 2001, 2003, and 2004).

11. Personal correspondence with the author.

12. I was helped greatly in writing this chapter by reading Joe Williams and Thomas Toch, "Extreme Makeover: Two Failing San Diego Schools Get New Start as Charters" (report written for Education Sector, a nonpartisan education policy think tank based in Washington, D.C.), http://www.educationsector.org/publications/extreme-makeover-two-failing-san-diego-schools-get-new-start-charters.

13. Ibid.

14. Ibid.

15. Ibid.

16. Vince Riveroll, interview by the author, May 2007, San Diego.

17. Ibid.

18. Williams and Toch, "Extreme Makeover."

19. Michelle Evans, interview by the author, May 2007, San Diego.

20. Williams and Toch, "Extreme Makeover."

21. Helen Gao, "Parents and Teachers."

22. Helen Gao, "New Charter School Requirement Draws Jeers," *San Diego Union-Tribune*, January 7, 2005.

23. Correspondence from Vince Riveroll to San Diego School Administrators Association, March 2005.

24. Riveroll, interview.

25. Maureen Magee and Helen Gao, "Popular Gompers Principal Loses Post," *San Diego Union-Tribune*, February 10, 2005.

26. Video of March 1, 2005, school board meeting. San Diego Unified School District.

27. Ibid.

28. Padmini Jambulati, "A Portrait of School Improvement Grantees," *Education Sector*, April 26, 2011, http://www.educationsector.org/publications/portrait-school-improvement-grantees.

29. Gompers Preparatory Academy video of graduation.

30. Jennifer Medina, "City's Schools Share Their Space, and Bitterness," *New York Times*, November 29, 2009, http://www.nytimes.com/2009/11/30/education/30space.html.

31. "Multiple Choice: Charter School Performance in 16 States," Center on Research on Education Outcomes, Stanford University, 2009.

Chapter 11

1. San Diego City Schools videotape of January 25, 2005, monthly principals meeting.

2. Helen Gao, "Bersin Given Emotional Ovation; Principals Pledge to Continue His Work," *San Diego Union-Tribune,* January 29, 2005.

3. "Superintendent Transition Document: 10 Strongest/Weakest Outcomes of Reform," Office of School Site Support, San Diego City Schools, June 2005.

4. Ibid.

5. San Diego Unified School District Board of Education video, January 2005.

6. Julian R. Betts, Andrew C. Zau, and Cory Koedel, "Lessons in Reading Reform: What Works" (report for Public Policy Institute of California, 2010), http://www.ppic.org/main/publication.asp?i=922.

7. "Q & A: Carl A. Cohn, Superintendent, San Diego Unified School District," *San Diego Union-Tribune*, December 4, 2005, http://www.utsandiego.com/uniontrib/20051204/news_lz1e4qa.html.

8. Maureen Cavanagh and Natalie Walsh, "Superintendent Grier Discusses His Pending Resignation" (transcript of interview with San Diego Superintendent Terry Grier), KPBS, August 26, 2009, http://www.kpbs.org/news/2009/aug/26/superintendent-grier-discusses-his-pending-resigna/.

9. Emily Alpert, "Would-Be-Superintendents Won't Blow Up the School District," *Voice of San Diego*, June 20, 2010, http://www.voiceofsandiego.org/education/article_0314a1c4-7ccf-11df-9509-001cc4c03286.html.

10. Frank Kemerer, Fred Galloway, and Lea Hubbard, "San Diego Unified School District Status Report: 2003–2009," University of San Diego, Center for Education Policy and Law, July 2010.

11. Ibid.

12. "State of the District Address, Richard Barrera, Board President" (speech), San Diego School District, San Diego, California, March 24, 2010, www.sandi.net/cms/lib/CA01001235/Centricity/Domain/457/2010stateofthedistrictaddress.pdf.

13. Alan D. Bersin, "Making Schools Productive: Growth in Student Achievement Must Be Education's Key Metric," *San Diego Union-Tribune*, June 5, 2005, http://www.utsandiego.com/uniontrib/20050605/news_lz1e5making.html.

14. Council on Foreign Relations, "U.S. Education Reform and National Security," Independent Task Force Report 68, 2012.

15. Unpublished essay.

died in May 2010, did not live long enough to see the completed book. He inquired about my progress every time I saw him and, when he was in the hospital just before his death, asked me if I'd brought him something to read.

—Richard Lee Colvin
Washington, D.C.
September 2012

About the Author

Richard Lee Colvin is a visiting fellow at the Woodrow Wilson National Fellowship Foundation. He is the former executive director of Education Sector, and previously directed the Hechinger Institute on Education and the Media at Teachers College, Columbia University. Under his leadership, the Institute created the Hechinger Report, a source of in-depth, nonpartisan journalism about education.

Previously, he wrote about national education issues for the *Los Angeles Times*, where he was a reporter and editor for fourteen years, and also wrote for the Associated Press. Additionally, he reported on education for the *Oakland Tribune* and the *Hayward Daily Review* in California.

Index